GERTRUDE BEALS BOURNE

Artist in Brahmin Boston

(1868-1962)

AF521836

by

D. ROGER HOWLETT

foreword by

PATRICIA HILLS

COPLEY SQUARE PRESS • BOSTON

distributed by

Northeastern University Press, Boston

First published in 2004 by

COPLEY SQUARE PRESS • BOSTON
169 Newbury Street
Boston, Massachusetts 02116

Distributed by
Northeastern University Press
Boston, Massachusetts 02115

Copyright ©2004 by D. Roger Howlett

All rights reserved. No part of this book may be used or reproduced in any manner whatsoever without written permission, except in the case of brief quotations embodied in critical articles and reviews.

Library of Congress Catalog Card Number:
ISBN: 0-9628143-1-8

First Edition
Printed in China by South China Printing Company Ltd.
on acid-free paper

ACKNOWLEDGEMENTS

Thanks to:
Thomas Blake; Peter W. Cohn, Jane Nylander; William B. Osgood; John W. Sears; Marilyn B. Wasserman; and special thanks to Margaret Hani, Assistant Professor of Art History, Simmons College, who generously shared her notes from her research on Gertrude and Frank Bourne made before many original source materials were destroyed. My mother, Dorothy T. Howlett, for a final galley proofreading that saved me from embarrassing mistakes.

Thanks to the following institutions and their staff:
American Art Museum, Smithsonian Institution, Elizabeth Broun, Richard Sorensen; Arts Club, Washington, D.C.,Vernon E. Gardner and Andre Stone;
Boston Public Library, Bernard Margolis, President; Janice H. Chadbourne, Kim Tenney, Evelyn Lannon, and Cecile Gardner, Fine Arts Reference; Sinclair H. Hitchings, Aaron Schmidt, Wiggin Print Room; Henry F. Scannell, Curator of Microtext and Newspapers;
Brooklyn Museum, Jennifer Lesslie;
Dublin Historical Society (NH), John Harris; Nancy E. Campbell; and Frank Consiglio;
East Haddam Historical Society, Charles Farrow; East Haddam, Connecticut, Karl Stofko, Town Historian; Episcopal Diocese of R. I., Mark Dirksen;Haddam Historical Society, Elizabeth Malloy; Harvard University Archives;
Ipswich Historical Society, Stefanie Muscat, Stephanie Gaskins, Patricia Tyler and Amanda Nelson;
Maine Historic Preservation Commission, Earl G. Shuttleworth, Jr.; Massachusetts Art Commission, Susan Greendyke Lachevre, Art Collections Manager; Milton Historical Society, Jeannette Peverly; Milton Public Library, Daniel Haacker; Museum of Fine Arts, Boston, Adria Bernier, Katherine Sanderson and Mary L. Sluskonis, Pat Loiko, registrar;
Newport Art Museum, Nancy Whipple Grinnell;
North Shore Art Association, Ted Tysver and Thomas O'Keefe;
Peabody Essex Museum, Salem, Massachusetts; Pennsylvania Academy of the Fine Arts, Cheryl Leibold, archivist; Philbrook Farm, Shelburne, New Hampshire, Ann Leger;
Simmons College, Trustman Art Gallery, Bob Oppenheim; Society for the Preservation of New England Antiquities, Richard Nylander;
Tourism Office and Convention Board of Gaspé, Mary O'Connor;
University of New Hampshire, Art Gallery, Cyndy Farrell;
William Vareika, Fine Arts, Newport, R.I., William Vareika.

The staff and Interns of Childs Gallery: Richard J. Baiano, Stephanie V. Bond, Cecily Brewer, Inez Chesler, Lesley W. Duncan, Joshua Eby, Juliana Gauron, Stephanie Kutylo, John W. Hamilton, Morgan C. Long, Courtney A. McGowan, Kimberly Merrill, Meghan Read, Judith O. Schulz and Miranda J. Vitello.

In the preparation of this book: Robert Sennett, for initial editing; Robert J. Gormley Editor-in-Chief, and Jill Bahcall, Associate Director, Northeastern University Press; Peter Lawrence, South China Printing; Gabriel B. Connolly for many of the digital images.

Patricia Hills for reading the manuscript and providing helpful suggestions and for her great kindness in providing an insightful foreword for this book. Other readers: Susan K. Cabot, Margaret Hanni, Christopher R. Mathias, Bettina A. Norton, Kenneth C. Turino, and Gail Weesner who saved me from many an error and provided insights and documentation.

Richard Bartlett, who provided design specifications, and thanks especially to Liam O. Toomey, Charles D. Childs Fellow 2003-04, who edited the manuscript and shaped its final form, laid out the book design, made most of the digital images, and worked with South China Printing and Northeastern University Press to put polish on the project.

Gertrude Beals Bourne's son, Philip Walley Bourne, was determined to make certain that her accomplishments were not forgotten. He commissioned a catalogue of her works and helped to sponsor exhibitions at Simmons College and the Essex Institute in Salem. He made carefully considered gifts of her work to major institutions and established the Bourne Art Trust to help preserve her legacy. This book is, in part, a result of his dedication. It is also a result of the continuing involvement of the Bourne family including Sallie Bourne Harrison, Carter Harrison, Mary Nicholson Bourne, Mrs. Philip E. Bourne, Jonathan F. Bourne, Carter Harrison, Jr., Peter Harrison, and the Bourne Art Trust. The Trust has been supportive of this volume in every possible way.

Among the institutions that hold works by Gertrude Beals Bourne in their permanent collections are: the National Museum of American Art, the Corcoran Gallery, the Museum of Fine Arts, Boston, the Brockton Art Museum, the Currier Gallery of Art, the Peabody Essex Museum, and the Danforth Museum of Art.

Every effort has been made to secure permission to use copyright material. We regret any omissions and will make appropriate corrections in any subsequent prints and editions.

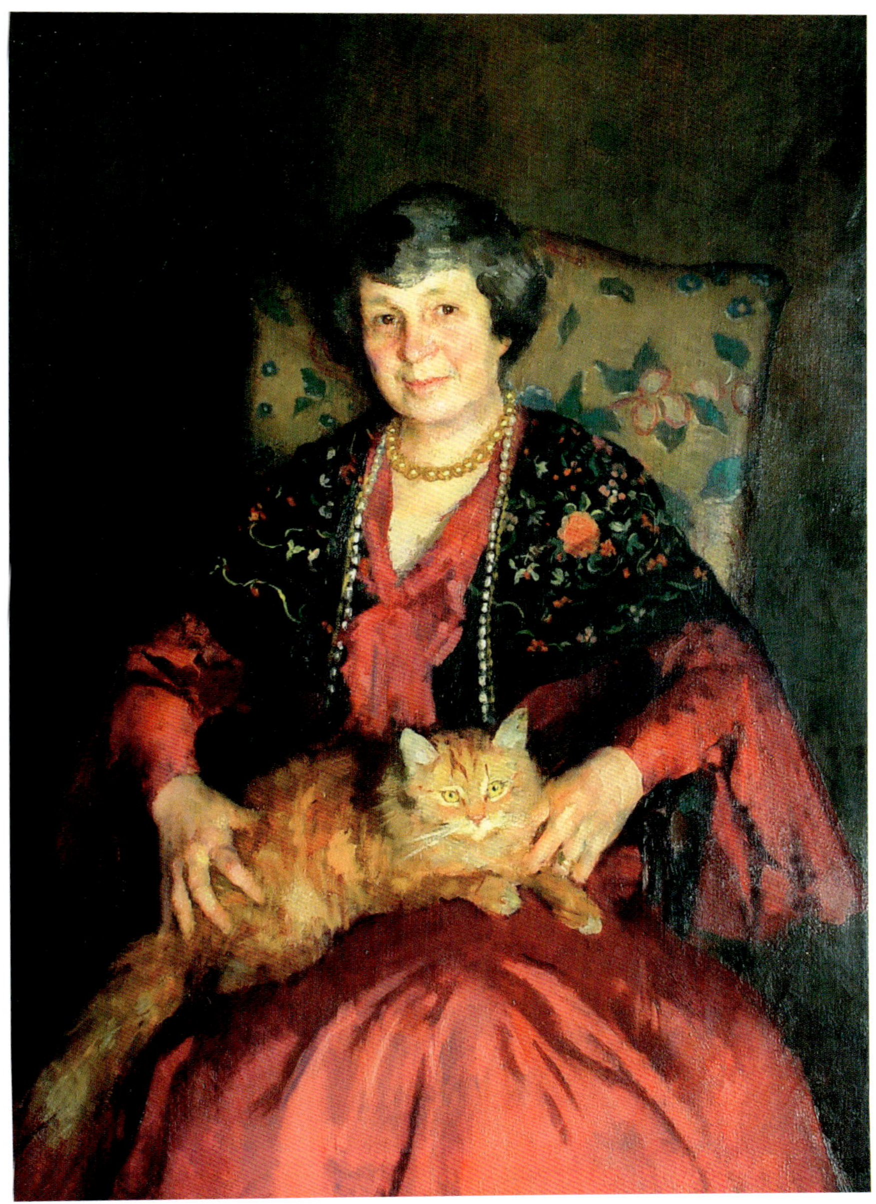

For my grandfather
Lyndon Jesse Howlett
Professor of Agriculture
Gardener
Antiquarian
Antiquer
and a founder of
The Men's Garden Club of America

Marie Danforth Page, American (1869-1940).
Gertrude and Galusha, 1935.
Oil on canvas, 50 x 40 inches. A portrait of the artist at age 66.
Private collection.

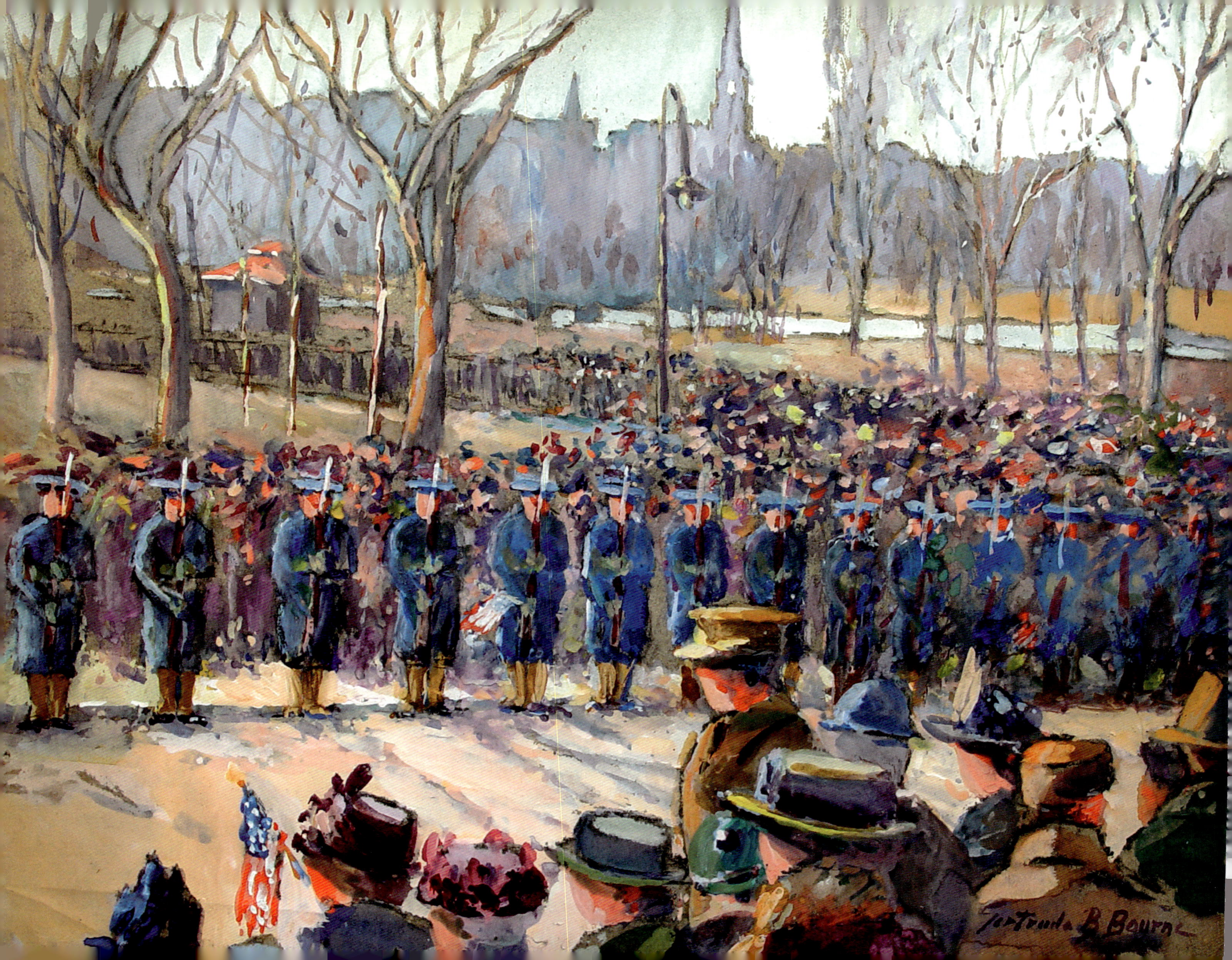
Gertrude B Bourne

CONTENTS

Marines Beacon Street Boston, February 24, 1919, 1919.
Watercolor and gouache on paper, 19 x 24 inches.
Boston fêted President Wilson on his return to the United States from France on February 24, 1919.
Courtesy of the Family of Philip E. Bourne.

AUTHOR'S NOTE

Gertrude Beals Bourne, like so many of her generation slipped from the consciousness of the public and scholars alike after the final exhibitions of her work and her death. The young Gertrude Beals was a child of privilege in one of the artistic and cultural capitals of the world. If Boston tended toward the self-congratulatory in the years when Gertrude was coming of age, it also had high expectations of its children. Women were able to pursue careers—especially in art. Gertrude's own great, great uncle, John Simmons, had left a legacy to found Simmons College to educate young women so that they could become independent. Unlike some of her female contemporaries, she chose both to have a career and to marry and have a son—to have it all. She seems to have been an early model of a liberated woman and to have succeeded in each of her duties.

Bourne did not leave published writings on her views on life or art. Much of what we know about her has to be inferred using her watercolors as manuscripts. Her son Philip was dedicated to the preservation of her work, reputation, and memory. However, in the 1980s as part of a storage space issue he had most of her paintings unframed and the original titles and labels were subsequently destroyed. Nevertheless, a good deal of reconstruction was possible. In the late 1980s a flood in the basement of Philip Bourne's house destroyed the contents of a trunk of her papers—letters, catalogues, and memorabilia from a lifetime of work. Fortunately Margaret Hani—now a professor of the history of art at Simmons College—had made careful notes on much of that material which she generously shared with me. In the chronology which follows the text I have indicated with an "*" that material which was drawn from Hani's notes and for which I have no other corroborating evidence. One issue that has arisen is the appearance of labels on surviving framed works where, in some cases, the institution where it was supposed to have been exhibited has no record of the work. This seems to indicate that the work was submitted to a venue but not accepted for exhibition.

There were three solo exhibitions noted by Hani that I have not been able to verify from newspaper or other accounts. The first two are the London exhibitions of the early 1920s at the Halcyon Gallery and the James Newman Gallery in Soho Square, and the other is an exhibition of Bourne's Moroccan works at the Boston Art Club following her visit to North Africa in 1927. Although I continue to believe that the exhibition took place, reading the *Boston Transcript* on a daily basis for 1927-29 has not identified a Moroccan exhibition for Bourne in its careful record of Boston exhibitions for the period.

In the fifteen years that Childs Gallery has worked with the Bourne Art Trust we have seen the acceptance of Bourne's work as a part of the body of watercolors by Americans from 1890-1940. The pioneering publications on Bourne by Margaret Hani for Simmons College and for the Essex Institute have considerably aided in reviving interest in Bourne and her work. It is my hope that this publication will continue consideration of Bourne as a bridge between Victorian and Modern watercolorists.

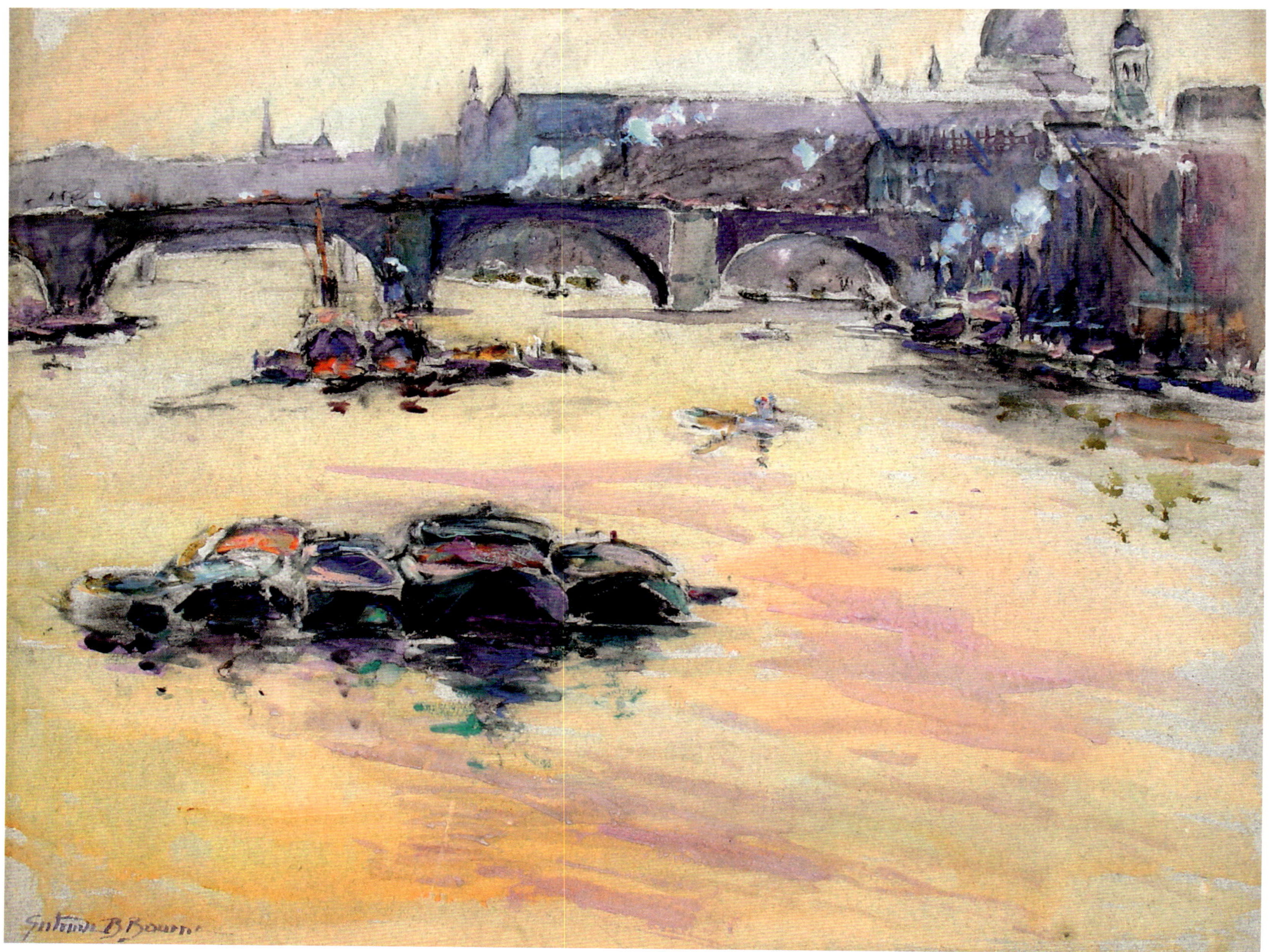

FOREWORD

'With much frankness, directness and crispness, with a good eye for color': Gertrude Beals Bourne as an Artist and Woman

One can imagine Gertrude Beals Bourne standing in the chill spring air, enveloped in layers of clothing, totally absorbed in focusing on the spots of color before her in the landscape or garden where she has set her easel. She dips her brush into the puddles of watered pigment squeezed out from paint tubes generally stored in her silver paint box and brushes pure color onto dampened watercolor paper. She probably will not show clouds or the sky in her composition, but instead will concentrate on the ways the elements of the landscape—trees, flowers, a pathway receding along a river—sparkle in the sunny quiet day. Perhaps she thought to herself, if indeed at such times there were room for such thoughts, "I am an artist. . . . That's what I do"—phrases of hers that ring in the memories of her descendants.

It is a mistake to think that the watercolors of Bourne, or of any other artist for that matter, are just fine arts objects to be exhibited and admired. Or that they are mere documents that give evidence of specific social histories—although they can certainly be interpreted as providing such evidence. From Bourne's viewpoint being an artist was what she would *do*. It was a process, a way of capturing those moments when she stood in front of a garden or architecturally interesting building or striking landscape and watched the sun brighten the natural hues. Experiencing the thrill of light and color, translating that three-dimensional reality into a composition on paper, coaxing the color from the brush was a process that took her out of her social role as daughter of a successful businessman, wife of an established architect, and mother to a growing son. It almost does not matter what she painted; to her, it was the act of doing it: "I am an artist...That's what I do."

London Bridge, 1923.
Watercolor, gouache, and charcoal on gray paper,
20 x 26 inches. Courtesy of the Bourne Art Trust.

Roger Howlett has written a fascinating biography in which we learn much about her family and the places where she lived.[1] She never went to art school, but she studied with the well-respected Boston artist Henry W. Rice and later with the New York artist Henry B. Snell. She traveled with her family to Europe on extended sojourns. We assume she went to the major art exhibitions in Boston during the 1880s and 1890s, where she would have seen the paintings of John LaFarge, John Singer Sargent, and Maurice Prendergast, Childe Hassam watercolors, J. Appleton Brown pastels, a lot of Claude Monet paintings, woodcuts by Arthur Wesley Dow, and an exhibition of Japanese art that Dow curated for the Museum of Fine Arts in 1896.[2] During this time she exhibited frequently at the Boston Art Club, a men's organization which did, however, include women in its exhibitions. In 1904 she also joined the newly formed artists' organization, The Copley Society, which admitted women on a par with men and where she would regularly submit watercolors for exhibition.

She insisted on and persisted in being an artist. When the family made a grand tour of Europe in 1892, she checked into the possibilities of studying at the well-respected Académie Julian, in which Boston artist Maurice Prendergast had enrolled the previous fall.[3] It was also known as a school where women could get training, and several Boston women had studied there.[4] When one reads that she did not seize the opportunity to study there, where she would have learned figure drawing, one suspects that Boston propriety intervened, since it might not have seemed proper for a young upper-class Boston lady to study unchaperoned in Paris. However, the art scene in Boston seemed to fill her needs.

By 1899 she took herself seriously enough to list herself in the *Boston Directory* as "artist," with a studio address at 264 Boylston Street. She was already in her 30s and a seasoned exhibiting artist, when in 1904 she married architect Frank Bourne, who would prove to be a husband supportive of her art career. Artistic himself, he and Gertrude counted among their friends the artists who lived in and around Beacon Hill. In 1917 and perhaps for a year or two more they rented a summer place in Ipswich, Massachusetts, from Arthur Wesley Dow. Although the birth of her son Philip in 1907 temporarily slowed her ambition to exhibit, one suspects that she probably continued painting her watercolors.

The big important exhibition for Bourne came in 1915 when The Copley Gallery mounted a show of twenty-one watercolors—views of architecture, gardens, and snow scenes. The reviews, reprinted here in Howlett's essay, were favorable. *The Boston Transcript* applauded the way the watercolors were painted "with much frankness, directness and crispness, with a good eye for color."[5] The reviewer especially liked her garden pictures, which "give Mrs. Bourne many welcome opportunities to indulge her predilection for bright, pure and brilliant color."[6]

It is not surprising that the garden pictures would stand out for special praise. She and her husband seem to have shared a delight in gardens. When they moved into 130 Mount Vernon, at the time of their marriage, Frank Bourne did some remodeling on the Tutor-revival cottage, including installing a Japanese garden. The name "Sunflower Castle," attached to the cottage, seems appropriate for a woman of Gertrude's sensibilities. "Castle" evokes the kind of privilege that was her social lot, and both "sun" and "flower" point to her sun-filled pictures of flowers. It was in her garden that she could create artistic and eclectic effects—installing potted plants to flank the fountain, painted concrete ducks to act as sentries, and window boxes to allow a profusion of flowers to cascade into the open spaces (p. 120). In the spring, as Howlett tells us, a "blaze of tulips" would greet visitors.

One of Bourne's greatest artistic endeavors was organizing the Beacon Hill Garden Club in 1928. As president for the first two years she rallied her neighbors to join in the efforts to make the tiny spaces in the backyards of houses gleam with green potted plants, flowers, trellises, garden furniture, bird baths, and other whimsies. The Club initiated garden tours the following year, which brought in income used to finance gardening projects for children. The tours have since become ongoing annual events. The Club also worked with the Massachusetts Horticultural Society, staging contests for their mutual benefit. Bourne and the other Garden Club ladies began to win ribbons for floral arrangements and handmade wreaths.[7] Bourne herself must have seen the tours as analogous to visiting exhibitions of paintings, with the added pleasure to the visitor of moving through three-dimensional space, breathing the perfumed-filled air, and basking in the sun (or the rain) that filled the tiny gardens.

During the 1920s Bourne continued to travel with her husband to paint touristic views of Europe and the more home-spun landscapes of New England, and to exhibit. As Howlett states in his essay: "Bourne always painted her surroundings and was a direct observer of nature." With a sharp eye for detail she matched a view or a corner of nature to the composition on her easel. Moreover, she did not seem to overintellectualize the process or become involved in the avant-garde debates over the relative merits of color versus drawing in painting.[8] This does not mean that she did not absorb influences from other artists or was not guided by the visual culture of postcards and travel book reproductions. For example, *Venice* (p. 84) seems composed much as would a tourist's picture postcard;[9] it is a view similar to one done in watercolor by Maurice Prendergast. And *Some Pumpkins* (p. 86), exhibited at the North Shore Art Association in Gloucester in 1928, shows the brightness of color and strong outlining of shapes that reminds one of the Ashcan artists John Sloan and Robert Henri, who had summered in Gloucester in previous years.

The death of her husband, Frank, did not seem to deter her painting activities. In 1937 she traveled to the Far West, through the Rockies and down into southern California. In the summer of 1939 she visited her son and his wife in Honolulu. Paintings from these trips were shown in exhibitions at Doll and Richards Gallery in 1938 and 1940, respectively. According to family memory, she simply did not quit as an artist. She was a lady—a well-respected matron living on Beacon Hill with both friends who were socially established and friends who were artists. But she was not a "lady artist." She saw herself as a professional with a long list of exhibitions. She kept her faith: "I am an artist . . . That's what I do."

PATRICIA HILLS
BOSTON UNIVERISTY

NOTES

[1] All factual information on Bourne comes from Roger Howlett, in this volume.
[2] This brief note of exhibitions in Boston was gleaned from Ellen Marie Glavin's dissertation, "Maurice Prendergast: The Development of an American Post-Impressionist 1900-1915," (Boston: Boston University, 1988) and Nancy E. Green, *Arthur Wesley Dow and His Influence* (Ithaca, NY: 1990), 8.
[3] Glavin, 19. Prendergast enrolled at Julian's in the fall of 1891. He also studied at the Académie Colarossi.
[4] For American women artists at the Académie Julian and Académie Colarossi, see Erica A. Hirshler,
A Studio of Her Own: Women Artists in Boston, 1870-1940 (Boston: Museum of Fine Arts, 2001), 76-78; and Kirsten Swinth, *Painting Professionals: Women Artists and the Development of Modern American Art, 1870-1930* (Chapel Hill, NC: 2001), 44-48.
[5] Quoted in Howlett, 67.
[6] Ibid.
[7] See Howlett, 90-96.
[8] See, for example, Charles Blanc, *Grammaire des arts du dessin*, trans. by Kate Newell Doggett as *The Grammar of Painting and Engraving* (New York: 1874) and Arthur Wesley Dow's teaching manual *Composition*, 1899.
[9] See postcard of the Piazza San Marco, 1897, reproduced in Nancy Mowll Mathews, *Maurice Prendergast* exh. cat. (Williams College Museum of Art, 1990), Fig. 12.

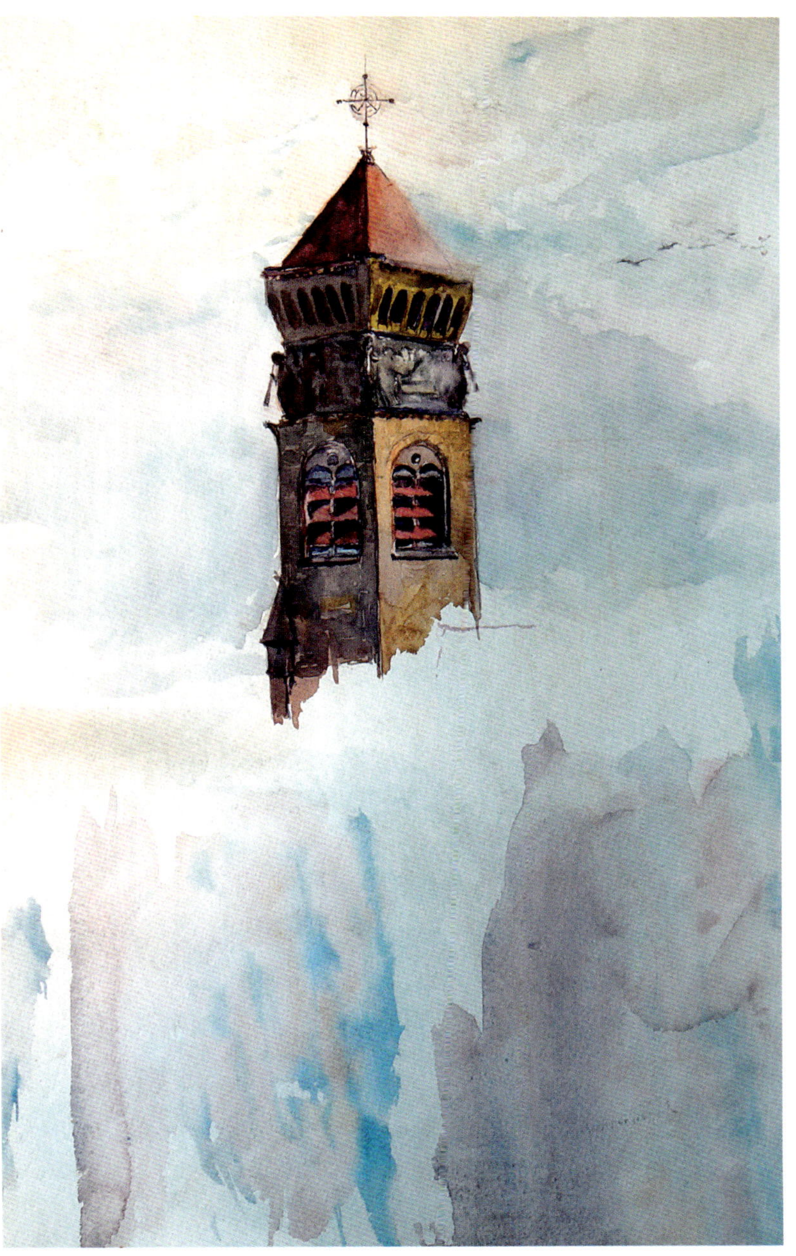

Tower of the First Baptist Church, Boston, c. 1890.
Watercolor on paper, 22 x 13 1/2 inches.
Located in the Back Bay at the corner of Commonwealth Avenue and Clarendon Street. It was built as the Brattle Square Church in 1871 and was designed by H.H. Richardson with a sculpted frieze by Frederic Auguste Bartholdi. The building was acquired by the First Baptist Church in 1882. Courtesy of the Bourne Art Trust.

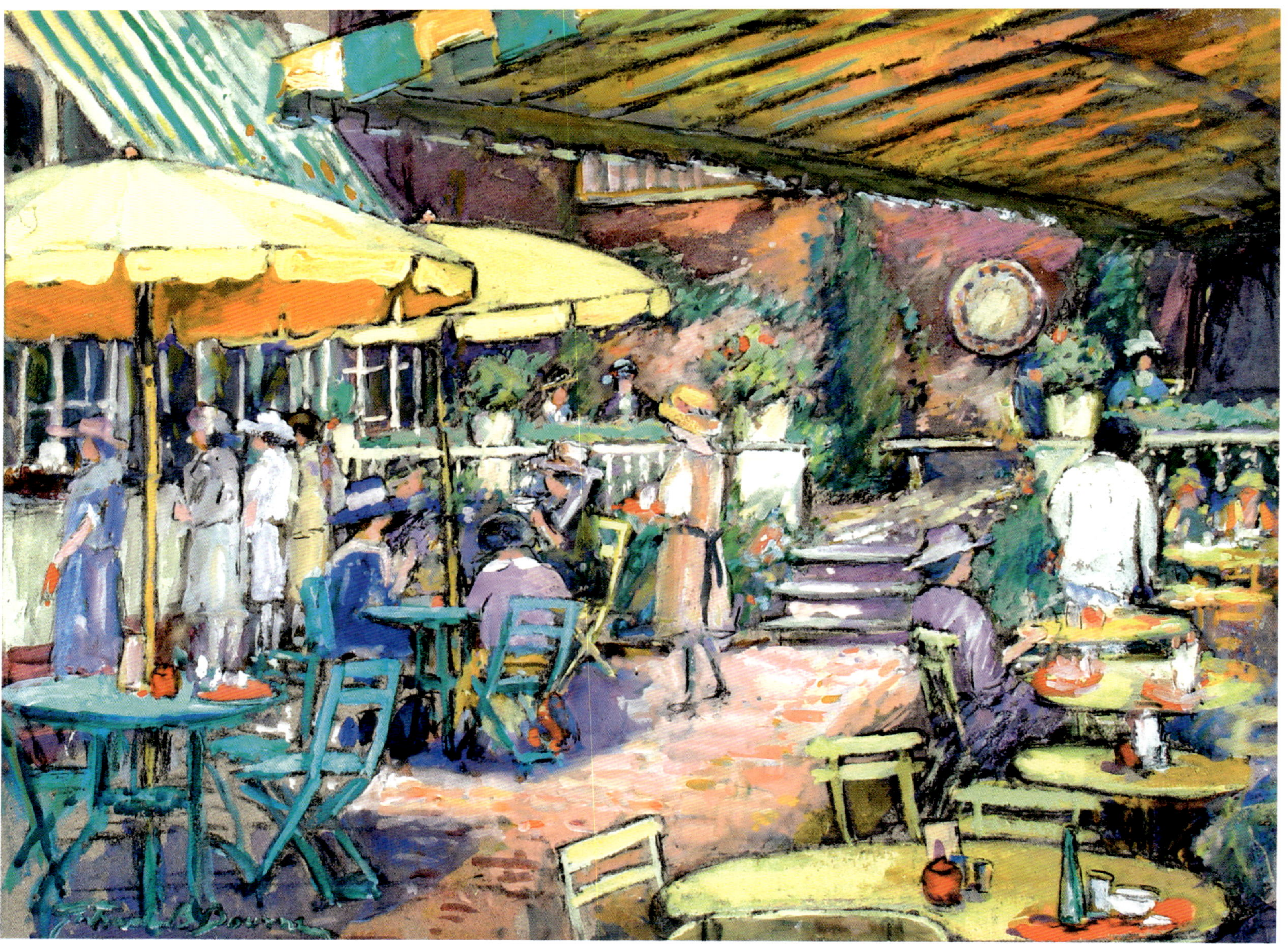

Garden of the Women's City Club (40 Beacon Street), c. 1925. Watercolor and gouache, 19 7/8 x 25 7/8 inches. Courtesy of the family of Philip E. Bourne.

PART ONE

THE BEALS OF BEACON HILL AND BACK BAY

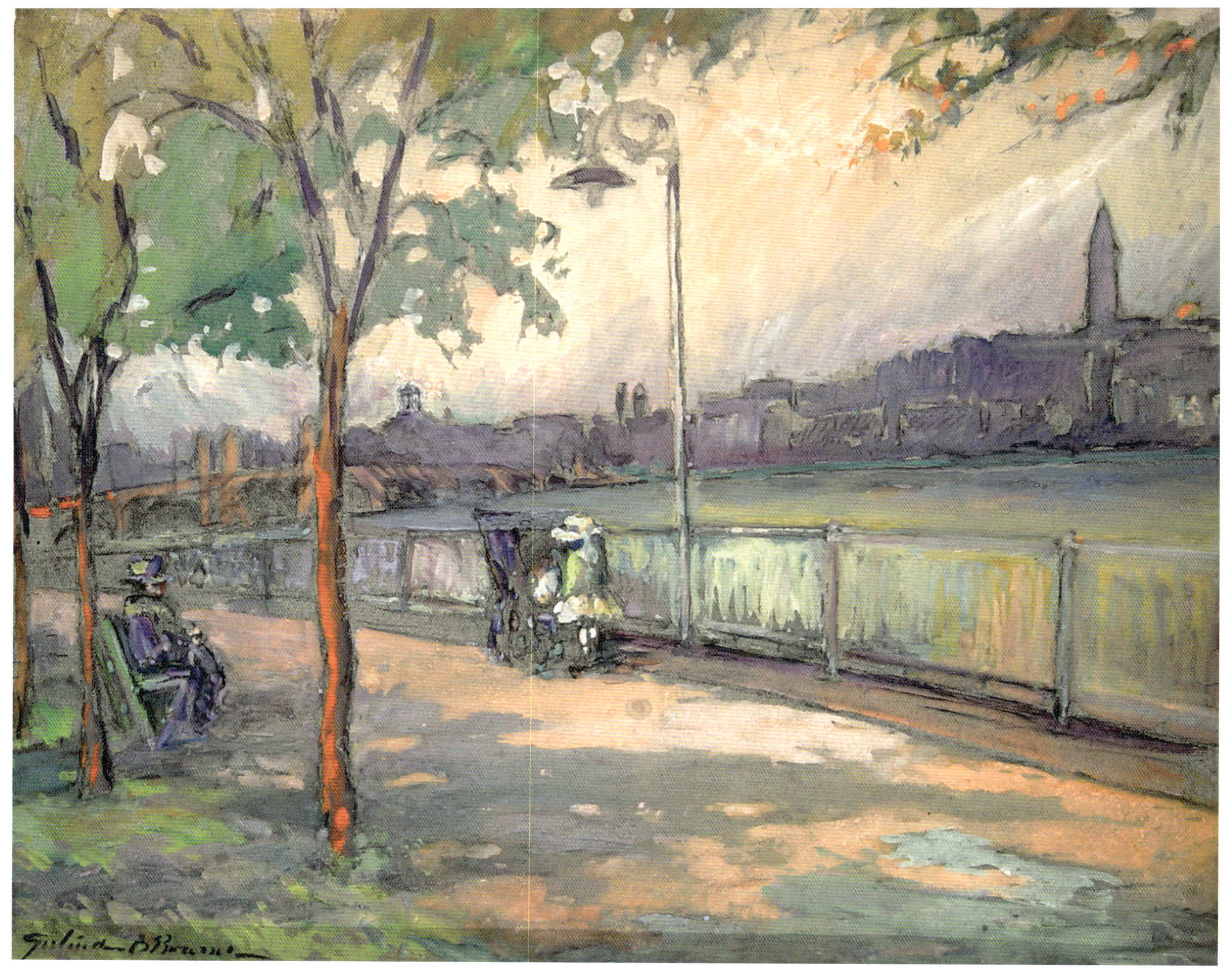

CHAPTER ONE

Family and Childhood Environment

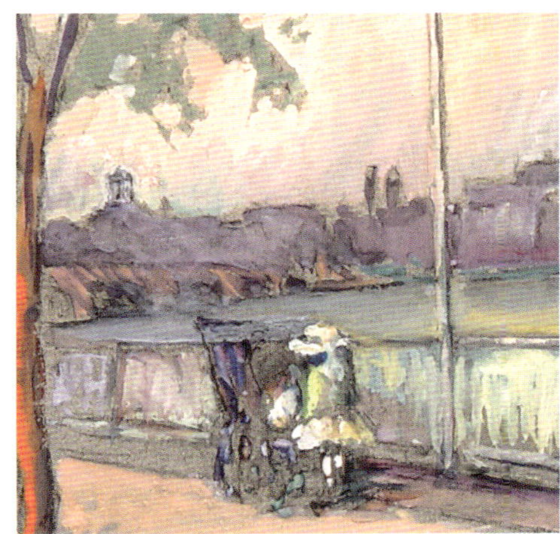

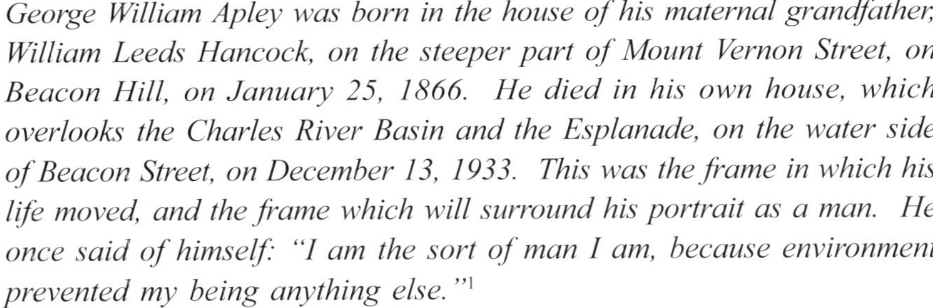

George William Apley was born in the house of his maternal grandfather, William Leeds Hancock, on the steeper part of Mount Vernon Street, on Beacon Hill, on January 25, 1866. He died in his own house, which overlooks the Charles River Basin and the Esplanade, on the water side of Beacon Street, on December 13, 1933. This was the frame in which his life moved, and the frame which will surround his portrait as a man. He once said of himself: "I am the sort of man I am, because environment prevented my being anything else."[1]

— John P. Marquand, *The Late George Apley*

Gertrude Beals Bourne inhabited the same sort of world as the "Late George Apley." The fictional George Apley and Gertrude Beals Bourne—the subject of this book—are virtual contemporaries. Bourne "outlived" Apley by more than thirty years, but each may be framed in the special environment of a narrow Brahmin society in Boston's Beacon Hill and Back Bay. Gertrude Beals Bourne and the fictional George Apley lived the same upper-class life, in the same environment, and each pressed the edges of a constraining social structure. The problem was set forth by John Marquand for Apley: "I have the most curious delusion that our world may be a little narrow."[2]

The question Marquand asks implicitly for Apley and we ought to ask for Bourne is: to what extent were their characters able to understand, break out of, or rise above the constraints of that society? How were they each limited by Brahmin Boston and how were they each able to take advantage of its resources? Marquand portrays Apley as born into its social elite and perfectly fitted to the expectations of Boston society. Bourne and her family were a little removed socially from the center of Brahmin society, which could translate into the desire to conform even more than Apley, or the ability to walk away from some of its chief dicta. She chose to marry outside of Brahmin society—not even a Harvard man; to establish her married household in a community of artists; and to form many of her lasting friendships among artists and architects. Yet she seems never to have lost a taste for imposing Brahmin standards on others: she set up one of the most respected Boston institutions with some of the most meticulous standards, the Beacon Hill Garden Club. The life of

View of the Charles River and the Esplanade from Cambridge, c.1915.
Gouache on gray paper, 20 1/4 x 26 3/4 inches.
Courtesy of The Bourne Art Trust.

Bourne may be set out with additional challenges: she was a woman in a man's society, she had to cope with an onrush of societal changes in the 1940s, 50s, and 60s, and she was serious about her life as an artist.

There were models before Bourne for life as a serious woman artist in Boston society that could not have been lost on her. Yet the majority of Boston women artists in the period of her artistic life—1890-1960—dabbled in art as an avocation, which made convincing her society of the seriousness of her chosen work much more difficult for Gertrude.

Gertrude Beals was born on May 21, 1868 into a comfortable upper-middle-class family on the periphery of Brahmin Boston.[3] At that time, the *Boston Post* reported that *Othello* was playing at the Boston Museum, that Miss Frances Anne Kemble was reading Schiller's tragedy *Mary Stuart* at Horticultural Hall, and that the New Orleans French Opera was performing Offenbach's *Orpheus* at the Boston Theatre. Property owners were given notice of the widening of Tremont Street from the Masonic Temple to the Providence and Boston railway station. The great medicinal virtues of Poland Spring water were touted.

The *Boston Post* reported in the same issue that, for their zeal in attempting to rid the country of President Andrew Johnson, the pro-Impeachment forces were coming in for criticism themselves: "Impeachment managers will rule and regulate the affairs of the whole country, public and private, if they can. Just now they are making ready to bring the Senate to trial for not having voted on Impeachment as they demanded." In the evening on the day of Gertrude Beals' birth General Ulysses S. Grant was nominated as the Republican candidate for President of the United States with Schuyler Colfax as his vice-presidential candidate. The southern states in reconstruction did not yet have full complements of representatives or senators in Congress or delegates in the political conventions, and Negro suffrage was a major issue with both radical and conservative politicians.

The *Boston Post* also announced a sale of paintings the following week which included works by Paul Weber, Frederick Rondel, Arthur Parton, T. C. Oliver, Edmond Darch Lewis, James M. Hart, Thomas Hewes Hinckley, S. L. Griggs, Benjamin Champney, A. F. Bellows. W.M. Brackett, George Loring Brown, A. T. Bricher, and J. Appleton Brown. With the exception of the latter painter, the group firmly represented the second generation of the Hudson River School. J. Appleton Brown, however, would become one of the most committed New England Impressionists. The works by these painters and their circle, along with European painters of the same generation, would find their way into the houses of Gertrude Beals' youth and help to form the first understanding of contemporary art for the young painter or art student.

Proper Beacon Hill

When Gertrude was born her father, Joshua Gardner Beals, was a junior partner in the family firm of Beals, Greene & Co., publishers of the *Boston Post*. His father William Beals, his uncle James H. Beals, and two members of the Greene family completed the principals of the firm. William Beals, Gertrude's grandfather, was described by R. P. Shillaber in the *Boston Post* in 1881:

> The counting room was presided over by Mr. William Beals, who as a newspaper financier was unsurpassed. He was always at his station in office hours, a man of the strictest integrity, but whose manner to those who did not understand him was not seemingly of a very gentle make, yet he was a man of sterling qualities, was liberal in his charities and never withheld his aid when help was needed. I am pleased to say this, for I had frequent occasions to test it. It is wonderful how the miserable find their way into printing offices, or it was so then: dead beat printers to be helped on their way home, dilapidated editors recovering from sprees, needing a little help, women seeking assistance for sick husbands at home. Lots of such cases came to us right along, as if the *Post* were regarded the home of all the

William Beals and Dolly Whitney Beals with their ten children. c. 1854. Joshua Gardner Beals stands prominently in the back row. Left to right standing: Harriet Matilda (Tuxbury), Joshua Gardner, Maria A. (Flagg), Emily Caroline (Mitchell), Francis Augusta (Baker); seated: James Henry, Elizabeth Bishop (Kendall), William Beals, Dolly (Whitney) Beals, William, Jr., Louise Annie (Weatherbee), John W. Courtesy Bourne Art Trust.

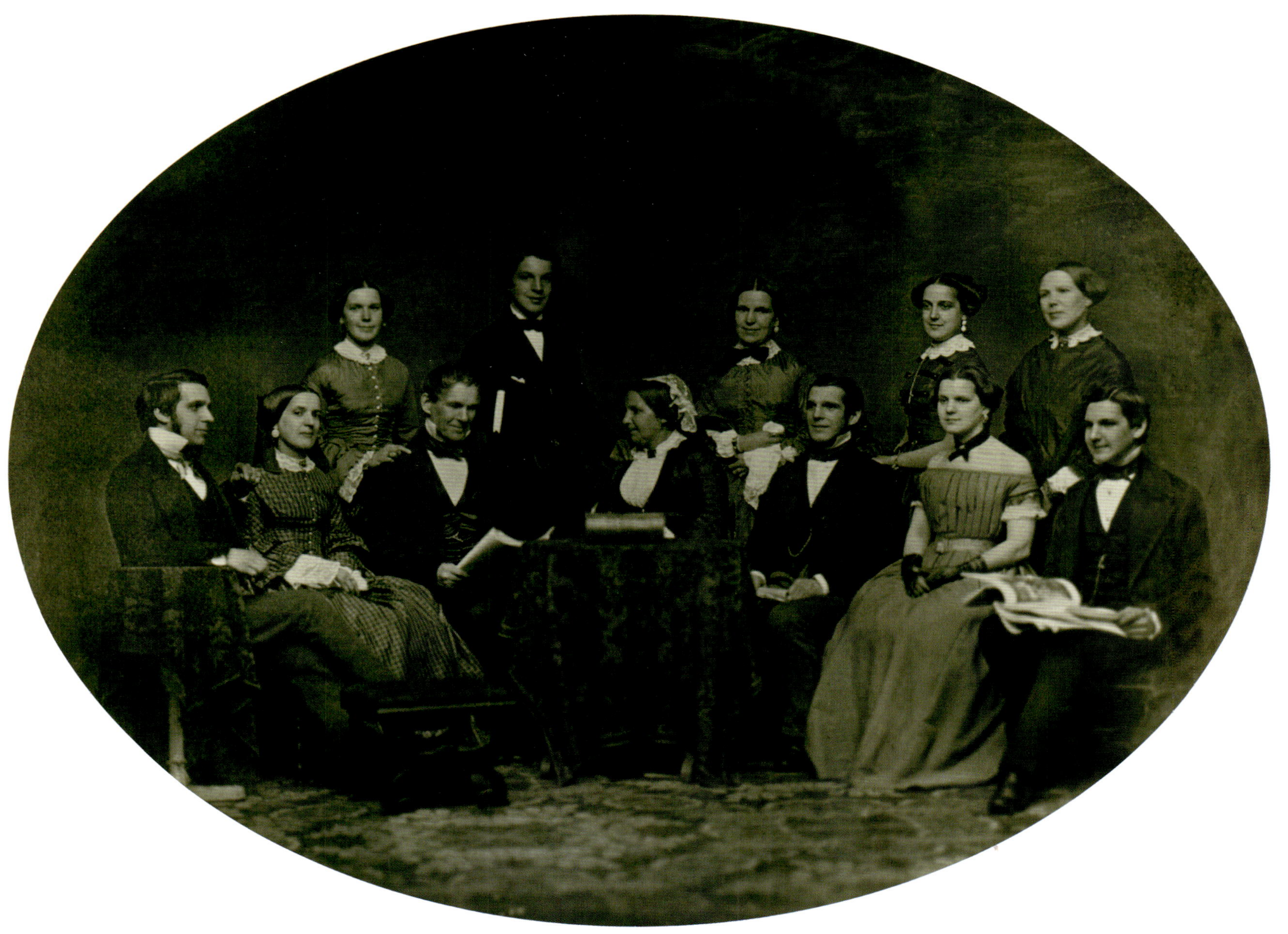

benevolences. On occasions of this kind it was my custom to go to Mr. Beals with my own statement of the case and ask his aid. He never refused me nor overwhelmed me with cross-questioning, but he gave without a word. He rarely spared me for blunders, which he abominated, but he would offset his severity by after kindness, and he won my profound respect.[4]

In this Dickensian atmosphere, Gertrude's father was born, was educated, and worked.

Joshua Beals was born in Boston August 25, 1836, the youngest of ten children. He was educated at Boston Latin School where he received a Franklin medal for scholarship,[5] he graduated from Harvard with the class of 1858 where he had taken the Boylston Prize for elocution in 1857, he entered Harvard Law School for one term in the autumn of 1858, and he then joined the *Boston Post.*[6] In 1861, he received an AM from Harvard. Fellow classmates at Harvard included the writer, Henry Adams, and the distinguished minister, Henry Wilder Foote. From 1859 until his marriage in 1865, Joshua Beals lived with his parents, William Beals and Dolly Whitney Beals, at 39 Hancock Street in Boston, just behind the Bulfinch's State House on Beacon Hill.

In 1865, Joshua became a publisher of the *Boston Post.*[7] On October 25 of the same year Joshua Beals and Edith Ware Simmons were married in the Congregational-Unitarian New South Church at Church Green on Summer Street in Boston. The Reverend Orville Dewey, who had served as minister of the church from 1857-1862, was invited back to the church to perform the Beals' ceremony.[8]

Edith Simmons was the daughter of George W. Simmons and the grandniece of John Simmons, both of whom worked in the clothing business. While her father was a successful businessman and owner of George W. Simmons & Co. clothing and furnishing goods, her great uncle John had been credited with founding the ready-made clothing business in the 1830s, by which he made a considerable fortune. He had begun in business with Edith's grandfather, Cornelius Simmons, who died in 1822. John's clothing business had grown to such a degree that, before 1844, he occupied the second floor of Quincy Market facing the water. Simmons was doing the largest wholesale clothing business in New England and had the first traveling sales agents in the West. Simmons invested his profits in Boston real estate which added to his fortune. He may be considered one of the pioneers in developing the Back Bay, having hired Gridley F.J. Bryant to design and erect for him numbers 1 and 2 Arlington Street in 1861.

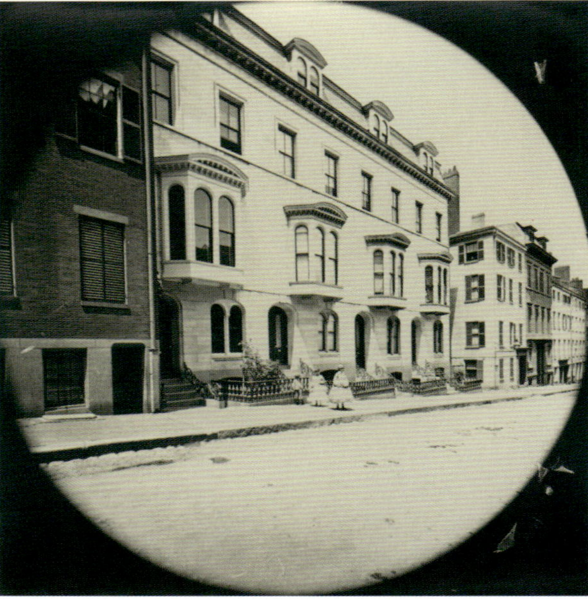

39, 37, 35, 33 Hancock Street, c. 1855-65. Joshua Beals grew up in 39 Hancock, the furthest left in the white complex. Photograph by J.J. Hawes. Courtesy of The Boston Athenæum.

In 1899, the trustees of John Simmons, following the directives of his will, founded Simmons College in Boston to provide free instruction and education for girls to acquire an independent livelihood. There is little question that even after his death in 1870, John Simmons held a major place in the consciousness of the entire Simmons family, including young Gertrude Beals.[9] Family respect for John Simmon's directives may have affected young Gertrude to believe that she could—and should—have an independent life.

George W. Simmons took a somewhat more local view in his clothing business, but one that was impressive enough. At the time of Gertrude's birth Simmons' flamboyance had made his "Oak Hall" business name synonymous with the first recognized brand name in ready-made clothing. He took full-page advertisements in the *Boston City Directory* indicating that the goods

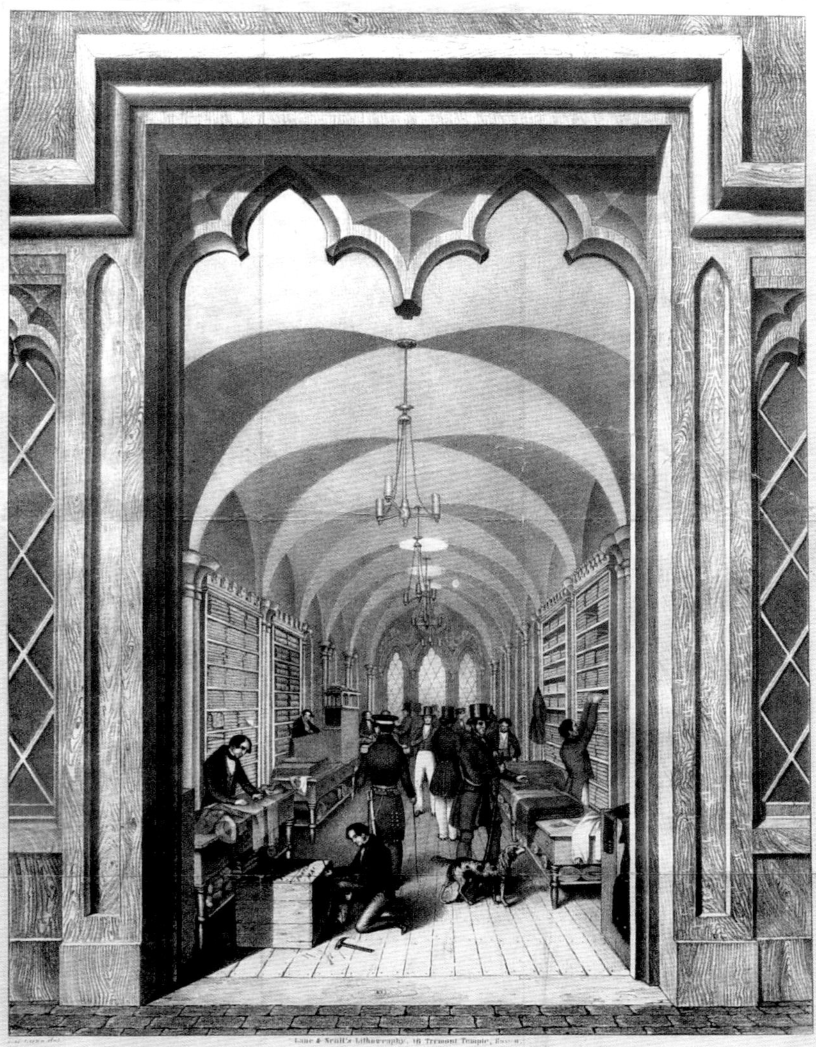

were "manufactured expressly for the New England Retail Trade." Oak Hall renown was wide. The noted author and poet, Oliver Wendell Holmes, Sr., used the ready-made clothes company's name as a simile; in order to show his faith that there would be an audience for verses, *The Old Man Dreams*, that were not written for an occasion or a particular person he used "Oak Hall".

> You will understand by the title that [the verses] are written in an imaginary character. I don't doubt that they will fit some family man well enough. I send it forth as "Oak Hall" projects a coat, on *a priori* grounds of conviction that it will suit somebody. There is no loftier illustration of faith than this. It believes that a soul has been clad in flesh; that tender parents have fed and nurtured it; that its mysterious *compages* or framework have survived its myriad exposures and reached the stature of maturity; and that the Man, now self-determining, has given in his adhesion to the traditions and habits of the race in favour of artificial clothing; that he will, having all the world to choose from, select the very locality where this audacious generalization has been acted upon. It builds a garment cut to the pattern of an Idea, and trusts that Nature will model a material shape to fit it. There is prophesy in every seam, and its pockets are full of inspiration. [10]

Perhaps, in using Oak Hall Holmes was returning the favor of appropriating an identity. Simmons had "borrowed" from Holmes' fellow-poet, Longfellow, when he purveyed poems as part of his advertisements that he attributed to "Professor Goodfellow." The attribution was not lost on Professor Henry Wadsworth Longfellow who wrote to his friend Sumner in the spring of 1850: "Simmons of Oak Hall has carried his poetic joke so far as to put my name at full length over his doggerel advertisement. I wish you would take such steps as may be necessary to stop this."[11]

Fitz Hugh Lane, American (1804-1865)
George W. Simmons' Popular Tailoring Establishment, Oak Hall, Boston**,** 1844. Drawn on stone by Fitz Hugh Lane. Lithograph by Lane & Scott, Boston. Courtesy of The Boston Athenæum.

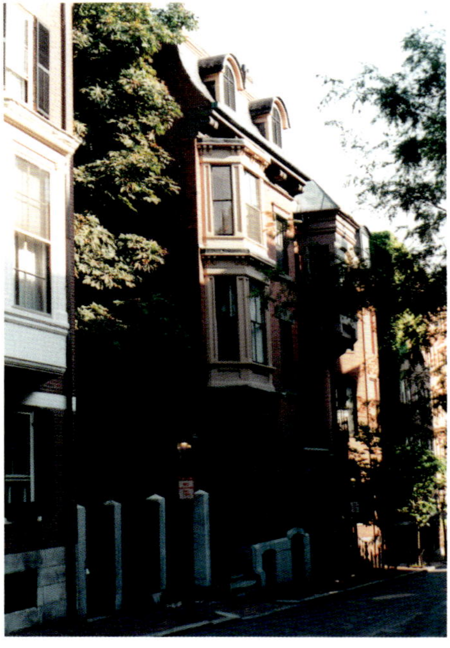

Simmons irritated more people in Boston Society than just Longfellow. He had come from Little Compton, R.I. and made his own social rules in Boston and at his summer residence at Nahant. His lack of social tact—which must have been palpable for his daughter, Edith, and the rest of the Simmons family—was expressed when:

A New York newspaper correspondent asserted that: The Nahantese drive fast and compress their nostrils, it is said, as they pass the place of 'that person Simmons,' presumably to express their displeasure." This is confirmed by the Palfrey ladies when they found themselves fellow-boarders in Bulfinch's with Simmons' daughter and son-in-law [perhaps John W. and Virginia Simmons Beals] in 1865. "I don't think we are likely to see very much of them," Mary Ann snobbishly remarked. That George Washington Simmons could care less was confirmed by the New York correspondent when he observed that Simmons "feeds hourly upon the displeasure and antipathy which he excites."[12]

In Boston, George W. Simmons and his wife, Frances, occupied a comfortable house on the south, the "proper," side of Beacon Hill at 6 Walnut Street. Beacon Hill in the 1860s was a circumscribed area with an active, if conservative, social life. Edith had been sent to the Sedgewick School in Lenox, Massachusetts for a proper education.[13] It was not difficult for a young man like Joshua from Hancock Street to find his way around Mt. Vernon Street to the door of 6 Walnut; the trail had already been blazed by Joshua's older brother, John W. Beals, when he courted and married Edith's older sister, Virginia. After marriage, Joshua Gardner and Edith Simmons Beals set up housekeeping at 8 Pemberton Square at the east side of Beacon Hill where Gertrude was born three years later. In 1869, they moved to 419 Beacon Street.[14]

The State House was then the center of Beacon Hill and the senior Beals' house was located just to its north, the Simmons' house just to its west, and Pemberton Square just to its east. And the Oliver Wendell Holmses, senior and junior, were living on the western side of Beacon Hill at 164 Charles Street. By 1868 nearly every Bostonian knew these lines of Dr. Holmes:

> The axis of the earth sticks out visibly through the center of each and every town or city ...[so] Boston is just like other places of its size;—only, perhaps considering its excellent fish market, paid fire-department, superior monthly publications, and correct habit of spelling the English language, it has some right to look down on the mob of cities. I'll tell you, if you want to know it, what is the real offense of Boston. It drains a large water-shed of its intellect, and will not itself be drained. If it would only send away its first-rate men, instead of its second-rate ones (no offense to the well-known exceptions, of which we are always proud), we should be spared epigrammatic remarks as that which the gentleman quoted...[viz.] *Boston State House is the hub of the solar system. You couldn't pry that out of a Boston man if you had the tire of all creation straightened out for a crowbar.* [15]

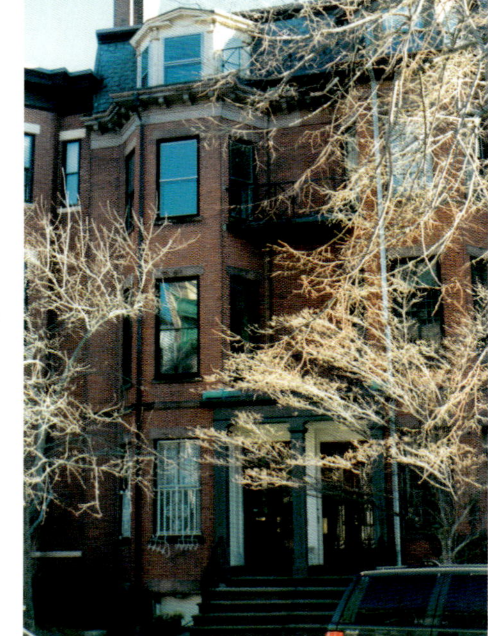

left: **6 Walnut Street**, c. 2000
right: **419 Beacon Street**, c. 2000

The Fashionable Back Bay

Old Boston of Beacon Hill, the North End, the downtown, and the waterfront had become crowded and, in places, overwhelmed by the growth of the city in the first half of the nineteenth century. Visionary plans for the improvement of roads, water supplies and the addition of a public garden were on a minor scale compared to the additions that would take place to the land area of Boston itself. The city in the next fifty years would grow by annexation, but Boston would also grow significantly by making land itself. Between 1857 and 1900 over 450 acres were added adjacent to Beacon Hill and the Boston Common by filling the back bay of the Charles River. Those families with older or newly increased fortunes and an interest in the amenities that new developments could provide, quickly opted for lots in the Back Bay.

The South End, which had been the subject of a similar project of filling tidal marshes before the Civil War, never achieved the status of the Back Bay. The fictional Apleys had been confronted by this problem. George Apley noted:

> [Thomas Apley, my father] bought this house on Beacon Street when the Back Bay was filled in, and this leads me to a single amusing instance of his unfailing business foresight.
>
> Shortly before he purchased in Beacon Street he had been drawn, like so many others, to build one of those fine bow-front houses around one of these shady squares in the South End. When he did so nearly everyone was under the impression that this district would be one of the most solid residential sections of Boston instead of becoming, as it is today, a region of rooming houses and worse. …One morning, my father, who had not gone down to his office at the usual early hour because he had a bad head cold, came out with us to the front steps. I could not have been more than seven at the time, but I remember the exclamation that he gave when he observed the brownstone steps of the house across the street.
>
> "Thunderation," Father said, "there is a man in his shirt sleeves on those steps." The next day he sold his house for what he paid for it and we moved to Beacon Street. Your grandfather had sensed the approach of change; a man in his shirt sleeves had told him the days of the South End were numbered.[16]

Thomas Apley's remarks reflect the judgements made by Brahmin society and the circle of wealthy Bostonians that young Gertrude knew—that the Back Bay would represent the area of the city for the residences of those that had achieved both social and financial respectability.

Gertrude's great-great uncle, John Simmons, was not the only Boston merchant prince who had constructed on this former marsh. On Beacon Street and on the wide, Paris-like Commonwealth Avenue, the wealthy Brahmin families and the newly rich alike vied for the correct lot and the correct and tasteful design for a house. The sunny side or north side of Beacon and Commonwealth were much to be preferred over the shady south sides. Corner lots were also at a premium. The names of the new owners of the houses with sunny exposures in the blocks of Beacon and Commonwealth closest to Beacon Hill showed a greater wealth and lineage than those owning other Back Bay properties. The wealthiest owners in the Back Bay engaged their own architects and had their houses built to their individual tastes.

Young Joshua Gardner Beals bought a house on the shady side of Beacon Street between Gloucester and Hereford Street, seven blocks from Beacon Hill that had been developed as a part of a seven-house project in 1869. Still, the Beals had a respectable new house in the Back Bay and on fashionable Beacon Street, even if it was a little far west.[17] The 29-year-old proprietor of the *Boston Post* and his 23-year-old wife hired Jane Campbell and Bridgett Zahne, 25 and 23 years of age, as domestic servants to live in and take care of the household.[18] The new residence of Joshua and Edith Beals was larger than that of either of their parents' Beacon Hill residences. After the death of her husband, Joshua's mother moved to 281 Dartmouth Street, and Edith's brother, George W. Simmons, Jr. moved to 5 Fairfield Street — both thus taking up Back Bay residences in the early 1870s.

Edith Beals might have been attempting to repair her reputation as the daughter of the publicly-pilloried George W. Simmons—an effort that apparently continued for the rest of her life. Edith seems to have wanted all of her children to make the 'right' friends under the 'right' circumstances; Joshua was less concerned.

The Great Boston Fire

The newspaper business in Boston, as in many American cities in the 1870s, was oversupplied with daily papers. The *Boston Post* was competing with the *Boston Globe*, *Boston Herald*, *Boston Advertiser*, *Boston Journal*, *Boston Times*, *Daily News*, *Traveller*, and *Transcript*. Beals, Greene and Company was also publishing the semi-weekly *Boston Press and Post*, and the *Boston Statesman and Weekly Post*. The greatest Boston story of the 1870s would affect the lives and fortunes of most every man and woman in the city for years to come. Undoubtedly, the four and one-half year old Gertrude would later remember it well.

On Saturday evening November 9, 1872 a fire began in a building on the southeast corner of Summer and Kingston Streets. It worked up Summer Street to Washington Street and then took the entire business district to the south and east, laying waste to everything until it burned out at the harbor.[19] In less than twelve hours the fire destroyed more than sixty acres of the financial and manufacturing district and $75,000,000 in property.[20] On November 14, G..W. Simmons placed a "Loss by Fire—Clothing Alone $4,000,000" advertisement in the *Boston Post*. Although Simmons' Oak Hall at 34 North Street was a number of blocks north of the fire, he used the opportunity to create a "fire sale"— a sale that may have been occasioned by either smoke damage or business acumen. The large loss may refer to other merchants and the advertising meant to direct buyers to his stock, which had survived.

The *Boston Post* at 44 Devonshire Street was the last building standing on the edge of the burned area — but the water which firefighters poured onto the building ruined much of the printing equipment and supplies and placed the publishers at a competitive disadvantage from which it struggled to recover.[21]

On Monday, November 11, the *Boston Post* bravely put out a broadside edition instead of its usual four pages. The next day's paper included a lengthy apology, possibly written by Joshua Beals:

> It is not with the purpose of parading our individual trials for commiseration in the midst of such great misfortunes on every hand; but as an apology due the public for the many shortcomings that appeared in our yesterday's issue, in to-day's and that will possibly appear for some little time longer, that we allude to the experience of the Post in the great fire. The flame that swept northward to Milk street, and thence made a detour of the new Post Office, to swoop upon the prey from which it was barred by the iron and granite of that building, crept up to our very walls. The Post Building alone stands on Water street, in the space from Devonshire eastward to the limit of the burnt district. That the building was saved at all is one of those occurrences we are accustomed to call miraculous.... By prompt action the fire was restrained within close limits and extinguished; but the composing room was left a ruin of shattered glass, plaster, and debris of roof and walls, the editorial and other rooms on the next floor beneath, and indeed even down to the lowest story, were drenched with water, and the building was, during Sunday, not only useless as a publishing office, but well-nigh uninhabitable. Moreover, although the presses were safe and the type had been conveyed to a place of security, the disarrangement and the inevitable mixing, the loss, and the destruction through hasty handling, rendered the material nearly useless. It was only by strenuous exertion, while walls were falling and the fire yet crackling close at hand, that a portion of the type was transferred again to the building, and the half sheet paper there set up and printed for yesterday's issue. It appeared, as does this, from within the guarded confines of the burnt district, with the smell of smoke upon it; and when our readers consider that our type foundries have gone, with so many other industries, and that the means of rehabilitation are made difficult in every direction they will perhaps appreciate why, although the Post Building has falsified all the predictions of Sunday morning, and still stands, the paper is somewhat curtailed in portions though uncrippled in spirit.[22]

This reversal in the prospects of the *Boston Post*, and his father no longer being a partner (he had died in 1870), undoubtedly contributed to Joshua Beals' decision to sell his shares of the *Post* in 1875. As part of the sale, the City of Boston purchased the old Post Building at the corner of Devonshire and Water

Streets for $325,000.[23] Later in 1875 the *Boston Post* and Beals, Greene and Company moved its offices to 17 Milk Street. This provided cash in the firm at a time when an outside buyer, The Reverend Ezra Dyer Winslow, made a bid for the *Boston Post*. He offered a small sum in cash for the *Post* and gave notes for the balance of the purchase price, which was completed through the sale of stock in a new company. Winslow was a slippery character who eventually left Boston and the United States ahead of a grand jury indictment and, by careful reading of extradition treaties, chose to settle in Buenos Aires and run a prosperous newspaper, *The Buenos Aires Herald*. By 1876 Beals, Greene and Company had ceased to exist.[24]

In light of subsequent troubles for the *Post* the Beals family seems to have been either remarkably foresighted or lucky in selling their interests at this time.[25] Trying to determine how much this may have meant in dollars to Joshua G. Beals versus the other members of the Beals and Greene families is impossible, but Joshua may have settled for a sum well into six figures at a time when a day laborer made a dollar a day.

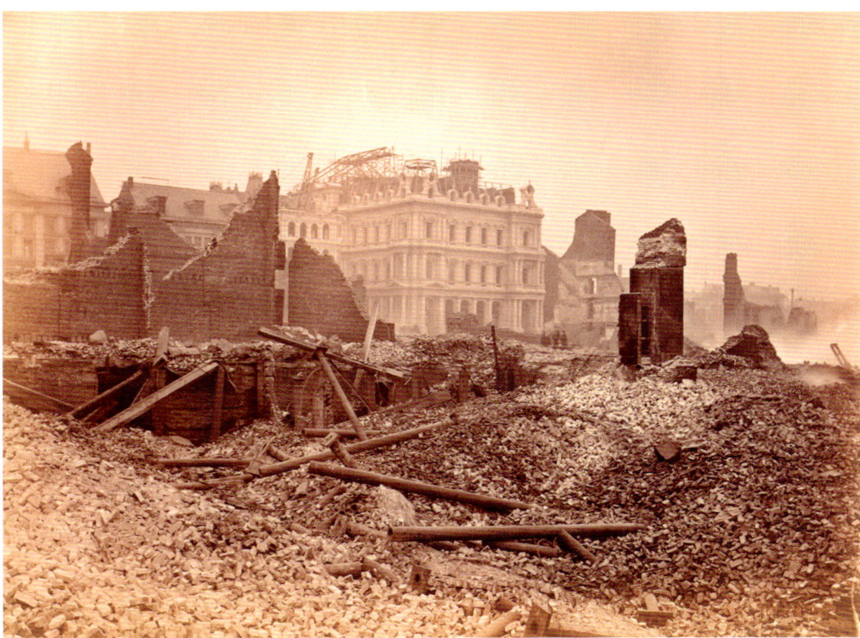

The New Post Office behind the rubble of the Great Boston Fire, 1872. The rooftops of the Boston Post Building can be seen just to the left of the Post Office. Courtesy of the Boston Public Library.

The Beals Move to New York

Following the deaths of his parents and the trauma of the fire Joshua may no longer have felt the need to remain in the "family" business or in Boston. After being out of business for a year and a half he formed the partnership of Beals and Foster with Edward W. Foster, a New York newspaper advertising agent who had been working with the New York Newspaper Union at 148 Worth Street in New York City. The newspaper unions consolidated advertising for businesses, giving advertisers a one-stop purchase for advertising in regional papers. Beals and Foster seem to have been the first to imagine a grand, national consolidation of newspaper unions—in effect a national advertising agency—and set themselves up to represent the unions as the unions represented the regional papers. Beals described that "they were the general agents of the New York, Chicago, Milwaukee, St. Paul, Cincinnati, and other 'Newspaper Unions.'"[26] Beals could have brought any necessary capital to the partnership. Joshua Beals appeared in the New York City Directory in 1878 at 41 Park Row as a newspaper-advertising agent—but refused to give his first name. Young Gertrude later remembered living in New York during this period with her parents and her eldest brother.

The next year Joshua's older brother, James H. Beals, Jr. (1823-1896), arrived in New York and became president of the New York Newspaper Union. Having the family represented as the head of Beals and Foster's most powerful client union was certainly an aid to success. Beals and Foster moved to 10 Spruce Street where they continued through 1880, when the firm was dissolved, and Joshua Beals and his family returned to Boston.[27] He was credited by at least one source with starting the New York Newspaper Union as well as developing a Boston branch "in which business, on his return to Boston, he was engaged until his retirement."[28] What may have happened is that Beals and

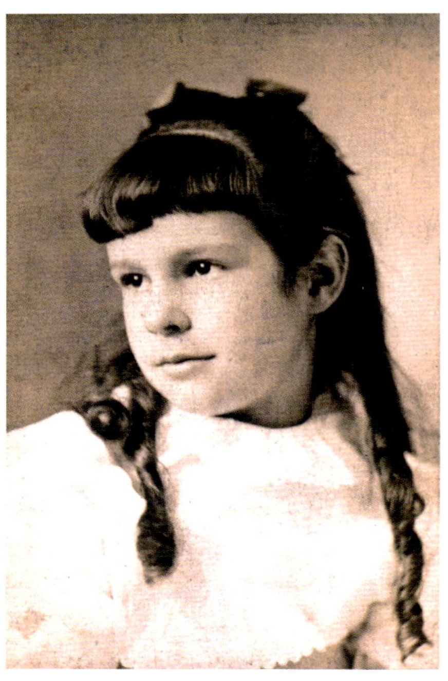

Foster folded their business back into the New York Newspaper Union with James H. Beals as a party to the deal. This would explain how Joshua may have had a financial interest in such a firm without having to be actively engaged on a daily basis.

In 1880 the Beals family re-established themselves at 419 Beacon Street. Joshua retired from active business, but seems to have maintained business interests which required him to travel and, for at least some of the 1880s and 1890s, to keep an office in New York.[29] Meanwhile, Edith and Joshua Beals had added two sons to the family, Gardner Beals, born January 14, 1873, and Sidney Lane Beals, born April 22, 1880. Joshua Beals joined several clubs: the Boston Athletic Association, the University Club of Boston, the University and Harvard Clubs of New York, and the New England Society of New York.[30]

A Boston Palazzo — Comfort and Culture

In 1886, the Beals family moved to 328 Dartmouth Street. The architectural historian, Bainbridge Bunting, wrote of this house and its neighbors:

> The most successful Academic Brick design (and perhaps the handsomest house in the whole Back Bay) was built in 1871 at 165 Marlborough Street. Designed by Snell and Gregerson for T. F. Cushing, but acquired soon after its construction by William C. Endicott… Standing on the northwest corner of Marlborough and Dartmouth streets, the house is part of a group of three closely related structures [165 Marlborough, 326 and 328 Dartmouth]. Although each house is a complete entity, the three units of design fit together to create an impressive whole. Seen from Dartmouth Street, the two end houses form pavilions which rise half a story higher than the center section, a relationship which is effected by a clever manipulation of floor levels. The end pavilions are marked by bay windows that are carried through to the cornice, and they are accented by a double dormer window plus a slight forward projection in the mansard roof. The pavilions serve to emphasize the self-contained quality of the composition. The entrance of number 328 has been inserted in the right octagonal bay in order to maintain a just balance with its pendant in the other corner. … The proportions throughout the whole group are so excellent and the relationships of its various parts are so skillful that one receives the impression that the building is much larger than it actually is.[31]

Although larger palaces were being built on Beacon Street and Commonwealth Avenue, the Beals family had a Back Bay house worthy of all but the largest social pretensions. Incorporating approximately 10,000 square feet with formal parlors and entertaining space, there was also sufficient room for Gertrude to have a separate studio for painting.

Although he had an office in New York, Joshua Beals had, in the 1880s, both the time and the money to travel with his family. Joshua had been successful in business and had invested

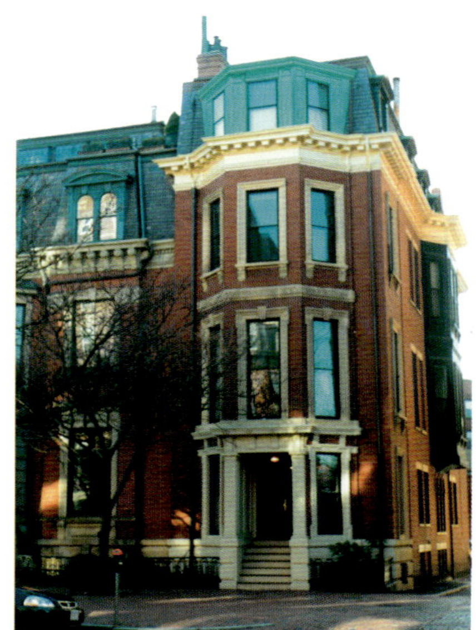

left: **Gertrude,** age 9.
right: **328 Dartmouth Street**, c. 2000.

his capital wisely. Edith's father George W. Simmons died December 13, 1882 as a very wealthy merchant and landholder of his generation,[32] and though he had five other living children, he passed a significant legacy on to his daughter.[33] A cultured and leisurely life had become a Boston ideal in the years following the Civil War. The initial fortunes founded on maritime trade and amplified by manufacture and investment had created a prosperity among Boston's social elite that permitted an aristocratic indifference to the pursuit of wealth or the appearance of work. Dr. Oliver W. Holmes words were published in 1886:

> What better provision can be made for mortal man than such as our Boston can offer its wealthy children? A palace on Commonwealth Avenue or on Beacon Street: a country-place at Framingham or Lenox; a seaside residence at Nahant, Beverly Farms, Newport or Bar Harbor; a pew at Trinity or King's Chapel; a tomb at Mount Auburn or Forest Hills; with the prospect of a memorial stained-window after his lamented demise, — is that not a pretty programme to offer a candidate for human existence?[34]

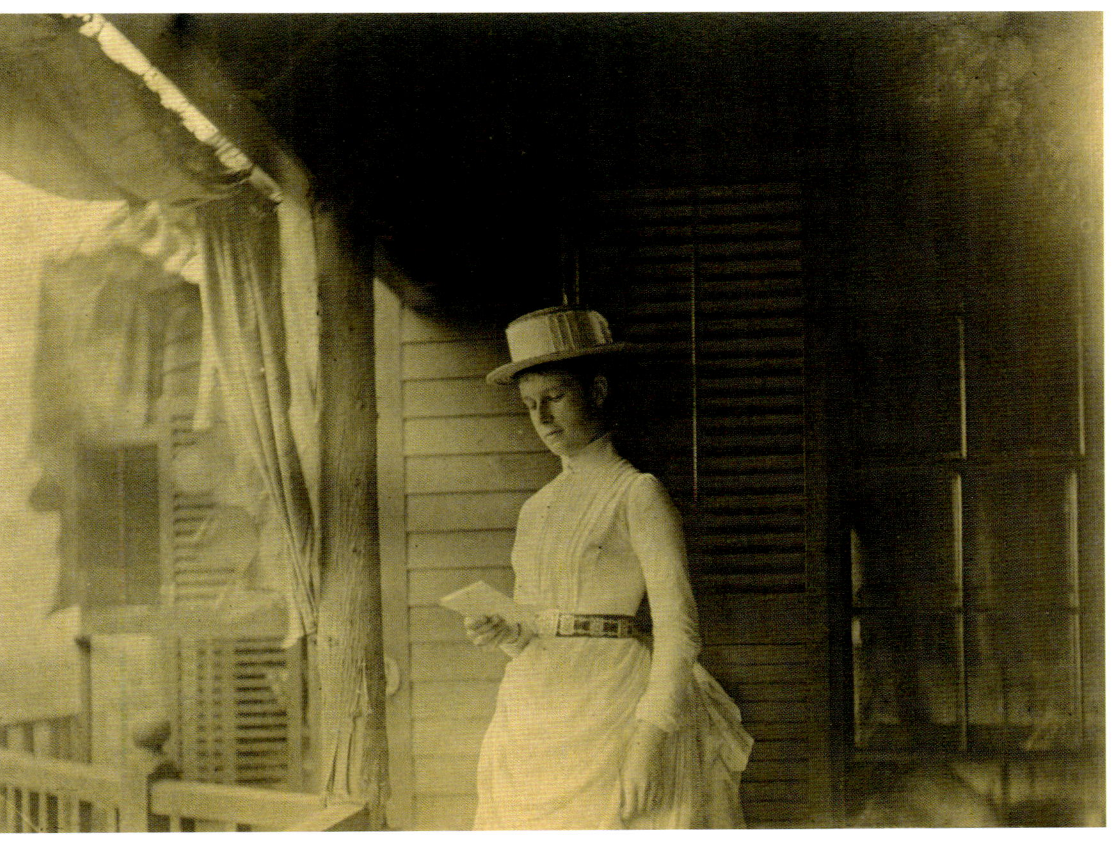

Gertrude, age 19, in Dublin, New Hampshire

For the Beals family a summer house in Nahant was soon added although it would seem that from 1882 to 1898, when a purchase of a portion of the Simmons' Nahant property was made by Joshua Beals, the use of a Nahant house was a courtesy extended to the late George Simmons' daughter by his estate.[35] Summer adventures seem to have been an annual event. Houses were rented. The family traveled to cultural capitals and natural wonders, and even experienced an elegant version of trekking in the back woods. Gertrude, and presumably the rest of the family, spent August of 1887 in Dublin, New Hampshire, which combined the vistas of rural New England with an elegant summer colony where elegant Bostonians such as Mary Amory Greene invited artists to join them in the summer. Greene, the great-grandaughter of John Singleton Copley, was then taking painting lessons from Abbott H. Thayer and would, the next year, build a house for him beginning his long residency in Dublin. While Thayer may have visited Dublin in the summer of 1887, it is also possible that Gertrude Beals was among the first young artists to summer in the region

Culture, or at least the appearance of culture, had become the great game. Even those engaged in the high finance of the 1880s such as Henry Lee Higginson, Joshua Beals' close contemporary, had a divided allegiance between business and culture. Higginson's first love was, perhaps, music, and if he could not be a player or composer, at least he could found the Boston Symphony Orchestra. Higginson had also traveled extensively in Europe since his first days at Harvard and such travel was considered a necessary part of a cultured Boston family's life.

The Beals, like Higginson, were Unitarians—the ultimate humanist successor to the Calvinist founders of New England. The philosophy extolled the virtues of good works and an excellent life, but was almost totally non-doctrinaire. They belonged to the Arlington Street Church at the corner of Boylston Street, about five blocks from the Dartmouth Street house.[36] Religion seems in the Beals' household, and later in the Bourne's, to have set a solid foundation of belonging within the community, but there is little evidence that either the Beals' senior or Gertrude took an active role in church life.

The Boston that Gertrude had re-entered from New York in the early 1880s was burgeoning, financially, physically, culturally, and artistically—and her family's house in the Back Bay placed her in the very center of it. Boston was a major art center in the late nineteenth century, with Copley Square as its heart. The Massachusetts Institute of Technology building where drawing and watercolor were taught was one block from Copley Square, the Museum of Fine Arts was directly on the square, and the Boston Art Club had broken ground one building off the square at Dartmouth and Newbury Streets (a little more than two blocks from the Beals' house) in 1881. The Boston Art Club had been founded in 1854 to bring together working artists, business professionals, and community leaders. It was the oldest art club in Boston and was in its heyday in the 1883-1909 period. The ratio in the club of businessmen to artists at this period was approximately seven to one.

One critic from *The Art Amateur* described the new club as: "Fronting on the grand square already surrounded by Trinity Church with its great tiled tower, the Art Museum with its broad terra-cotta bas-reliefs, the new "Old South" with its lofty campanile and Byzantine lantern, and blocks of towering French apartment houses the new art club will be emphatically "de son temps," a monument to the sumptuous "solid" period in which old Boston is settling down to luxurious enjoyment of the well-earned fruits of generations of thrift, enterprise, industry and cultivation." The club was budgeted at "not far from a hundred thousand dollars. Is there another art club anywhere in the New World or the Old?" It promised to provide "the luxurious privacy of the club proper and the public use of the gallery for periodic exhibitions."[37]

Other construction projects for the arts abounded in the Back Bay of the 1880s. At the same time as the building of the Boston Art Club there was the simultaneous construction of a grand gallery in the Back Bay for the Massachusetts Charitable Mechanics Association, "an immense structure, no less than six hundred feet long, built of brick and stone which will include, besides the art gallery, a great hall for meetings and concerts."[38] The construction began in 1883 on the new building for the Massachusetts Normal Art School, which had been founded in 1873 to train public school teachers in art and later expanded to offer courses for artists. The new building opened in 1886 on the corner of Newbury and Exeter Streets. And the Boston Public Library was begun on Copley Square in 1887. The School of the Museum of Fine Arts had opened next to the museum in 1877, and the Cowles School of Art had just opened in 1883 on Dartmouth Street.

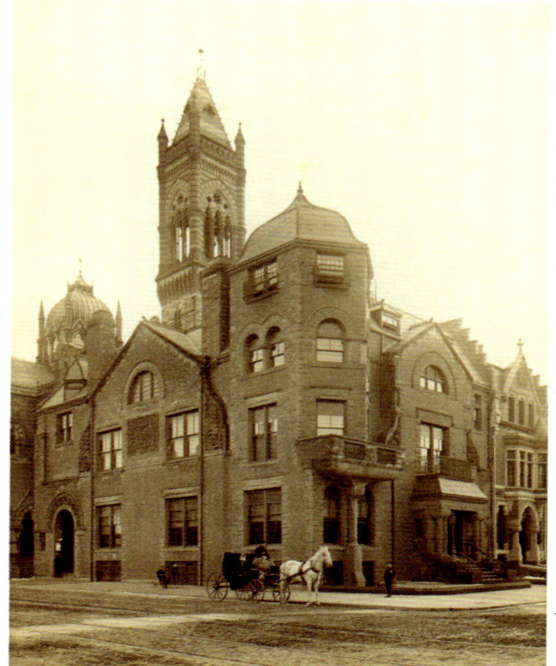

Boston Art Club, c. 1883
Showing the corner of Dartmouth and Newbury Streets.
Courtesy of The Boston Public Library.

Impressive exhibitions were planned and executed in Boston of the 1880s. Impressionism was the newest style to reach New England, and it was adopted by both collectors and artists with enthusiasm. Gertrude Beals should have seen the Foreign Exhibition of 1883 which included hundreds of paintings by French, Italian, and Spanish artists. Claude Monet (*Custom Station Dieppe*; *My Garden*; and *Tide at Varengeville*), Edouard Manet, Eugene Boudin, Camille Pissarro, Pierre Auguste Renoir and Alfred Sisley were included. These might have been the first works by French Impressionists that Gertrude had ever been able to see. By the late 1880s Bostonians of the Beals' set in the Back Bay were buying works by Monet and Boudin. Boudin was given a one-man show at the J. Eastman Chase Gallery in May 1890, and Monet was given his first non-commercial exhibition at the St. Botolph Club in 1892. Childe Hassam, who had been studying in Paris and had adopted the style of the French Impressionists, was given a first watercolor exhibition at Williams and Everett in Boston in 1882 and a second there upon his return from his first trip to France, in 1884.

Painting or modeling in clay was an accepted social accomplishment as well as a way of making a living. Many Bostonians of old and respected Brahmin families, as well as the general population in Boston and other parts of the country, accepted the principal that art in general, and painting in particular, was an acceptable pursuit for a young man or woman. The "Athens of America" was in an unprecedented period of construction and many of the buildings erected in the area of Copley Square housed galleries for art exhibitions or classrooms for teaching art in a period when Gertrude would have been making decisions about a career in painting.

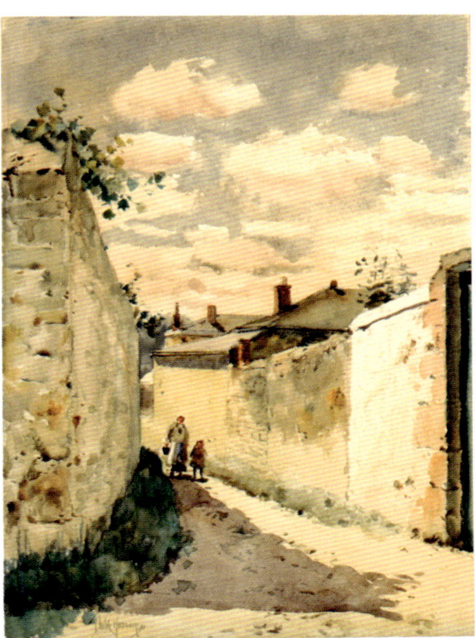

Childe Hassam, American (1859-1935)
Street -- Auvers-Sur-L'Oise, 1883.
Watercolor on paper, 12 x 8 15/16 inches. Courtesy Childs Gallery, Boston.

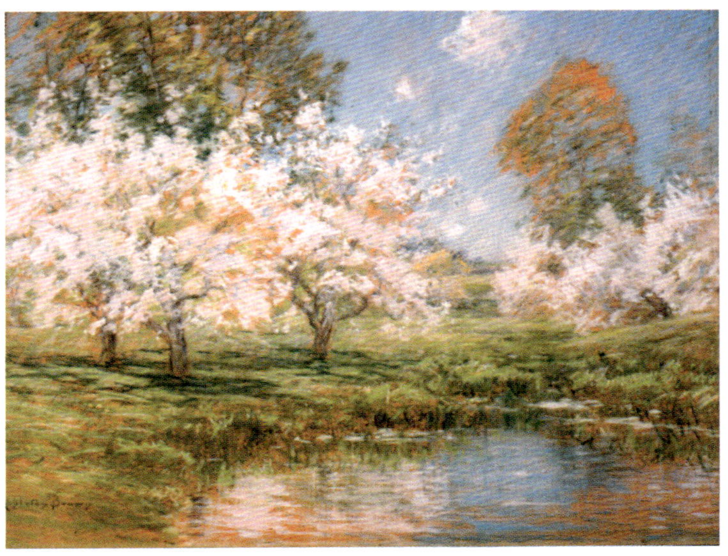

J. Appleton Brown, American (1844-1902)
Apple Blossoms, c. 1890.
Pastel on board, 18 x 21 1/2 inches. Courtesy Childs Gallery, Boston.

The Back Bay was a work in progress during this same period. Lots had been sold for both public and private development, and some had been built upon while others remained vacant. But the new construction had, by today's standards, an unusual feature: the Back Bay, as well as Beacon Hill and the South End, was filled with artists' studios. If after 1886 Gertrude had a studio in the Dartmouth Street house, she was by no means unique. Large buildings were built incorporating studios as a major part of their rental space, and many private houses had upper floor studios either for rent or for the artist of the household. Today, walking through these areas of Boston, one has only to glance up at the north sides to see the tall studio windows of the ateliers of the past. The larger edifices included the Harcourt Studios, the Studio Building,

St. Botolph Studios, the S. S. Pierce Building, and the Grundmann Studios (named after the first artist-director of the School of the Museum of Fine Arts), adjacent to the Museum of Fine Arts and Trinity Church. The Grundmann Studios was the site of the meetings of the Boston Art Students Association, which gave an annual festival in Grundmann Hall; and the square was the site of the Artists' Ball.

Boston Women: Education and Opportunity

We know that the Simmons family had a deep commitment to education—including female education. Her father and brothers went to Harvard, and her mother had gone to the Sedgwick School in Lenox, Massachusetts. Although we know little about Gertrude's formal academic schooling, two books in the Bourne family give clues. In the flyleaves of *Rosa* by Madame Elise de Pressensé, published in 1874 in French "with a French and English vocabulary," young Gertrude shows her attachment to the book with her pencilled couplets (which appear in the flyleaves of this book). We can posit that she was studying French by age six or a little later. In the front flyleaf of *Outlines of the World's History*, published in 1879, is Gertrude's signature, the 419 Beacon Street address and the inscription "'83 - '84 / Miss Ireland's School-." Since the Beals were at 419 (again) from 1880 to 1886 and Miss Catherine I. Ireland listed her school in the Boston City Directory from 1881, we can suppose that fifteen year old Gertrude was studying world history and other subjects at Miss Ireland's School at 9 Louisburg Square on Beacon Hill during 1883 to 1884. We might surmise that Gertrude studied with Miss Ireland through the early 1880s. If she was studying on Beacon Hill at age fifteen and sixteen, she probably did not go away to finishing school as had her mother. She was almost certainly tutored and given private lessons in French and piano—and later could not understand why each skill would not be an accomplishment within the education of any young lady. In 1888 Gertrude turned 20 and had acquired the finish of a young Boston woman of the educated and prosperous classes. In the first years of the nineteenth century, drawing—often including watercolor—had been a part of a young lady of Gertrude's social standing's education. It is not clear if Gertrude had the chance to learn to draw as a part of her general accomplishments. Opportunities for "schoolgirl work" in drawing and watercolor were in decline, but other opportunities were replacing them.

In Boston, in the latter 1880s, for the first time there was not only art education available to women—since at least 1850 a succession of schools and instructors, including the Lowell Institute, the School of Design (1851), William Rimmer, William Morris Hunt, Helen Mary Knowlton, the School of the Museum of Fine Arts Boston, the Massachusetts Normal School of Art, and the Cowles School of Art—but there was also a growing belief that women could be successful artists on the same footing with men.[39] In 1889 the Boston City Directory listed, in addition to the Cowles School and the Massachusetts Normal School, 28 private teachers of drawing and painting. And the result of the new opportunities for the teaching of women as artists could be seen at the galleries of Williams and Everett in February of 1888 when fifteen women—all former Hunt pupils—showed their work.[40]

It is difficult to determine just when young Gertrude began to wish to be an artist. As noted above, the teaching of young women in Boston by serious painters had been given greater respectability by William Morris Hunt from the late 1860s until his death in 1879. Hunt had taken on many promising young women; some were destined to become Sunday painters, but some, like Helen Mary Knowlton, were to become professional artists and teachers in their own right. By the late 1880s a number of women painters and sculptors were making their way as artists as a respectable means to (in the words of John Simmons) "acquire an independent livelihood."

Situated only two brief blocks down Dartmouth Street from the Joshua Beals' house, the Boston Art Club's new home was a tangible art presence in the neighborhood that would prove, over a forty-year period, to be the most consistent and visible venue for Gertrude's paintings. The club seems in retrospect, however, to have had a curiously ambivalent policy towards women and women artists in particular. Only gentlemen could be members, but ladies could exhibit. Gentlemen members and their gentlemen guests could enter the club and view exhibitions at any time, whereas ladies were invited to view

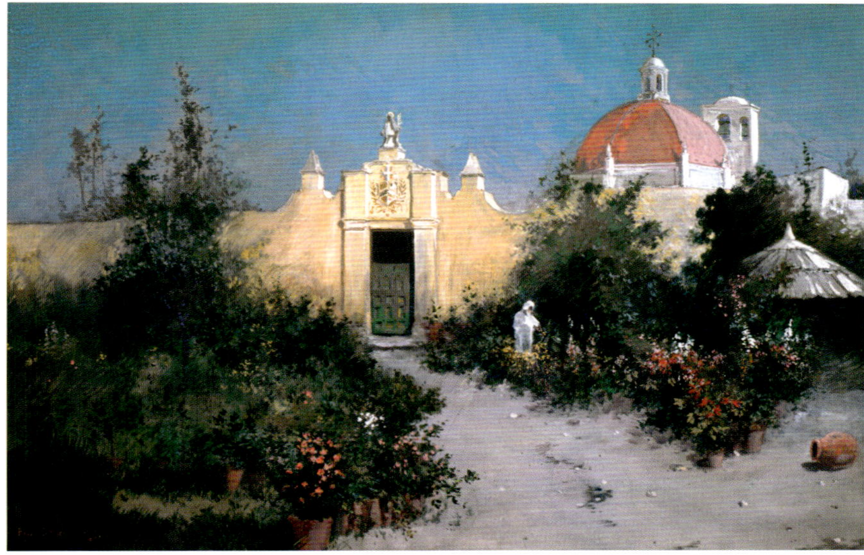

Ross Sterling Turner, American (1847-1915).
Old Church, Mexico, 1898.
Watercolor and gouache on paper, 17 1/2 x 26 1/2 inches.
Turner's prominence within Boston's artistic community, his use of gouache with watercolor, his extensive travel for subject matter, and his combining of gardens and architecture all may well have affected Gertrude Beals choices in medium and subject.
Courtesty Childs Gallery, Boston.

exhibitions accompanied by a gentleman member during openings and "when and as the House Committee may from time to time direct."[41]

We may infer that these rules were in effect from an early date; although women members were allowed at the beginning in 1854, they were excluded at the time of the adoption of the charter and constitution in 1873. The two entrances were undoubtedly planned as a part of the clubhouse in 1881, but no codification of the rules was placed in "House Rules" until 1912. This change was almost certainly a result of the perceived need by 1912 to regulate both men and women, as suffragettes were advocating for women's rights and access, and for the vote. The 1912 "House Rules" stated that gentlemen could use the main entrance on Newbury Street, but ladies, or ladies accompanied by a gentleman, would use the 'ladies entrance' on Dartmouth Street. Thus, while the club clearly admitted that women artists could be talented professionals and their works could hang in the general juried exhibitions alongside the works of men, they were not equal and most certainly were separate. We may suppose from later characterizations of her personality as both strong and opinionated, that Gertrude had more than one comment on that policy.

The Boston Art Club was not the only artists' society in the Back Bay. There were also the male-only St. Botolph Club (1880), known for its sophistication, innovation, and exclusivity; the Paint and Clay Club, which attracted many younger artists; and the male-only Boston Society of Water Color Painters (1888). The Boston Art Students Association (1879) was originally formed by alumni of the museum school, but in 1891, it opened its membership to non-alumni, and in 1901 changed its name to the Copley Society. The Association of Boston Artists (1880) aided its artist members in selling paintings, and the New England Manufacturers' and Mechanics' Institute (1879) ran annual fairs in the 1880s and 1890s with an ambitious art department.

The only club that was founded as a women-only society was the Boston Water Color Club, formed in 1887 as a counterpart to the Boston Society of Water Color Painters. In 1896 it admitted men. Gertrude Beals would have noted this women-only watercolor club and it could have contributed at a formative age to her appreciation of watercolor. In an interesting comparison between the men-only Boston Society of Water Color Painters and the Water Color Club "Greta" wrote in *Art Amateur* in January of 1889:

> This has been a month of water-colors here. The Boston Water-color Society, which is composed of thirty or so young painters of established reputation, makes a pretty, cheerful, and in every way pleasant and creditable exhibition. Seriousness and ability mark nearly every work. Things are generally carried out to finish in a clean, thorough, accurate and yet not niggled or labored style. Some visitors have thought they discovered a tendency to the English manner of water-color. But it seems to me distinctive from that—although neither kaleidoscopic in brilliancy, like the Roman, nor impressionistic and watery, like the French, nor literal and brown, like the Dutch—as the American

Elm from the English elm. It is an excellent combination or compromise of qualities, apparently the judicious choice of men mature enough in technique to choose a manner for themselves from conviction. …(F. Childe Hassam sends from Paris a smart every-day figure of the streets) …

Besides this there is a water-color exhibition also current at the same time by the Water-color Club. This collection is composed entirely of ladies work and of ladies who are "somebody" in society for the most part—Susan H. Bradley, Gabrielle D. Clements, Mary McG. Dalton, Kate Greatorex, Katherine Lane, Mary K. Longfellow, Louisa B. Mason, Helen B. Merriman, Mary Minns Morse, Eleanor W. Motley, Elizabeth F. Parker, Ellen Robbins, Sarah C. Sears, M. Silsbee, Emily D. Tyson, Sarah W. Whitman and Elizabeth B. Duveneck. Here are a considerable number more pictures than in the men's club exhibition, and three times as much dash, emphasis and sensation, but also, alas! the inequality and hit-or-miss sketchiness so notably absent in the other; and thereby hangs a revelation of much of the wherefore of things ineffable in art. Many things would be utterable in art if their creators only *knew how* to utter them! The less one knows the more one dares ofttimes; the less one can really do, the louder, under some circumstances, must be one's assertion that one could do it if one cared. But this show is immensely interesting and amusing, and judging the work of lady amateurs in it as amateur work is creditable in the highest degree. There is even something of public pride and moral glow to be felt in the presence of the evidence here displayed that not all the dwellers in the great houses at Nahant, at Beverly Farms, at Lenox, or at Newport dawdle their mornings away in bed and their afternoons in carriages, or that they have eyes only for colors and forms of flowers and clouds, and are interested only in studying the ways of the latest lions and leaders in society, and note nothing of the sweetness of childhood or the profoundly significant traits of human nature high and low alike…The flowers are for the most part broadly and sumptuously painted characterized with true poetic and artistic feeling, and some of the landscapes and marines are strong and effective. *But there is nothing that men do that is not done by women now in Boston.*[42]

The final sentence is now oft-quoted but without the irony that the author intended. Young Gertrude Beals could have gleaned many things from Greta's review: that watercolor was developing a distinctive style in the hands of Americans in general and Bostonians in particular, that women were able to compete with men and show "three times as much dash, emphasis and sensation" as the men, but she could also glean the cautionary tale that women amateurs could drag down the respect that critics and the public might have for the works of women professionals. In addition, Greta praised the flowers, landscapes, and marines in the Watercolor Club that would become the staple subjects of Gertude Beals Bourne. Her mother, Edith Beals, might have found another message in Greta's review: that "ladies who are *somebody* in society", social lions, could exhibit watercolors together and that, should Gertrude wish to be a painter, she might respectably exhibit with such a group.

The rise in interest in watercolor in Boston as a separate medium coincided with Gertrude Beals' return from New York. By 1892 a reviewer in the *Boston Transcript* would assert that "the ability of the American painter to make a pretty and satisfactory watercolor has enormously grown in the last decade." For the first time in 1881, the Boston Art Club formalized the division of its two major annual exhibitions into a January-February oil painting exhibition and an April-May watercolor exhibition. To some degree this placed watercolor on the same level (albeit separate) with oil painting. At the same time a few major artists were making history in the changes that they were effecting to the concept and construction of watercolors.

The Beals would have been back in Boston from New York in time to have seen the exhibition of Homer's Cullercoats watercolors at the J. Eastman Chase Gallery in February of 1882. This was followed in December of 1883 by "Water Colors by Winslow Homer" at Doll and Richards in Boston, and "Studies in Black and White" at Doll and Richards in November-December of 1884. In 1886 Doll and Richards again showed Homer in "Paintings by Walter Gay and Water Color Drawings by Winslow Homer." In March of 1890 she could have seen eight Homer watercolors at the St. Botolph Club, lent by Edward Hooper. Again, at the same venue in December of 1891 she could have viewed five Homer watercolors as part of a loan exhibition. During this nine year period Homer and American watercolor had changed. "They are pictures and not sketches" one critic observed of the Tynmouth watercolors. Theodore E. Stebbins, Jr. wrote, "A major break in Homer's approach came in the mid-1880s...[he] began to portray the outdoors with an ever freer and transparent method. Increasingly he came to use pure colors from the tube, and despite care and sensitivity, even an admirer such as Mrs. Van Rensselaer found his colors lacking in 'suavity,' calling them 'rude, violent, almost brutal.'"[43]

Dodge Macknight (1860-1950) was just being noted for the first time in the same period. His work in watercolor in France in 1887-88 showed that he was one of the earliest adopters of a brilliant, even shocking palette which would qualify for the 'rude, violent, almost brutal' comments about Homer's work. Macknight's first public showing was at Doll and Richards gallery in Boston in January-February 1888 and the *Boston Transcript* reported that he was "a man with great courage of his convictions...[and his work was] shining with intense, dazzling brilliancy." Not everyone, not even Macknight's father, approved of the direction that his work had taken. The following year even the *Transcript* opined that the artist should avoid compositions which "set the observer's teeth on edge."

Evidence from her own work, however, demonstrates that Gertrude took note, and within a decade Macknight's work began to be an influence on her own. In addition, she would find inspiration in the paintings and watercolors of Arthur Wesley Dow, Ross Turner, John La Farge, Claude Monet, and John Singer Sargent, all of whose work she could view in Boston in the late 1880s and early 1890s. In order to pursue watercolor seriously and to build her skills toward a career as a professional artist, she first needed to find a teacher.

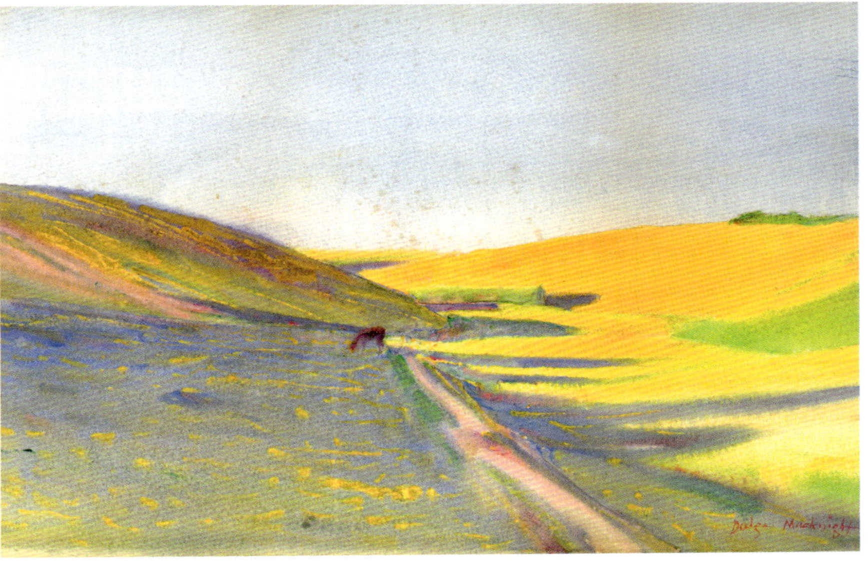

Dodge Macknight, American (1860-1950).
***Gorse in Bloom,* 1887-1888.**
Watercolor on paper, 11 3/4 x 18 5/8 inches. This is one of the earliest examples of Macknight's shocking Modernism. Courtesy Childs Gallery, Boston.

NOTES, Chapter One

1 John P. Marquand, *The Late George Apley* (Boston: Little, Brown and Company, 1937), 3.
2 Ibid., 176.
3 Commonwealth of Massachusetts, Division of Vital Statistics, Boston, Delayed Certificate of Birth, issued November 4, 1930. Registered Vol. 144, p. 105, No. 7452. "Gertrude Beals [born at] 8 Pemberton Sq. [to] Joshua G. [and] Edith W.(Simmons) Beals. Residence 8 Pemberton Sq. [father's] occupation Newspaper publisher." There has been some controversy over Gertrude Beals' birth year. Most published sources list her birth year as 1867. I believe her delayed birth certificate and her father's Harvard "Class of 1858" Third Triennial Report, issued in 1868 which states, "A daughter, Gertrude, was born 21 May, 1868", to be authoritative.
4 R. P. Shillaber, "Personal Reminiscences," Boston Post Semi-Centennial Supplement, 9 November 1881.
5 "Boston Advertiser," July 15, 1914 (obit); *Harvard Graduate Magazine*, 1915 (obit.), clipping files at Harvard Archives.

[6] *Harvard College Class of 1858 Report*, 1861, 1868, 1878, 1880, 1898. (Note: Dr. Oliver Wendell Holmes delivered the Boylston Prize Dissertation [Medical] in 1838 – nineteen years before Joshua G. Beals).
[7] Ibid.
[8] *Beals Family Bible*, given to Joshua G. Beals on the day of his marriage, October 1865, by his father (handwritten notes). Harvard Graduate Magazine, March 1915 included the information: "their wedding ceremony [was] the last performed in Church Green on Summer Street."
[9] Henry Rowe, *Ancestry of John Simmons* (Cambridge: Riverside Press, 1933), 61-68.
[10] Oliver Wendell Holmes, Sr., *The Autocrat of the Breakfast Table* (New York: Dutton, 1970), 65.
[11] Stanley C. Patterson and Carl G. Seaburg, *Nahant on the Rocks* (Nahant, MA: Nahant Historical Society, 1991), 227.
[12] Ibid., 227-228.
[13] "Mrs. Edith W. Beals Dead," *Boston Transcript*, 9 August 1927.
[14] *Boston City Directory*, 1870. Before 1870 either his house is unstated or, confusingly, is listed in 1868 "Joshua G. boards 8 Pemberton square."
[15] Holmes, Sr., *Autocrat*, 125-27.
[16] Marquand, 25-26.
[17] Bainbridge Bunting, *Houses of Boston's Back Bay: An Architectural History, 1840-1917* (Cambridge, MA: Belknap Press of Harvard University Press, 1967), 409.
[18] *United States Census*, 1870, ward six, Boston, Suffolk County, Massachusetts, p. 37, lines 2-6.
[19] Henry Rowe, *John Simmons*.
[20] Russell B. Adams, Jr., *The Boston Money Tree* (New York: Thomas Y. Crowell Company, 1977), 197. (The cost of the fire was more than one billion in 2004 dollars.)
[21] Herbert A. Kenny, *Newspaper Row: Journalism in the Pre-Television Era* (Chester, CT: Globe Pequot Press, 1987).
[22] *Boston Post*, 12 November 1872, 1.
[23] "Boston Post Estate," *Boston Post*, 31 March 1874, 3. (The purchase price was approximately $5,176,160 in 2004 dollars.)
[24] Kenny, 19. The Beals family appears to have been wise in selling out to the Greenes. Quarrels between Colonel Greene and his son Nathaniel H. Greene over how the Post should be run during the Grant administration depression led to the Post being sold in 1891. Boston City Directory, 1871-1876 indicates the changing ownership of the Post.
[25] The Rev. Ezra Dyer Winslow purchased the Boston Post in 1875 and this may have also been a part of the pay-out to the Beals family. Albert P. Langtry discusses the sale and subsequent perfidy by Winslow. Fortunately, although "Beals, Greene & Company, continued a nominal connection with it, which was to terminate when terms of sale had been fully complied with … no member of the firm retained any control or responsibility." Albert P. Langtry, *Metropolitan Boston: A Modern History Volume II* (New York: Lewis Historical Publishing Co., 1929), 553-57.
[26] *Harvard Class of 1858 Report*, 1898 (Boston: Alfred Mudge & Son, 1898).
[27] *New York City Directory*, 1876-1881.
[28] *Harvard Graduate Magazine*, March 1915.
[29] Diary of Sidney Beals, entry of September 21, 1892, "went to Papa's office (134 Lenard St) in the elevated railway." Harvard Archives "graduates cards" #B 1629 "in 1880 retired from active business."
[30] *Harvard Graduate Magazine*, March 1915.
[31] Bunting, 178-181.
[32] Department of Labor Statistics "Historical Value of the U.S. Dollar in 1991 constant dollars."A calculator of 1.35 to convert 1991 DLS dollars to 2003 DLS dollars was provided by the economist Christopher D. Mooz using information from the DLS web site.
[33] Suffolk County Massachusetts administration #68, 19 February 1884, 719. Simmons's estate listed real estate assets of $255,560 and liquid assets of $103,971(approximately $7,250,000 in 2004 dollars). Real estate included 6 Walnut Street and 299 Beacon Street in Boston, two properties in Nahant, and other real estate in Chelsea, MA, Andover, MA, and Sheldon, VT. He also had personal property showing that he had collected paintings, prints, sculpture, and silver. Distributions to his six living children and a grandchild began in 1884 and continued until after 1894.
[34] Oliver Wendell Holmes, Sr.
[35] Margaret Hani, *An Essex County Collection*, 13.
[36] "Mrs. Edith W. Beals Dead," Boston Transcript, 9 August 1927.
[37] Greta, "Greta's Boston Letter," *Art Amateur*, vol. 5 (July 1881), 30+.
[38] Ibid.
[39] Erica Hirshler, *A Studio of Her Own: Women Artists in Boston – 1870-1940* (Boston: Museum of Fine Arts, 2001), 9-55.
[40] Ibid., 28.
[41] #15. Upon written application of a member, the House Committee will issue a card admitting ladies of the immediate family of such member to the use and privileges of the Ladies' Department. For the purposes aforesaid a special blank shall be used, the same to be obtained at the office. The House Committee, within its discretion, will issue cards of admission to ladies who may not be of a member's immediate family. Any card issued under this rule may at any time be recalled and cancelled by said Committee. A member shall be responsible for any and all indebtedness contracted by the holder of a card of admission issued upon his application, the same to be charged to his account.
#17. The Ladies' Department shall be opened when and as the House Committee may from time to time direct, and ladies accompanied by a member shall be admitted thereto. A lady holding a card of admission shall be entitled to the use and privileges of said department. She may be accompanied by a lady or ladies not holding such cards. She shall, when not accompanied by a member, enter in a book kept for such purpose, her own name, the name of the member appearing on her card, and the name or names of any guest or guests accompanying her. All order checks shall be signed by the holder of such card with her own name and that of the member who applied for the same. No gentleman guest under this rule shall be introduced oftener than once in thirty days, and the holder of a card of admission shall ascertain whether such intended guest has been introduced during the previous thirty days.
#18. Upon the written request of a member the use of the Ladies' Department may be secured for not more than one day, in which case gentlemen accompanying such ladies must register as guests of the Club. The member applying as aforesaid shall be responsible for all charges.
#19 No refreshments of any kind shall be served in the Ladies' Reception Room, or to a member in any part of the Ladies' Department unless accompanied by a lady.
#20. Ladies shall be admitted to the Club-house by the Dartmouth Street entrance, and they shall not be admitted to any part of the Club-house other than the Ladies' Department, except as permitted by the House Committee."
By 1914 the Boston Art Club added a new House Rule:
#16. Members unaccompanied by ladies shall enter and leave the Club-house by the Newbury Street entrance." While these rules may be seen as quaint, very restrictive and oppressive of women, they may also be seen in the light of a successful new women's movement that was supported by a significant number of men, that would triumph in 1920 with the XIX Amendment to the United States Constitution and have a belated triumph in the change of the rules of the Boston Art Club in the early 1930s back to the original policy of admitting women members. The women's movement in 1914 necessitated the codification of rules that were seen as rapidly eroding.
[42] Greta, "Art in Boston," *Art Amateur*, vol. 20 (January 1889), 28. [This author's italics in the final sentence.] Greta was a pseudonym for the well-known Boston correspondent of the Art Amateur, whose identity is still unknown.
[43] Theodore E. Stebbins, Jr., *American Master Drawings and Watercolors* (New York: Harper & Row, 1976), 241. The quote from Mrs. M. G. Van Rensselaer, an art writer for many American publications, was from her *Six Portraits: Della Robbia, Correggio, Blake, Corot, George Fuller, Winslow Homer* (Boston and New York, 1911), 180.

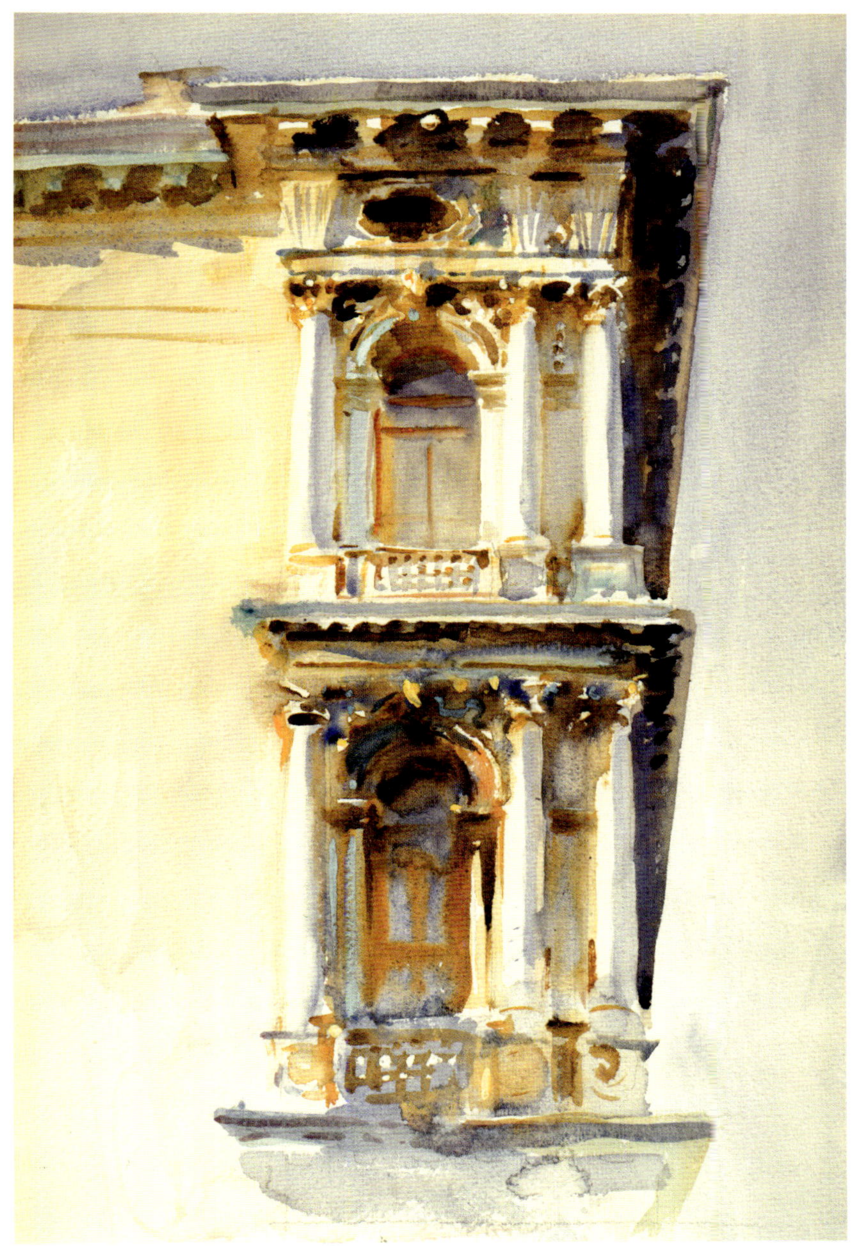

John Singer Sargent, American, (1856-1925).
Palazzo Rezzonico, c. 1904.
Watercolor and pencil on paper, 20 x 12 3/4 inches.
Private Collection, courtesy of Childs Gallery, Boston.

By the 1890s Sargent's skill in watercolor was established in Boston. He had first visited Venice as a teenager and in 1880 set up a studio in the Palazzo Rezzonico, the building depicted here. He returned to Venice many times. In this watercolor Sargent's adherence to the "blue shadow" school that later permeated Boston watercolor is clear. His later watercolors also formed a teaching tool for Gertrude in the mid-1910s when she copied a number of them at the Museum of Fine Arts, Boston.

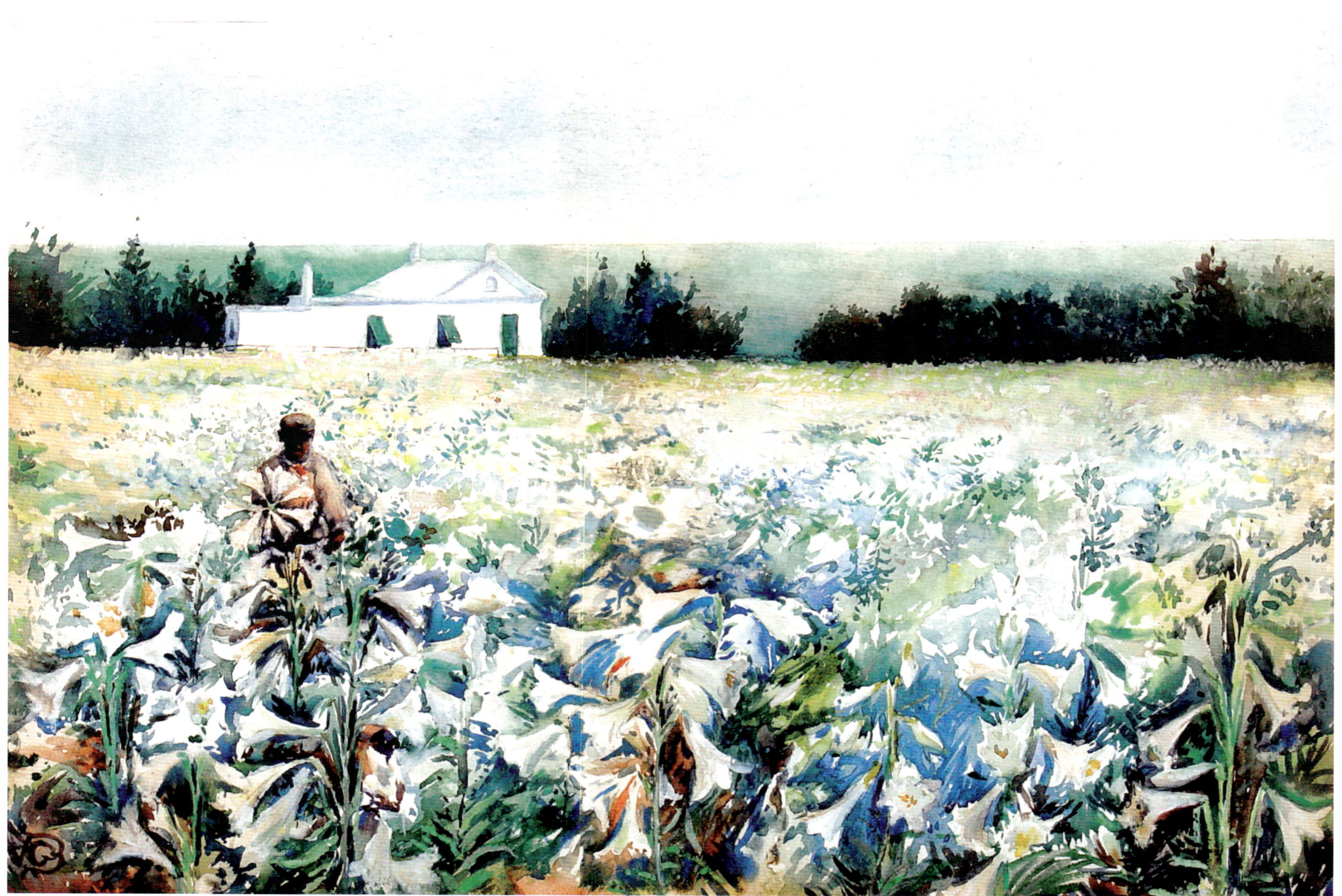

CHAPTER TWO

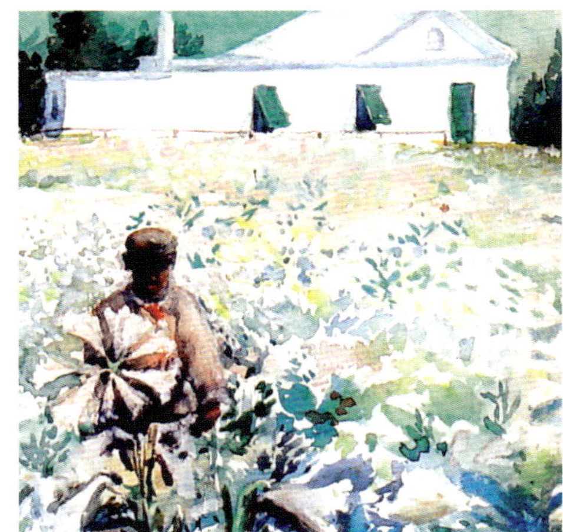

A Career as an Artist Begins

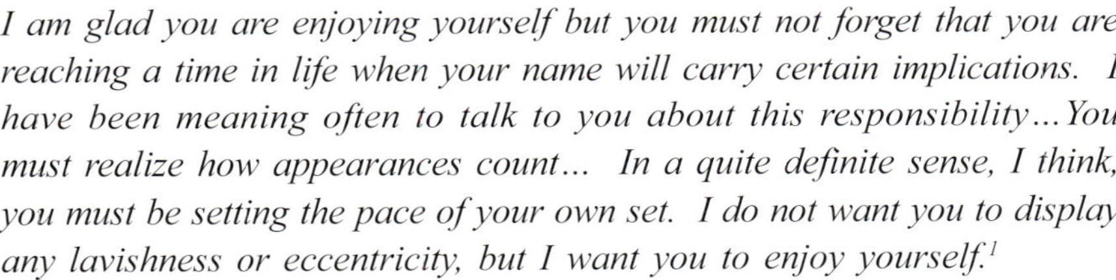

I am glad you are enjoying yourself but you must not forget that you are reaching a time in life when your name will carry certain implications. I have been meaning often to talk to you about this responsibility...You must realize how appearances count... In a quite definite sense, I think, you must be setting the pace of your own set. I do not want you to display any lavishness or eccentricity, but I want you to enjoy yourself.[1]

Thomas Apley to George Apley, January 1888
— John P. Marquand, *The Late George Apley*

As she turned twenty, Gertrude Beals, already a young woman with some educational accomplishments, social standing, and a Boston upper-class view of the world, challenged some of the normal expectations that Boston Brahmin society had for her. Rather than seek a proper marriage with one of the young men of Boston society, which her father's wealth and background would almost certainly have promised and which we must believe her mother planned and hoped for, Gertrude stayed within the bosom of her family and embarked on a career as a professional artist.

A Cottage by the Sea, Bermuda, 1897-98.
Watercolor on Paper, 9 1/2 x 21 1/2 inches.
Exhibited: Boston Art Club, April 1898.
Private Collection

In the late 1880s or very early 1890s Henry W. Rice (1853-1934) became Gertrude Beals watercolor teacher. With the availability of schools with regular curricula in the Back Bay it is interesting that Gertrude chose the more traditional route for training as an artist: private studio lessons. Rice was born in North Pownal, Maine and had come to Boston by 1875 where he was listed as a carriage painter. Later, however, he studied with the notable watercolorist and teacher Ross Turner and by 1888 was listing himself as "artist" at 18 Highland Street, Boston Highlands. Turner himself had been one of "Duveneck's Boys," studying under Frank Duveneck and William Merritt Chase at the Royal Academy in Munich in the late 1870s and early 1880s.

Turner taught privately and at the Massachusetts Institute of Technology. His watercolor technique was assured and he was a regular exhibitor in Boston and at national and international exhibitions. Turner was able to instill in Rice much of the craft of his technique; Rice was, although not as widely-known as Turner, a respected member of the Boston art community. In 1888 Rice began to exhibit at the Boston Art Club, and he continued to show in the annual April

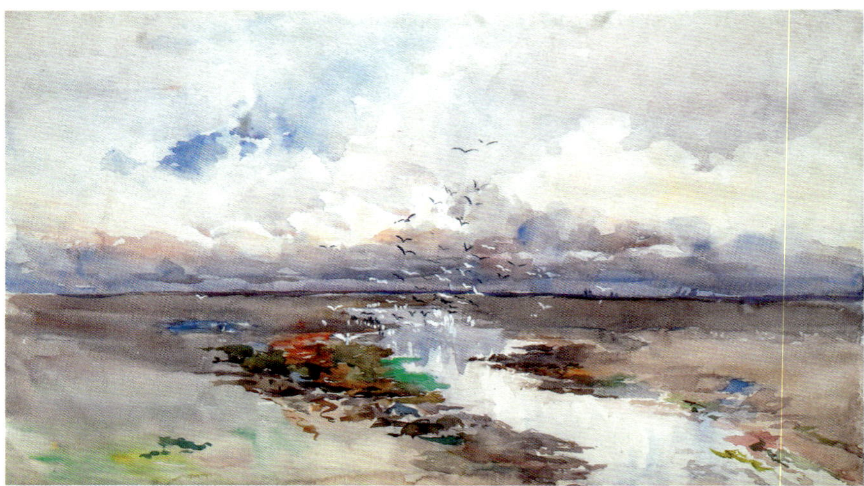

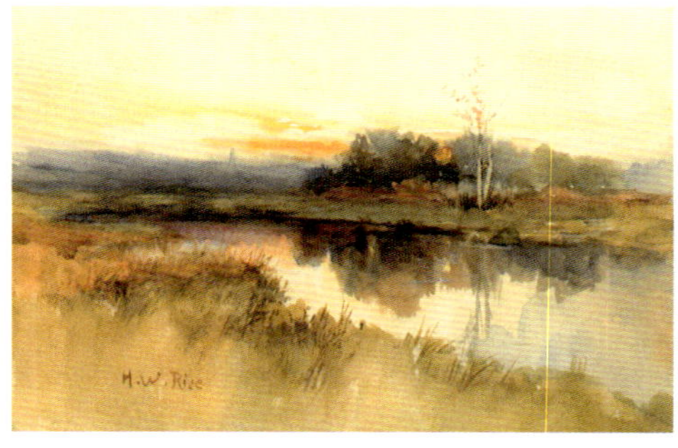

above: ***Seagulls and Tidal Flats,*** c. 1900. Watercolor and gouache on paper, 10 1/2 x 18 inches. Courtesy of the Bourne Art Trust.

right: **Henry W. Rice, American (1853-1934).** ***Reflections in Autumn,*** c. 1895. Watercolor on paper, 7 x 10 inches. Courtesy of Childs Gallery, Boston.

watercolor exhibitions every year through 1907. His devotion to watercolor—he never exhibited an oil painting at the Boston Art Club—may also have been a factor in choosing Rice.

In selecting Rice as a teacher, proximity to the Beals residence may have been a deciding factor. Beginning in 1889 or 1890, until the demise of the building by fire in 1904, his studio was in the Harcourt building at 23 Irvington Street — the present site of Copley Place and the Back Bay Marriott Hotel. Gertrude would have had a short walk down Dartmouth Street through Copley Square to reach his studio. If proximity were an issue, we might also ask why Gertrude (or her family) did not elect to pursue a more regular and formal course of instruction at the equally near School of the Museum of Fine Arts, the Cowles School of Art, or the Massachusetts Normal School of Art. Perhaps Gertrude, or her family, believed that private instruction, which had already been a part of her education, would be more effective than a schoolroom. And so, although education for women in a regular course of instruction was now readily available in Back Bay Boston institutions, Henry Rice would lead Gertrude Beals into the mysteries of becoming a professional watercolor painter. His own work paralleled her later works in subject and technique with views of Mt. Washington in the snow, a New Hampshire sap house, and views of the coast of New England. He emphasized landscape and was not very interested in figures. The Boston critic A. J. Philpott wrote immediately following Rice's death: "He loved the Mountains of New Hampshire. He loved the New England coast…He loved water colors, the transparence and freshness of them, and he became a master of this medium in the "pure wash"—the most difficult and the most beautiful method of handling such colors. He could blend his colors in wash and get every subtle tone gradation. He had the pictorial sense. His point of view; his arrangement in forms and design; his sense of light, shade and color, were all in perfect harmony."[2] Gertrude Beals' first instructor would teach her the fundamentals of watercolor in pure wash and subtlety in blending of colors and realizing form, shading, and depth. Soon she would be ready to show what she had learned.

Gertrude Beals' first exhibited watercolor was *Azaleas*, at the Boston Art Club watercolor exhibition from April 4 – 25, 1891. At the same exhibition, Rice exhibited *October* and *Near the Sea*. The review in the *Boston Evening Transcript* noted: "Perhaps we ought not to notice the fact that New York has contributed somewhat to the result, but the Boston portion is very good, showing advance on the part of nearly all of the exhibiting artists… Turning to the right, we find H. W. Rice's admirable sketch of *October Trees*, truthful and vigorous."[3] Henry B. Snell was one of the New Yorkers to whom the reviewer referred. He had exhibited previously at the Boston Art Club's watercolor exhibition in 1887 and would exhibit nearly every year after 1891 until 1909. He was reviewed oddly in the same article: "Snell's *Ocean Tramp* is a weird and rather wicked-looking picture." And in a follow-up article the reviewer continued: "H. B. Snell's *St. Stephen's, Cornwall* [is] an exact rendering of

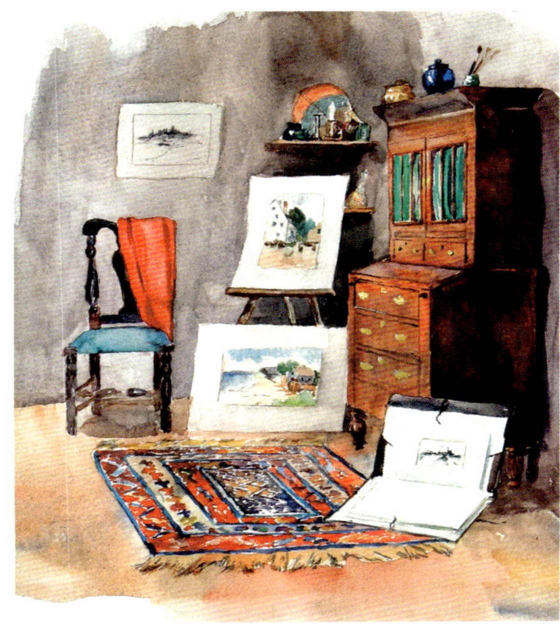

an old English Church…Snell's *Church Tower* [is] an original and pleasing sunset scene in Cornwall, England, land beloved just now of painters."[4] Snell was later to be Gertrude's other acknowledged teacher and in this first exhibition, she could compare her work with her teachers', and their works with each other's. A possible impetus for Gertrude's beginning to exhibit at the Boston Art Club was that her uncle, George W. Simmons, Jr., was a businessman member of the club by 1890, a membership he continued to 1895.[5]

The following year, 1892, she exhibited *Geraniums* at the Boston Art Club watercolor exhibition, April 2 –23. Here a *Transcript* reviewer noted:

> The ability of the American painter to make a pretty and satisfactory watercolor has enormously grown in the last decade, and where one man knew how to do it in 1882, an army of men and women can now perform that feat without apparent effort. The three hundred pictures in the galleries of the Art Club are not all equally good, of course, but the general character of the work is noticeably professional and workmanlike compared to what it was a few years ago. Watercolors have for some time been a sort of fashion,

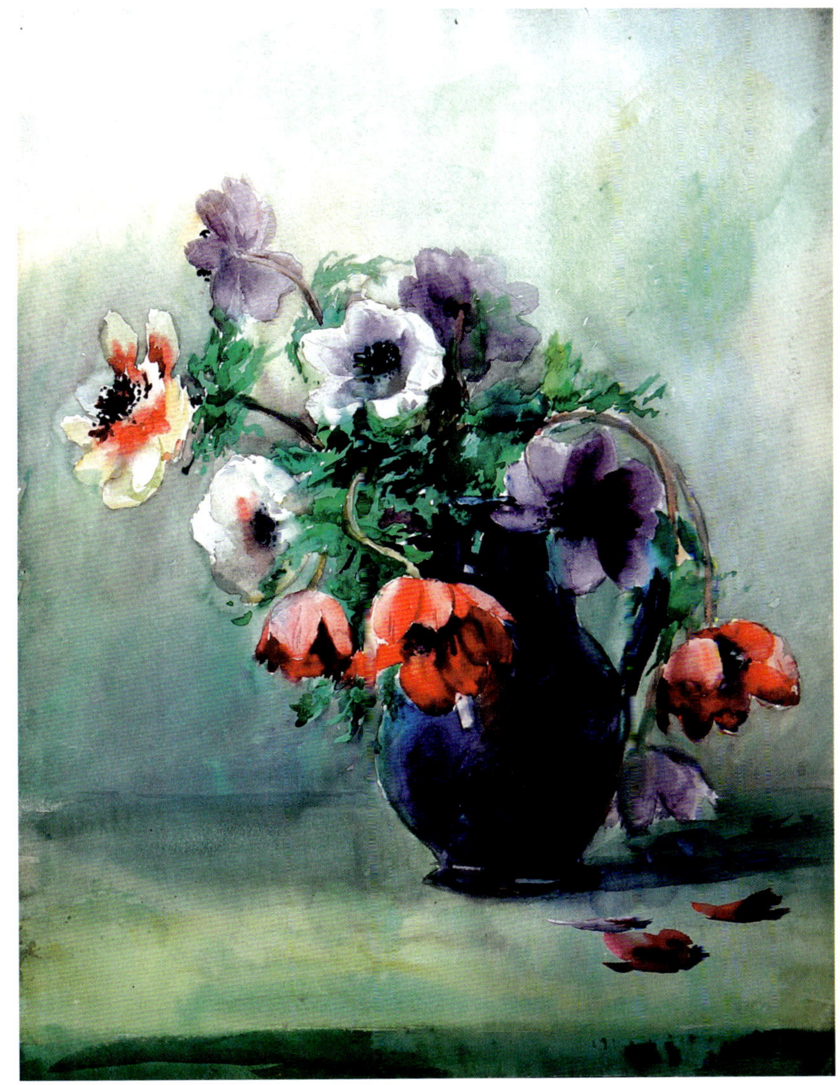

above: ***Anemones in a Blue Vase,*** c. 1895. Watercolor on paper, 19 1/2 x 14 3/8 inches.
left: ***Desk and Study (328 Dartmouth Street),*** c. 1890. Watercolor on paper, 13 1/2 x 12 1/4 inches.

and their vogue has resulted in an astonishing increase in their quantity as well as an improvement in their quality. ... The watercolorists who should shine the brightest in a crowd (such as Childe Hassam, George Smillie, Francis Murphy, S.P.R. Triscott) are easily outstripped by many less-known competitors."[6]

While Beals may not have been singled out for praise, she could have included herself in the "many less-known competitors." She may have been increasingly confident that in selecting watercolor as her medium she was in the forefront of a movement that was gaining in critical and public acclaim. The next month, Gertrude gave two watercolors to the Grundmann Studio Building Fund, *Roman Anemones* which sold for $15 ($300 in 2003 dollars) and *Old House Marion* which brought $18 ($370)[7]. These are Gertrude's first recorded sales. While these watercolors were on exhibition, the Beals family left for Europe.

Many Grand Tours

The importance of travel to Gertrude's life and career is indicated by considering that more than one half of her total oeuvre was painted while she was traveling, often to exotic locations. In the last quarter of the nineteenth century the Beals family traveled regularly to Europe. During a time when artists struggled to get to Paris and other capitals of European culture to see the great works of the past in galleries and to view new works in the salons, Gertrude had been, by the age of twenty, on a cultural sight-seeing trip that would have been the envy of Boston artists more than twice her age. In 1897, at the age of 51, William Partridge Burpee—a fellow exhibitor at the Boston Art Club and newly established Boston painter—wrote home of his first trip to Europe, that it "has equaled my anticipation, and this is much, for my anticipation has been augmented by years of waiting."[8] Similarly, Arthur Wesley Dow, who would later be part of Gertrude's circle of acquaintances, struggled in the early 1880s to put together the money for study in Europe—he finally arrived in Paris for the first time in October 1884.

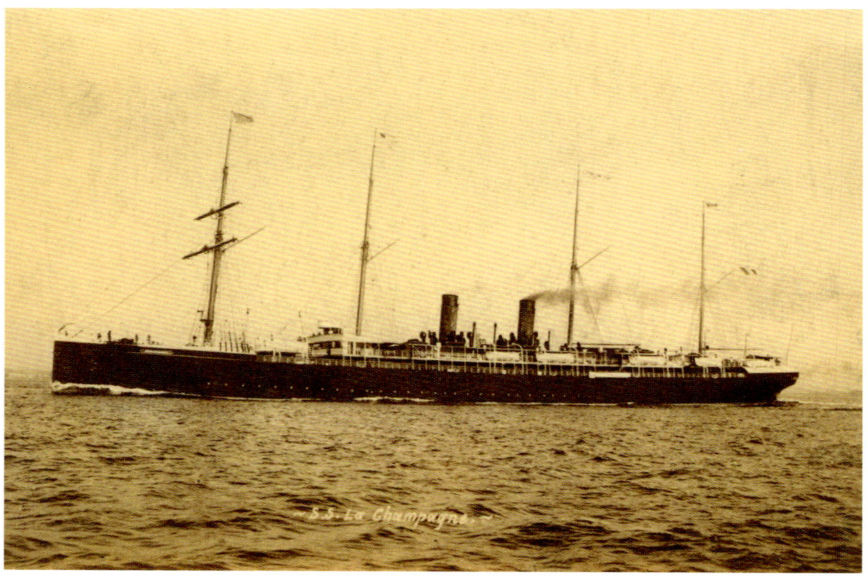

The French steamer, La Champagne, *sailed from New York on May 7, 1892, carrying Edith, Getrude, and Sidney Beals, and their friends, the Thorndikes.*

By 1888 the Beals family had made a lengthy trip which included London, Paris and Geneva. They were back again for the summer of 1892, which was well documented by Gertrude's twelve-year old brother Sidney in a diary kept from May 6 through September 18. Sidney's descriptions form a guileless insight into not only the physical accommodations of upper class travel, but also into the attitudes of the travelers. The entire family, Joshua, Edith, Gertrude, Gardner, and Sidney boarded the train from Boston to New York where Joshua took a room at the University Club. After supper the family went to the docks where Edith, Gertrude, and Sidney got settled in their stateroom on the French mail steamer *La Champagne.* Family friends, Mrs. Quincy Thorndike, her daughter and son, Richard, were on board and would see the Beals in many locations in Europe. Mrs. Thorndike of 175 Marlborough Street, Boston was the widow of the artist, George Quincy Thorndike (1827-1886).[9] Joshua and Gardner, then a Harvard junior, would join the others after taking a later steamer. On May 15 the three Beals arrived in Le Havre and stayed in the Hotel Frascati, which Sidney reported was "thought to be the best hotel there." This was to be a trip of first class accommodations and in nearly all cases the best there was to be had. Sightseeing was done at a relentless pace. Culture and history were actively pursued.

"Good Americans when they die, go to Paris," wrote Dr. Oliver Wendell Holmes, "...Paris is a heavenly place after New York or Boston."[10] On May 16 after a train trip from Le Havre, the three settled into what Sidney described as "our old Hotel Chatham 17 –19 Rue Daunou off Rue de L'Opera" in Paris. They stayed there through June 22. On their first full day in Paris, the Beals trooped off to the Salon of the Champs Elysees, which they compared to the Salon of 1888 and noted paintings by Detaille and Vibert. Later the family went to the auction sale of Georges Petit, where they did not make a purchase but Sidney reported the prices of the paintings as $100 to $600. The next morning Gertrude had her brother get her a painting permit for the museums while he was obtaining one to take photographs. They then went to the Palais du Luxembourg where they liked the paintings, especially those by Meissonier, better than those at the Salon. The day was completed with a trip to the Pantheon and the Musée Cluny.

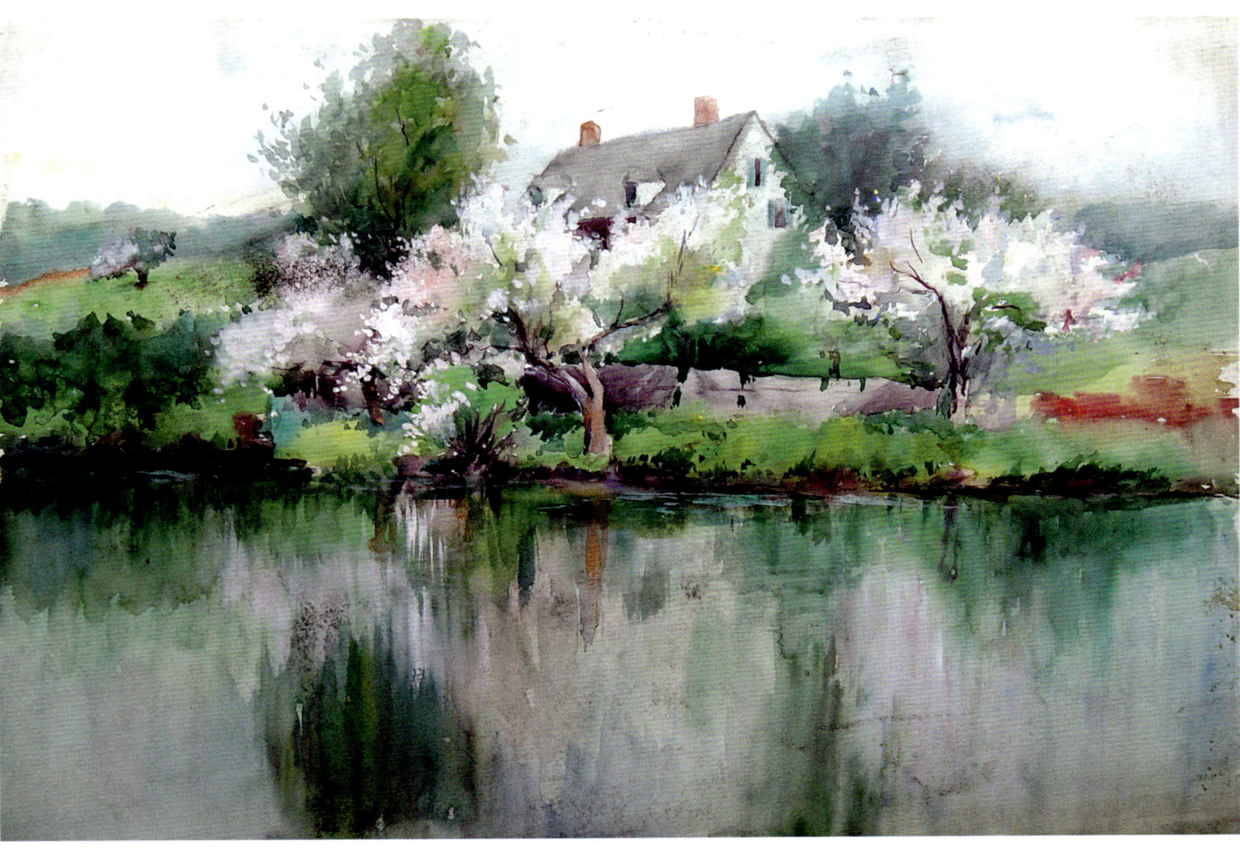

Apple Blossoms and Reflections, 1890-95. Watercolor and gouache on paper, 14 x 20 inches. This Impressionist watercolor relates in subject and style to similar works by J. Appleton Brown and Ross Turner.
Courtesy of Childs Gallery, Boston.

On May 19, they went to see an exhibit of paintings by Marie Bashkirtseff (1859-1884), the Russian painter. Bashkirtseff's diary, *The Journal of Marie Bashkirtseff,* had been published in English only two years earlier and her radical ideas about feminism and restrictions on educated women in the arts inspired a generation of women to resist intellectually, if not to actually rebel against the norms of their society. Seeing the Bashkirtseff exhibition, when Bashkirtseff had died eight years before at about the age that Gertrude was on this trip, may have caused her to reflect on similarities and differences in their lives and artistic philosophies. Baskirtseff was the perfect model of a

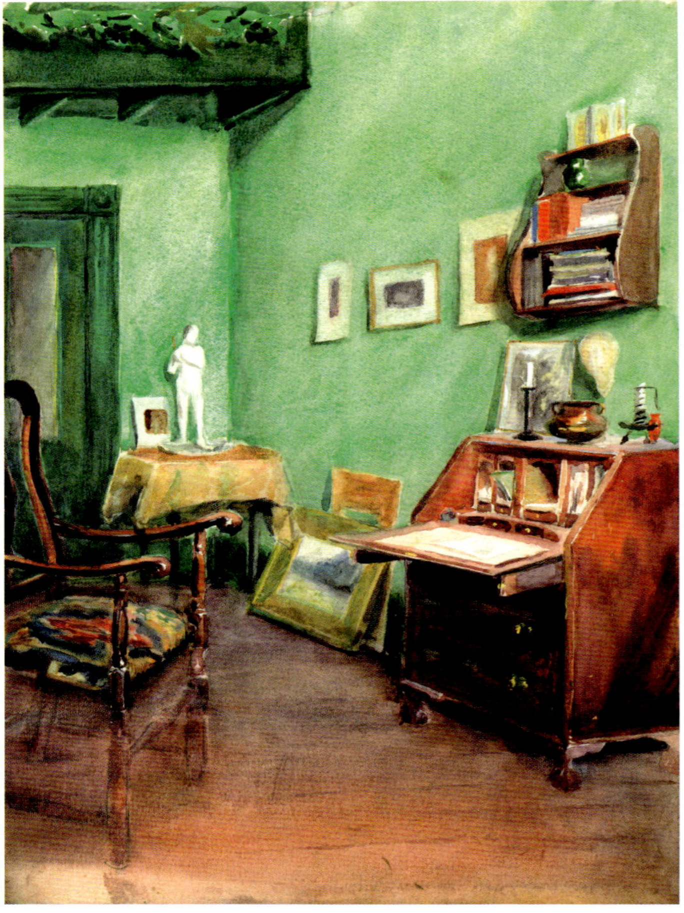

left: ***Green Studio Interior,*** c. 1895. Watercolor and gouache on paper, 14 x 10 inches. Courtesy of Childs Gallery, Boston.

right: ***Clock Tower — Dinan,*** *July 2, 1892*. Watercolor on paper, 19 5/8 x 12 1/2 inches.Signed: "DINAN/ G.B." Exhibited: Boston Art Club, April 1893. Courtesy of Childs Gallery, Boston.

below: Dinan - La Tour de l'Horloge. Photograph from Sidney Beals' Diary.

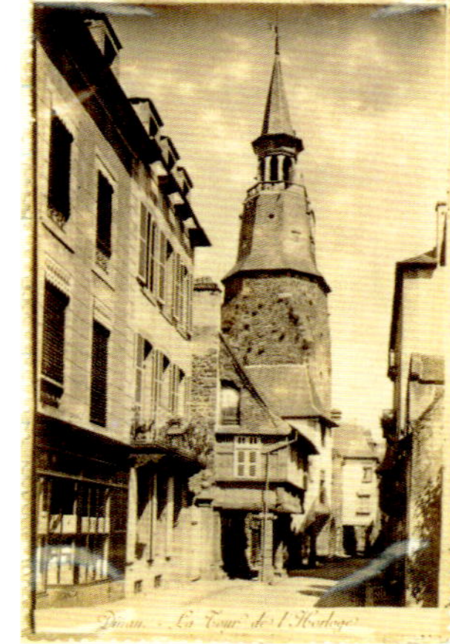

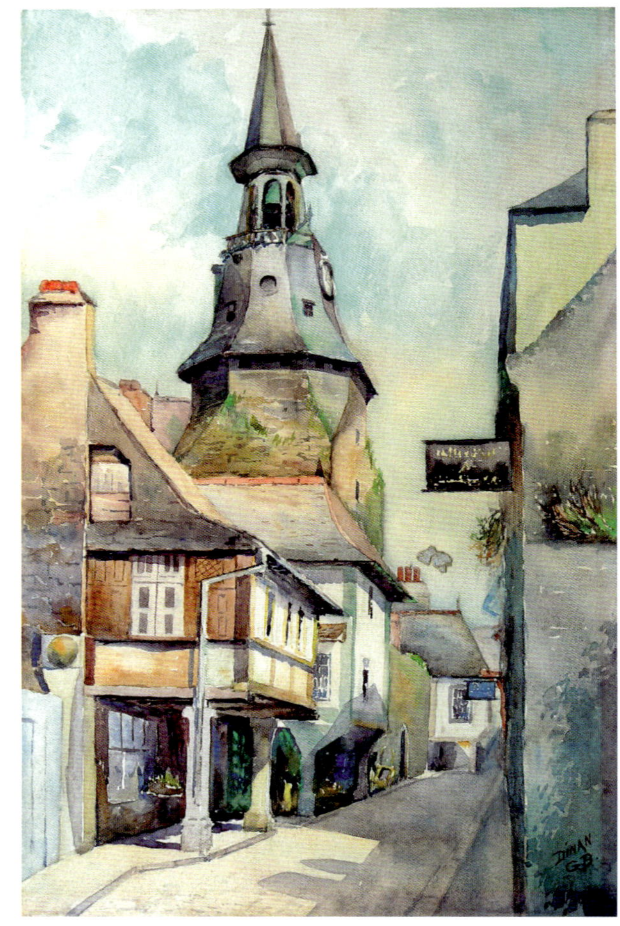

romantic woman artist as her life combined aristocracy, privileged birth, beauty, art, travel, romance, death, tragedy, and world renown. She studied in Paris at the Académie Julian and exhibited more than professional admiration for one of her teachers, Jules Bastien-Lepage. Excepting her early death, could Bashkirtseff's independent and forceful life as a woman artist from a privileged family form a model for Gertrude?

On Friday May 20th they spent the morning in the Louvre, had lunch at the Palais Royale, and spent the afternoon at the Salon of the Champs de Mars. They noted that there were two salons this year since one would not hold all the pictures. Clearly there was no coincidence or accident that proper Bostonians arrived in Paris at the height of the exhibition season and that they were viewing and reporting on as many events as possible. Here in Paris in 1892 Gertrude could see and discern the rift in the art world in its capital, between the academic styles favored by the old salon and the newer ideas of the Impressionists. She had already had the opportunity to see works by Monet, Pissarro, Boudin and others in Boston, but here she could see and feel the division between old and new. As she formed her style over the next two decades she would opt for the new as she saw it in Paris in 1892.

On May 24 Gertrude went to the Académie Julian, saw a group of paintings by Ribot, and had a long talk with Rodolphe Julian (1839-1907). Julian had founded his school to be independent of the French government and the rigid structure and examinations of the École des Beaux Arts. He accepted women on the same footing as men and his school was very popular with foreigners—especially Americans. The École des Beaux-Arts would not accept women until 1897. Everyone interested in American artists in Paris, and especially American women artists in Paris, in the final quarter of the nineteenth century would like to have the transcript of that long talk. Was Gertrude inquiring about enrollment and classes? If so, why did she decide to forego a place at the Julian and continue her work the following year in Boston? On June 12 they were back to view the sale at Georges Petit where they admired four Meissoniers that were sold. The next day Gertrude and Edith went to see the house where Meissonier had lived at Poissy.

The Beals were living very well in Paris; perhaps Edith Beals preferred to travel in more luxury than Joshua Beals required. Sidney's friends Richard Thorndike and Fred Sears, his "most intimate friend" (whose grandfather, Thomas Jefferson Coolidge, had just been appointed United States Ambassador to France), each had private carriages and seemed to have acquired even more of the accoutrements of travel than Edith Beals did. Sidney recorded on May 21, "When I came home to lunch I found a note asking me to the theatre from the Thorndikes. The Thorndikes called for me at 8:15 in a private carriage or rather a carriage which they had hired for a month and looked like a private." Both the Thorndikes and the Sears allowed their children the use of their carriages and invited Sidney and other members of the Beals family on their sorties in and about Paris. There was a great deal of dining back and forth at each other's hotels, and Richard Thorndike and Sidney took French lessons together most days from Mme. Herling. This closeness of the community of Boston travelers was re-created in *The Late George Apley*:

> It is the intense congeniality of our own society which has its inception in a unique community of ideas resulting in a common attitude toward life. When the individuals of one group find a complete peace and happiness and fulfillment in the association with one another, why should they look farther? This, I think, explains an evident but completely wholesome element of our self-satisfaction. It explains why so many residents of Boston flock together when abroad, instinctively seeking the relaxation gained from each other when confronted with an alien environment—why Boston has her own hotel in New York City and in London and on the right bank of the Seine. Yet, let us repeat, this congeniality bears in it no element of superiority toward or dislike of the world around it.[11]

The Beals, Searses, Thorndikes, and Coolidges convened, dined, studied, amused themselves, and stayed together. There were American and Boston hotels in Paris: the Chatham, Rastadt, Binda, and the Westminster. Boston society in abbreviated form was alive in Paris.

After more than a month in Paris at the Hotel Chatham, Edith Beals, with Gertrude and Sidney, went to Normandy, Brittany, and the Channel Islands with the eventual object of meeting the rest of her family arriving at Le Havre. On June 22 Edith, Gertrude, and Sidney Beals left Paris for St. Malo. They immediately went on to Mont St. Michel where they stayed only one night, although Gertrude and Sidney drew and painted. They then left for the Channel Islands, visiting Jersey and Guernsey through June 30. They returned to St. Malo and went the next day up the Rance by boat to the medieval town of Dinan. Sidney's diary indicates that not only was ample time spent appreciating art, but that he and Gertrude both spent time sketching and painting. This may have been Sidney's first foray into watercolor painting and his sister's debut as a teacher of watercolor for her younger brother. On July 2, according to Sidney, "Gertrude and I got up early and went sketching after breakfast. We sketched the horloge. We did the same in the afternoon. The boys as they came out of school crowded around so that we couldn't do anything." On July 4th, their last full day in Dinan, Sidney recounted, "We drew again today — this time I bought a paint box for 5 frs. We did an old door and a shrine in it… The school boys bothered us again today." On the 5th they returned to St. Malo and went on to the Grande Hotel at Dinard where the Thorndikes were staying. Gertrude was equipped with a sunshade and a device to hold it while she was painting, for Sidney notes that, " she also found she had lost a thing to hold her sunshade while sketching, but I told her a shovel would do as well and so it did."

After a week of bathing on the beaches of Dinard, they returned to Paris on the 12th of July. The next day they all went to Rouen where they spent Bastille Day and toured the cathedral. Sidney recounted, "It was the most wonderful carving I ever saw. All the outside was lace work with statues over the door. This photograph does not give justice to it. … Coming out of the church Mamma asked of a person whom she met where St. Ouens church was. She took us there and she told us that she used to be Mrs. Thorndike's maid." They seemed to be following the peripatetic Thorndikes everywhere. After witnessing the many games and celebrations on the 14th, the next day the Beals' took the train for Trouville where they settled in on the beach at the Grand Hôtel de Paris. The next day, they moved to Le Havre and on the 17th were met by Joshua Gardner Beals and young Gardner who had just arrived on *La Bourgogne* from New York. On the 18th Gertrude and Sidney went down on a boat to Trouville and "painted some sailboats with blue, yellow, green and all-colored sails that were anchored in a clump." On the 19th Sidney reported on transatlantic accommodations: "We also went on *S.S. La Bourgogne* and saw Papa's palatial room compared with ours — as his was often used for six people (his no. was 258 to 266). Also the room that Mama and Gertrude will come back on." On the 20th the entire Beals family arrived in Paris.

With the presence of Joshua, things changed slightly. What had been their "old Hotel Chatham" suddenly became too luxurious. According to Sidney: "In Paris Gardie and Gertrude went for the letters while we took the carriage to Hotel Rastadt 4 Rue Daunou the same street Hotel Chatham is on. We didn't go there on account of its being so expensive." Sidney was impressed the next day when they went to visit Fred Sears "who has hired a house on 58 Avenue Marceau with his grandfather Mr. Coolidge, who has recently been appointed minister to France… We then went to 4 Rue Villejust where I had a talk with Mme Herling [his tutor] who was very glad to see me. I told her she might give me a lesson tomorrow. She said she had been teaching the Forbes of Boston." After a round of visits to the Louvre, plays, and spectacles, the family left for Geneva on July 27th. They returned to the Grand Hôtel de la Paix where they had stayed four years earlier. After breakfast they went out on errands that included taking their watches to the shops where they had been purchased on the prior trip to be cleaned; this was followed by the purchase of six and one-half dozen pairs of gloves.[12] On the 29th Gertrude unpacked her sketching things and went by steam train to Chene. "In the car we met another person who was going sketching at Chene. She showed us a very pretty little pond there with trees overhanging and fine shadows. It was about a mile from where we stopped and Gertrude and I would never [have] thought of going there." On the 30th Sidney wrote, "Gertrude and I went to Grosh Canal where we went to the Horticulture and he gave us permission to paint his hollyhocks. It was the second painting I ever did and [it] turned out pretty well."

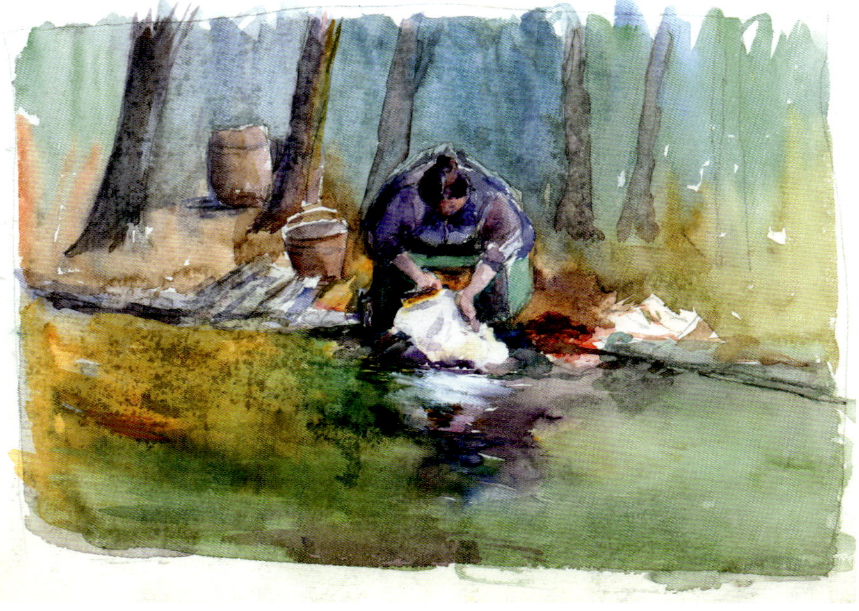

Blanchisseuse, 1892.
Watercolor and gouache on paper, 9 1/2 x 13 inches (image) 19 3/8 x 13 1/2 inches (sheet). A work that relates directly to French Impressionist watercolors by Pissarro, Renoir, and others.
Courtesy of the Bourne Art Trust.

In the beginning of August the family moved through Lausanne, Basel and Strasbourg where they "walked to Hotel National but it was crowded, so we went to Hotel Pfeifer which is a second class hotel although very good." After a day each at Baden-Baden, Heidelberg, and Frankfort, they arrived on August 6th at Schwalbach where they stayed at the Duke of Nassau Hotel intending to take the waters for the cure. The regimen started in the morning with a bath at 90 degrees for 15 minutes in water with high iron content. After lunch Sidney reported, they had to drink the water, "which tasted horridly, but after several [you] couldn't tell the difference. I drank one glass full then walked ½ hour then took another glass the way the doctor told me. We had to get a glass of our own and pay a certain amount to have a number put on it and be allowed to drink. I had to drink twice every day." This routine continued until Joshua and Gardner departed on Wednesday the 17th to go down the Rhine and eventually to London. Edith then made the shocking discovery when "Gertrude…was told that Schwalbach was the very worst place for the complexion and as a good many others had told her so also, we took a carriage with our trunks over to Schlangenbad. At Schlangenbad we stayed at the Hotel Victoria where we were given two fine rooms with a balcony." There they returned to the baths and the waters in a more elegant environment than that which suited Joshua. Schlangenbad seems to have been a bit more fashionable than Schwalbach and they even witnessed the arrival of Queen Isabella "the ancient queen of Spain" who, Sidney noted "got stuck getting out of the carriage as she is so fat." Gertrude got a pain in her side, which Gertrude began to think "was getting to be a cancer." Although she was feeling better, Gertrude chose to remain at Schlangenbad when Edith and Sidney departed to follow the rest of the family down the Rhine. On September 9th Edith returned to Paris, presumably to the Hotel Chatham. Gertrude probably joined her there before the two returned to America on *La Bourgogne*.

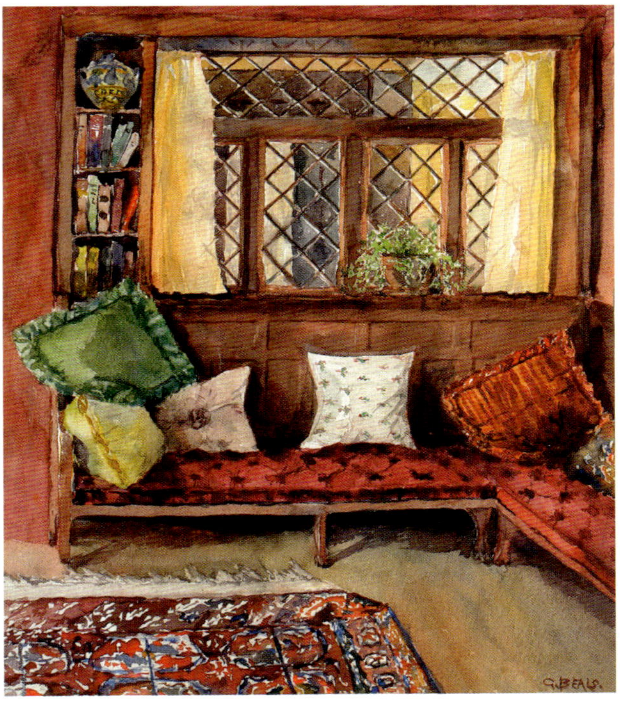

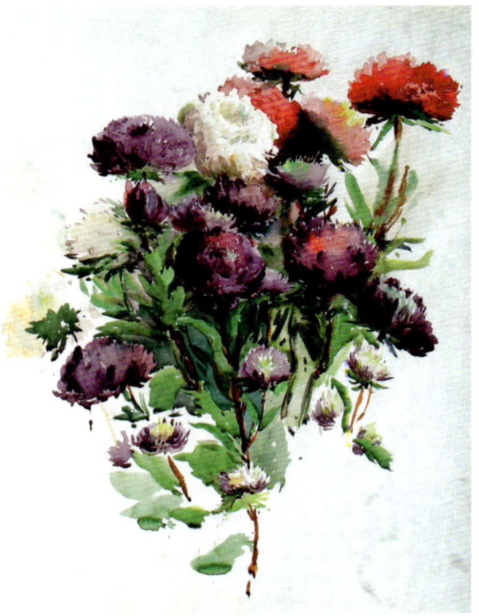

above: ***Gothic Interior with Cushions,*** c.1899. Watercolor on paper, 13 1/4 x 12 inches. Courtesy of Childs Gallery, Boston.

above right: ***Bouquet of Asters,*** c. 1895. Watercolor on paper, 20 x 14 inches. Courtesy of Childs Gallery, Boston.

What would Gertrude's circle of friends in Boston have thought of her on her own, presumably without chaperone, left at Schlangenbad to live, however briefly, independent of her family? Notwithstanding Gertrude's being a young woman of twenty-four, an unmarried young lady of her social standing would not generally have been left alone in a European resort. Edith Beals

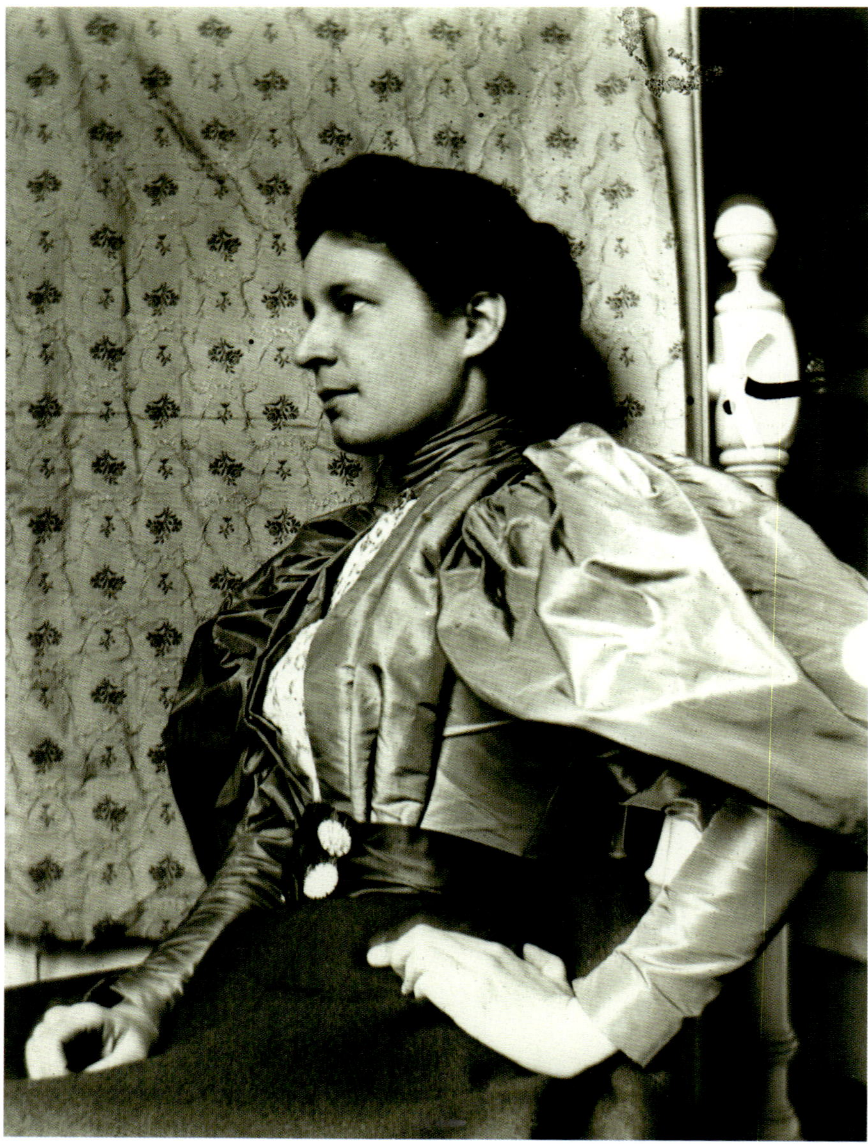

Gertrude Beals, c. 1900. Courtesy of the Bourne Art Trust.

must have felt confident that Gertrude was responsible, independent, sensible, and trustworthy to have been able to leave her on her own at Schlangenbad. One wonders to what extent the "pain in her side" was an excuse to stay on without the rest of the family. Later in life Gertrude would surprise and shock family and friends with her unconventional solutions to travel problems and arrangements—she once went to jail when no other room was available. Liberty in Schlangenbad was arranged with the complicity of her mother. Did this time, spent in Europe away from Boston, her family, and her friends, convince Gertrude that a season alone at the Académie Julian was not for her? Other evidence from her later life would suggest the opposite. Gertrude was independent, strong-willed, and happy to be left alone to paint.

Although the summer of 1892 was undoubtedly a highlight of the summers of the 1890s, the evidence suggests that Gertrude was a participant in regular family summer travel for education, culture, rest, and relaxation. A major European jaunt seems to have occurred every four years or so. Did Gertrude and her family meld with Europeans as they traveled and gain insights into the cultures of the peoples that had built, painted and sculpted the cultural artifacts that they so admired? Or would they have reflected as did George Apley:

> Here I am reaching the end of my trip through Europe. I have seen much of England and not a little of France, but I have been impressed by a similarity existing between almost every scene, the reason for which I think I chanced upon today. It seems to me that all this time a part of Boston has been with me. I am a raisin in a slice of pie which has been conveyed from one plate to another. I have moved; I have seen plate after plate; but all the other raisins have been around me in the same relation to me as they were when we all were baked.
>
> It is strange that instead of gaining much impression of different cultures, we have succeeded in transferring our own culture momentarily upon every place we visited. We had no wish to lose our identity and we did not lose it. We have succeeded in interposing a barrier of polite conversation, dealing principally with relatives and personalities, against the facades of the cathedrals, the collected works of the masters, and the walls of Chinon. When we were not doing this we were quoting from observations made by

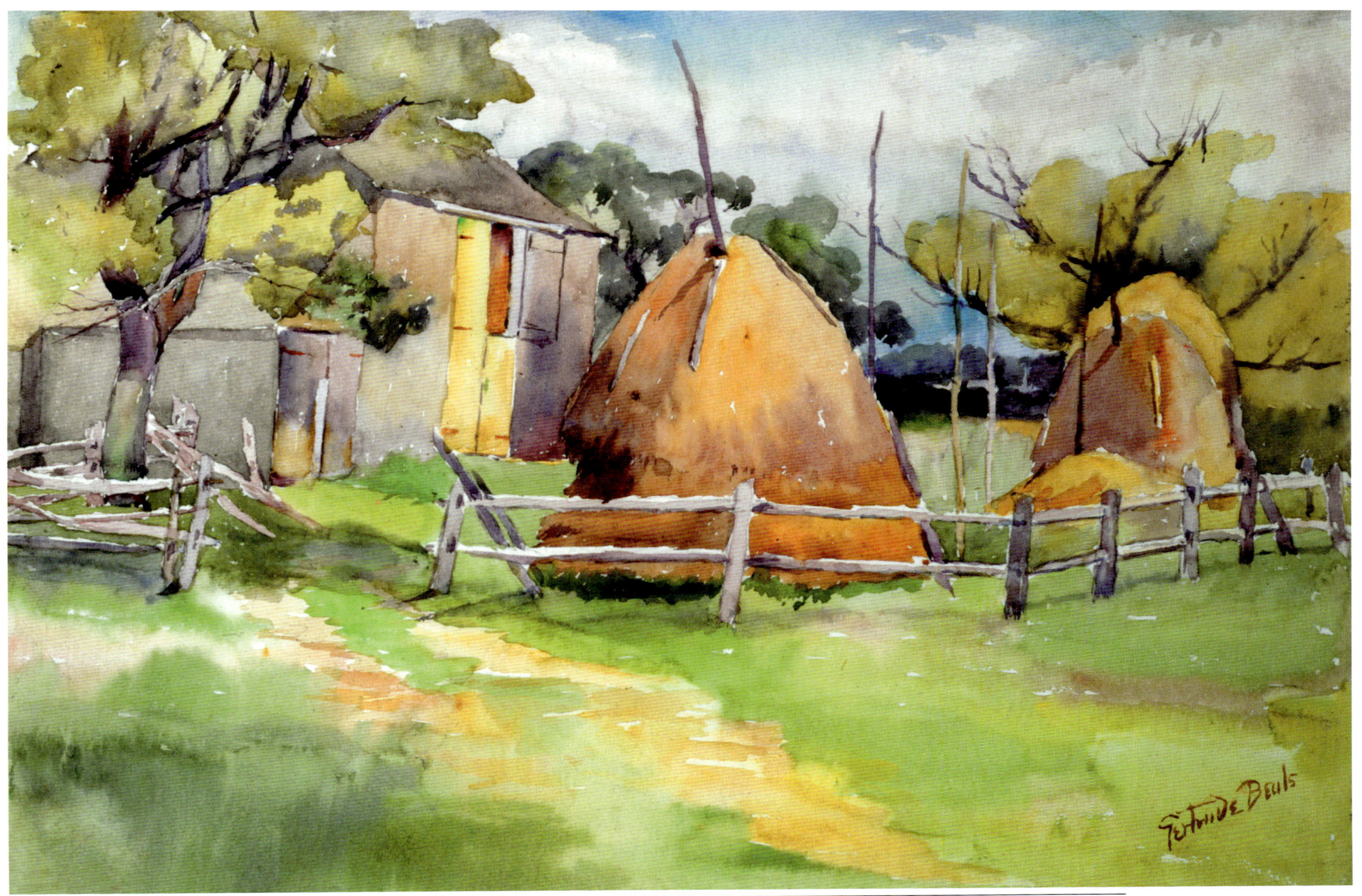

Haystacks, Autumn, c. 1895. Watercolor and pencil on paper, 13 1/8 x 19 1/4 inches. Courtesy of Smithsonian American Art Museum.

our own poets and scholars and thus we have the world through a local haze. This has had a strange effect on me. This effect is composed of a desire to escape plus an admiration for our tradition… I have seen more of Boston than of Europe. By and large, I have seen a great deal of Boston since I was born.[13]

From Sidney's meticulous record of the 1892 trip there is nothing to indicate that Gertrude formed any friendships with Europeans or was encouraged to do so.

The first trip abroad where Gertrude exercised her new skills as a watercolorist may well have been 1892, and she exhibited the fruits of this trip at the Boston Art Club in April of 1893. *Arches and Shrine — Dinan* and *Clock Tower — Dinan* (p. 38) are undoubtedly the pictures that Sidney described Gertrude painting on July 2nd and 4th of 1892.

Travel continued to be an integral part of Gertrude's formative years. In the summer of 1893 the Beals family spent part of the summer at the Islesboro Inn at Islesboro, Maine. Bostonians had long considered Maine to be their backyard and often spent the entire summer there. There was also a spirit of adventure among the more affluent of Boston in seeing the American wilderness, even if they saw much of it from a certain level of comfort. Departing the Islesboro Inn on August 23, the Beals took the steamer *Lewiston* to Bangor and up the Penobscot River where they noted the many lumber schooners in the river. They then had to take train cars, changing at Foxcroft for one attached to a freight train, for Greenville, where they stayed at the Moosehead Inn. On August 25th, they got on a boat at 7 am to go up Moosehead Lake to Northeast Carry to have lunch, then returned to Greenville and departed the next day for Montreal. Sidney, the diarist, again recorded that, "after a nasty day's travel … arrived at 4 o'clock. We had our trunks examined and then went to the Windsor Hotel." On August 28th they left by boat for Quebec City. The Beals returned to Montreal in September and October 8th took the steamer *Passport* through the locks and lakes necessary to pass up the rapids and through the 1000 Islands to stop at Kingston and finally disembark at Toronto on October 10th. They went on to spend the 12th at Niagara Falls and then took the train to return to Boston. The Maine and Canada trip made a

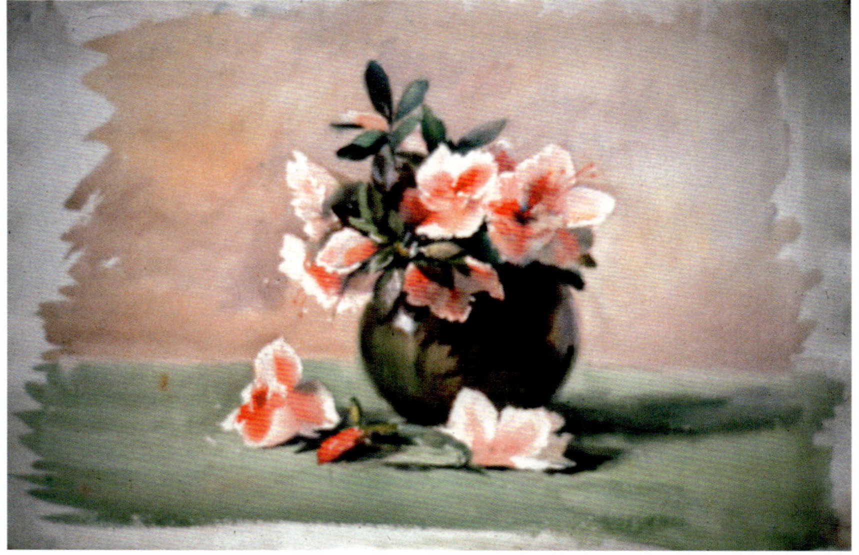

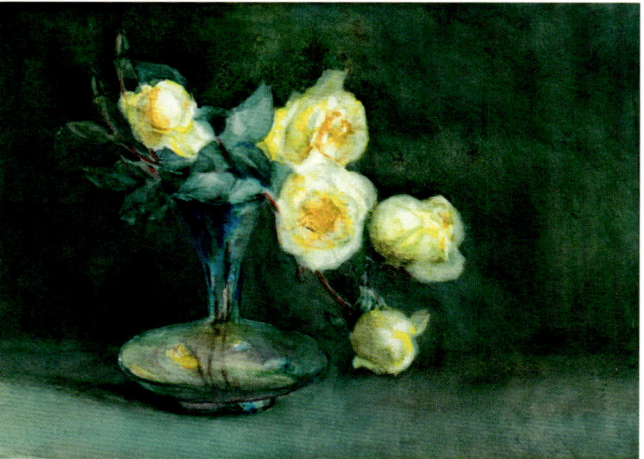

Azaleas in a Green Glass Bowl, 1890-95.
Watercolor on paper, 16 x 23 inches. Private Collection.
below: **John La Farge (1835-1910), *Yellow Roses in a Blue Glass Vase***, c. 1879. Watercolor and gouache on paper, 11 1/8 x 15 1/2 inches. Courtesy of Willaim Vareika Fine Arts, Ltd., Newport, R.I.

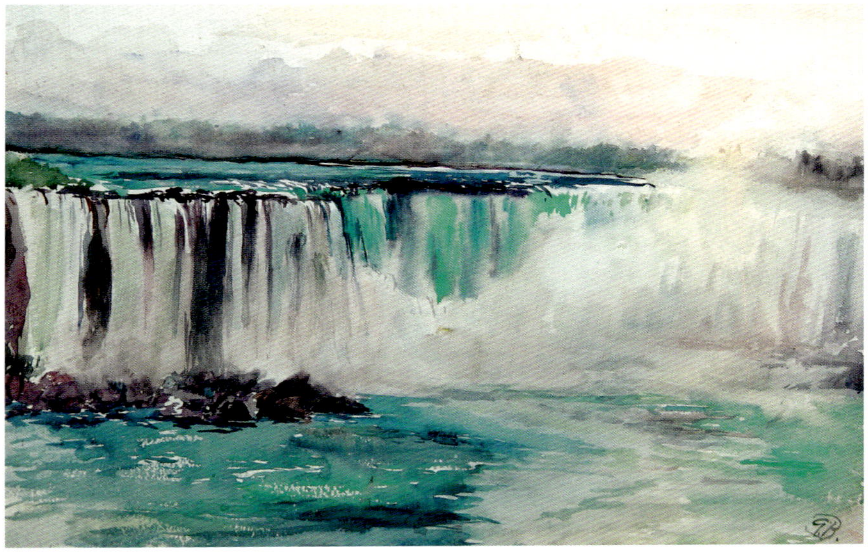

above: ***Niagara Falls***, 1893.
Watercolor and gouache on paper, 11 3/4 X 18 inches. Courtesy of Childs Gallery, Boston.

right: ***Garden in Shottery—Larkspur and Poppies,*** 1899.
Watercolor on paper, 14 x 10 inches. Signed Gertrude Beals. Shottery is about one mile outside of Stratford-on-Avon. Courtesy Childs Gallery, Boston.

counterpoint to the rather more luxurious travel of the prior summer. Gertrude developed a taste for more adventurous and exotic travel as she matured, even if the circumstances allowed for less comfort than the grand tours of her youth.

The European trip of 1892 had allowed her to paint ancient and picturesque architecture, as well as flowers and gardens, all of which would hold a place in her subject matter for the rest of her life. But, the intense vistas of northern woods in the Maine and Canada trip of 1893 provided subjects that were of equal fascination to her, and which would appear in the Norwegian mountain paintings of 1902, the New Hampshire mountain and winter forest paintings beginning around 1914, and the Cascades and Canadian Rockies paintings of the late 1930s. The fifteen years from 1888 to 1903 also saw Gertrude develop subjects of gardens and floral still life in addition to exotic and wild mountain landscapes and ancient buildings.

During the 1890s Gertrude Beals developed a confident style in the handling of watercolor. She combined techniques that Henry Rice taught her with style that she observed in the watercolors in current exhibitions by Ross Turner, Childe Hassam, and John LaFarge. LaFarge seems to have been especially influential in her floral still life paintings. The jewel-like puddling of watercolors in brilliant and opalescent effects in simple floral still life was a main stay of LaFarge's work in the 1880s and was for Beals as well in the 1890s. Turner's lush gardens gone half-wild overgrown with flowers also seem to be a model that continued in Gertrude's work throughout her career. She learned to use washes well, allowing colors to flow into one another, and to respect the white of the paper. Yet while many of her contemporaries used only transparent watercolor, her teacher, Rice, Turner, and LaFarge all employed gouache and opaque watercolor when it was needed for emphasis. Gertrude learned this technique and employed it as well. While much of her work in the 1890s employs brilliant color, it is carefully controlled and derived from fairly conventional beliefs as to colors seen in nature. Her style of application of paint was well within the boundaries of Impressionism as practiced by a watercolorist such as Hassam. She would later employ Modernist techniques learned from observing works by Dodge Macknight, her friends Maurice and Charles Prendergast, and her sometime landlord Arthur Wesley Dow. She would also have had the opportunity in February 1904 to see the great Whistler memorial exhibition in Boston. Many of the prominent

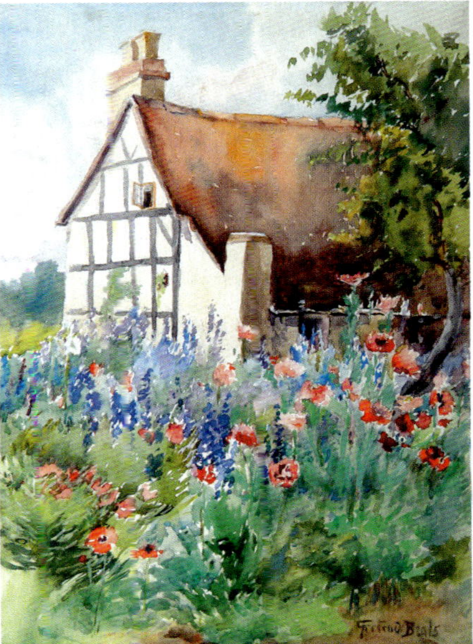

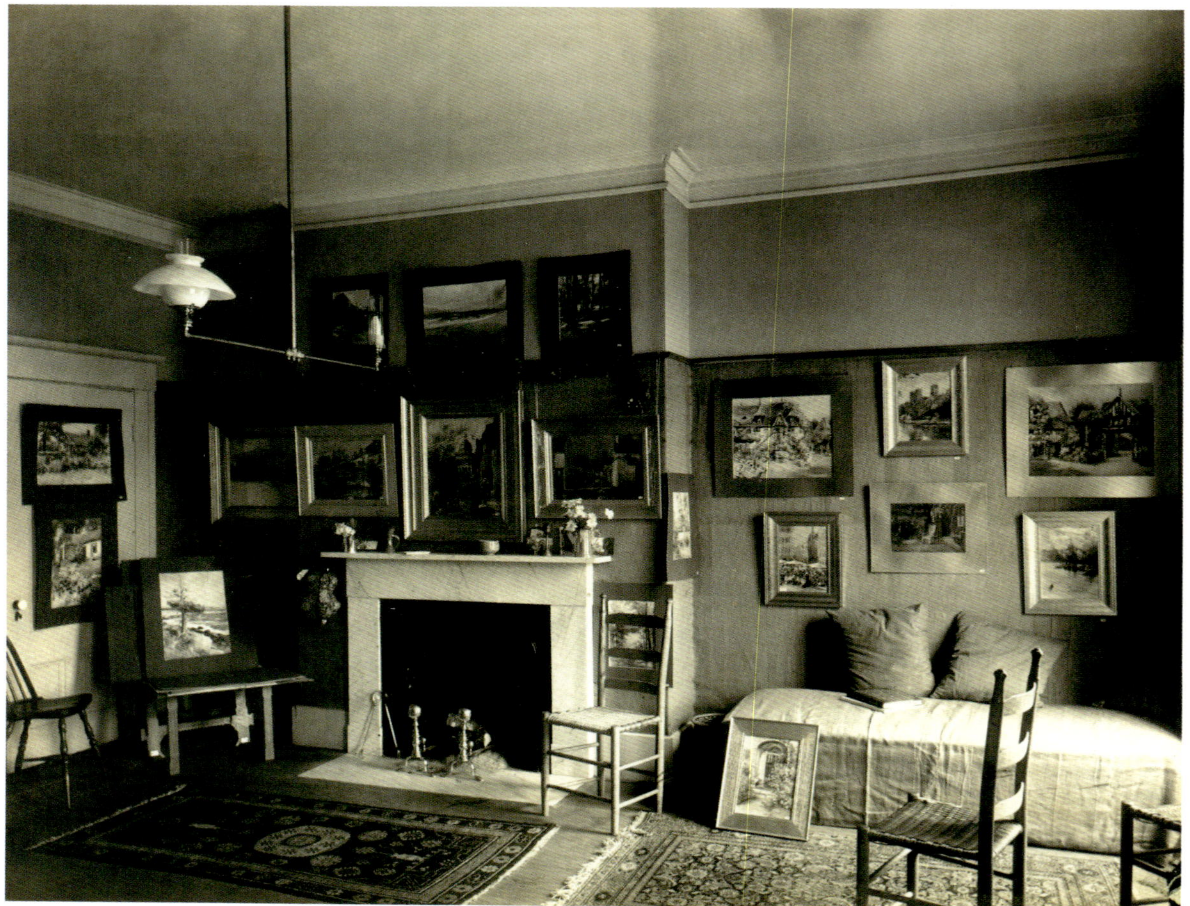

Interior of Joshua Beals house at 328 Dartmouth Street, 1902-03.
Gertrude's paintings adorn the walls shortly before her marriage.

collectors in Boston, New York, Paris, London, Philadelphia, and Chicago were either organizers of or lenders to the show. There were about 150 oil paintings, watercolors, and pastels as well as about 225 etchings and a large collection of lithographs and drawings. It was styled by the *Boston Transcript* as "the exhibition of the year" in which "the collection of Mr. Whistler's works is the largest, the most important, and the most representative ever brought together."[14] Although Whistler's influence in Gertrude' work might not be evident before 1910, she would later show that she had seen and digested his ideas, especially for nocturnes.

Summer travel in New England may have become less frequent for the Beals family after 1898, when Joshua purchased a large section of his father-in-law's summer estate at Nahant on the coast just north of Boston. The settling of the estate of G. W. Simmons included the sale of his "large tract of land belonging to the Simmons estate located in Nahant… It was divided into seven parcels" which were purchased by four buyers—including Joshua G. Beals for an aggregate of $42,250.[15] It may, however, have begun Gertrude's adventures as an independent traveler.

Gertrude Beals' confidence as an exhibitor grew, and she began to show at the Boston Art Club regularly in the April watercolor exhibitions through 1907. Although there are no detailed records of Gertrude's whereabouts in the late 1890s and early 1900s, she traveled over the next several years to Bermuda (1897 or early 1898), Nantucket (1898), England (1899), and Norway (1902), which resulted in a series of watercolors that were exhibited at the Boston Art Club. While she may have been accompanied by a family member or a friend on these excursions, Gertrude, alternatively, may have embarked on the first of her many independent travels in search of material for her art. She exhibited *June* in April 1895; *A Cottage by the Sea, Bermuda* (p.32) in April 1898; *In Old Nantucket* in 1899; *In Clovelly*, and *Anne Hathaway's Cottage* in April 1900; and *Valders Valley, Norway* in April 1903. Gertrude may have been especially delighted to place a work near Winslow Homer's *Inland Water—Bermuda* in

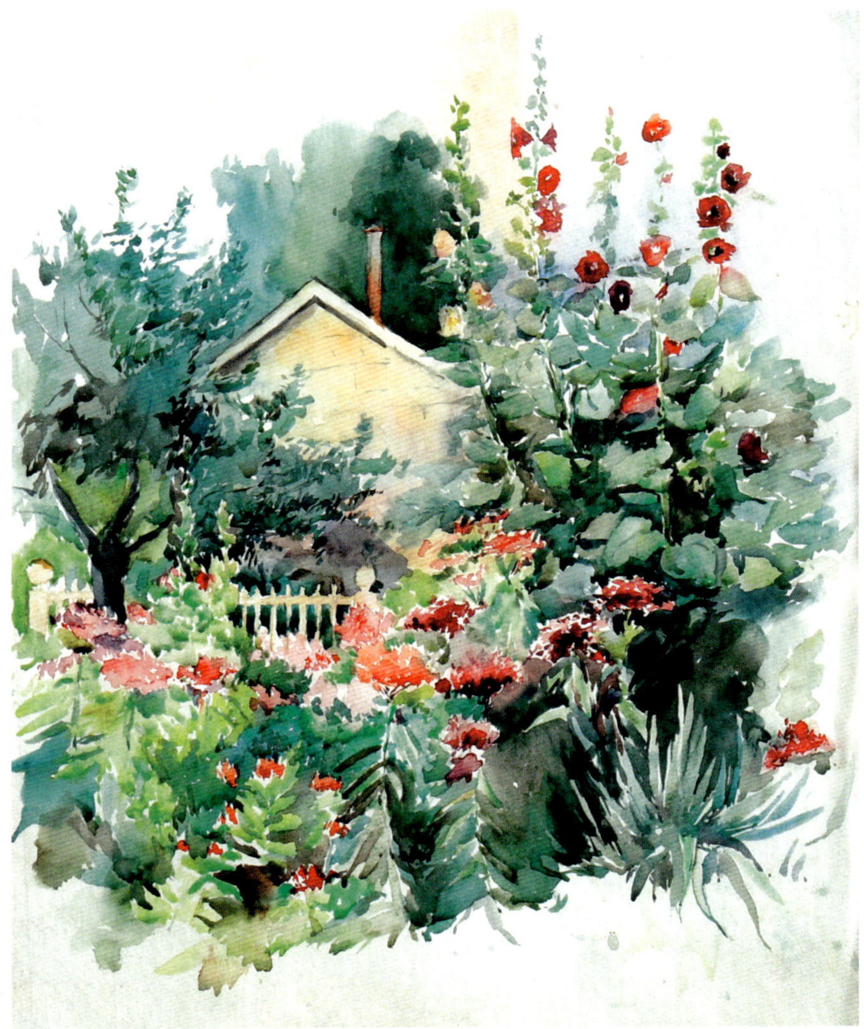

above: ***Cottage with Hollyhocks,*** c. 1895. Watercolor on paper, 20 x 14 inches. Henry Rice and Ross Turner's garden subjects rapidly became Gertrude's. Courtesy of Childs Gallery, Boston.

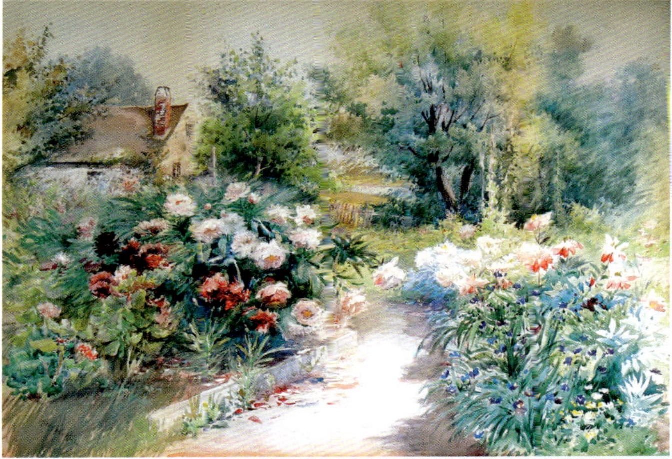

right: **Henry W. Rice, American (1853-1934).** ***A Garden Walk***, c. 1895, watercolor and gouache, 19 3/4 x 27 3/4 inches. Private Collection.

the 1903 Boston Art Club watercolor exhibition, and she could compare his work to her own Bermuda entry of 1898.

She also exhibited her first picture at the American Water Color Society, *Doorway, Dedham*, in their 35th annual exhibition in New York April 21 through May 4, 1902. Henry Snell had six watercolors in that exhibition, and Bostonians were well represented. Susan H. Bradley, Rhoda Holmes Nichols, Sears Gallagher, and Childe Hassam submitted works. Edmund H. Garrett sent two works of subjects in Clovelly, England, the same picturesque North Devon village where Gertrude had painted a few years earlier. She was beginning a career as a watercolorist beyond the regional restrictions of Boston. At the age of 30, she took a separate studio at 254 Boylston Street and listed herself in the Boston Business Directory as "artist" while maintaining her residence with her parents at 328 Dartmouth Street. But, after this single listing in 1899, despite a growing exhibition career, she did not appear again as an artist in the Boston City Directory. We might speculate that her parents could have disapproved at so public a presence as listing her address. In 1904, however, she became a member of the Copley Society, an organization of artist-members that had grown out of the alumni of the School of the Museum of Fine Arts. Very possibly Edith Beals was more concerned with the appearance of propriety for a young woman of a certain social class and upbringing than she was for her daughter's professional advancement as an artist. The implication may be that Gertrude was chafing—as a woman in her thirties—at the restrictions imposed on her by her parents while living at home, and that taking a studio, listing herself as an artist, and joining an artist's society represented major steps toward personal and artistic freedom.

This period of increasing professional independence coincides with Gertrude's younger brothers finishing their education and leaving the Beals' household. Gardner Beals graduated from Harvard College with the class of 1894 and received his law degree (LLB) from Harvard in 1897; her youngest brother, Sidney, graduated from Harvard College with the class of 1901 and received his law degree from Harvard in 1904. Gertrude's comfort level with family arrangements and restrictions, with Edith's worries about propriety, may have been brought to crisis when Gertrude was left as the only child remaining in the household. Gertrude may also have foreseen a life as a spinster-artist caring for aging parents—a duty that she may have witnessed among her spinster-artist peers.[16] Unmarried daughters of social standing, living with their parents in the early twentieth century would have been expected to care for them, if they needed care, and to defer to them if they did not.

NOTES, Chapter Two

[1] John P. Marquand, *The Late George Apley* (Boston: Little, Brown and Company, 1937), 108-09.
[2] A. J. Philpott in *Exhibition of Water Colors by the Late Henry W. Rice, Dec. 9-28*, Robert C. Vose Galleries, Boston (undated c. 1934).
[3] "The Fine Arts: The Boston Art Club Watercolors Exhibition-First Notice," *Boston Evening Transcript*, 9 April 1891, 6.
[4] "The Fine Arts: The Boston Art Club Watercolor Exhibition-Second Notice," *Boston Evening Transcript*, 13 April 1891, 3.
[5] *Boston Art Club, Constitution, Bylaws and list of Members*, 1890; *Boston Blue Book*, 1892-95.
[6] "The Fine Arts: The Annual Watercolor Exhibition at the Boston Art Club." *Boston Evening Transcript*, 4 April 1892, 6.
[7] Department of Labor Statistics "Historical Value of the U.S. Dollar in 1991 constant dollars." A calculator of 1.35 to convert 1991 DLS dollars to 2003 DLS dollars was provided by the economist Christopher D. Mooz using information from the DLS web site.
[8] Burpee letters, Nov. 7, 1897, Cadiz, to Mrs. N. A. Burpee (his mother). William Partridge Burpee Papers Archives of American Art.
[9] *Cabin Passinger List, French Mail Steamer La Champagne, from New York to Havre, Saturday, May 7th, 1892* (New York: Companie Générale Transatlantique, 1992); *The Boston Directory* (Boston: Samson, Murdock & Company, 1892), 1339; Clara Erskine Clement and Laurence Hutton, *Artists of the Nineteenth Century and their works* (Boston: Houghton Mifflin and Company, 1880), Vol. 2, 294; Henry T. Tuckerman, *Book of the Artists* (New York: James F. Carr, 1966), 567. G. Quincy Thorndike, native of Boston, graduate of Harvard, resident of Newport, R.I., returned to Boston in 1885 and died at age 59. His painting was called, "so thoroughly French in style and motive that his pictures require naturalization before being popularly welcomed at home."
[10] Holmes, Sr., *Autocrat*, 127.
[11] Marquand, 50-51.
[12] According to Jane Nylander, we should not be surprised at the quantity. In the 1890s nearly every occasion required a lady to be outfitted with white kid gloves, which did not remain white for very many outings.
[13] Ibid., 101-02.
[14] "Whistler's Great Works," *The Boston Transcript*, 23 February 1904, 2.
[15] "Real Estate," *Boston Advertiser*, 24 August 1898, 5.
[16] Erin Pipkin, "'Striking in its Promise': The Artistic Career of Sarah Gooll Putnam" in *The Massachusetts Historical Review*, Vol. 3 pp 89-115 (Boston: Massachusetts Historical Society, 2001). Pipkin says of Putnam (1851-1912) concerning her situation in the mid-1880s: "A single woman dependent on her family for emotional and financial support, Putnam was liberated from the full-time demands of marriage and motherhood but also obliged to arrange her supposedly free schedule around the needs of her parents, siblings, and the large social network that overlapped with her extended family."

PART TWO

SUNFLOWER CASTLE

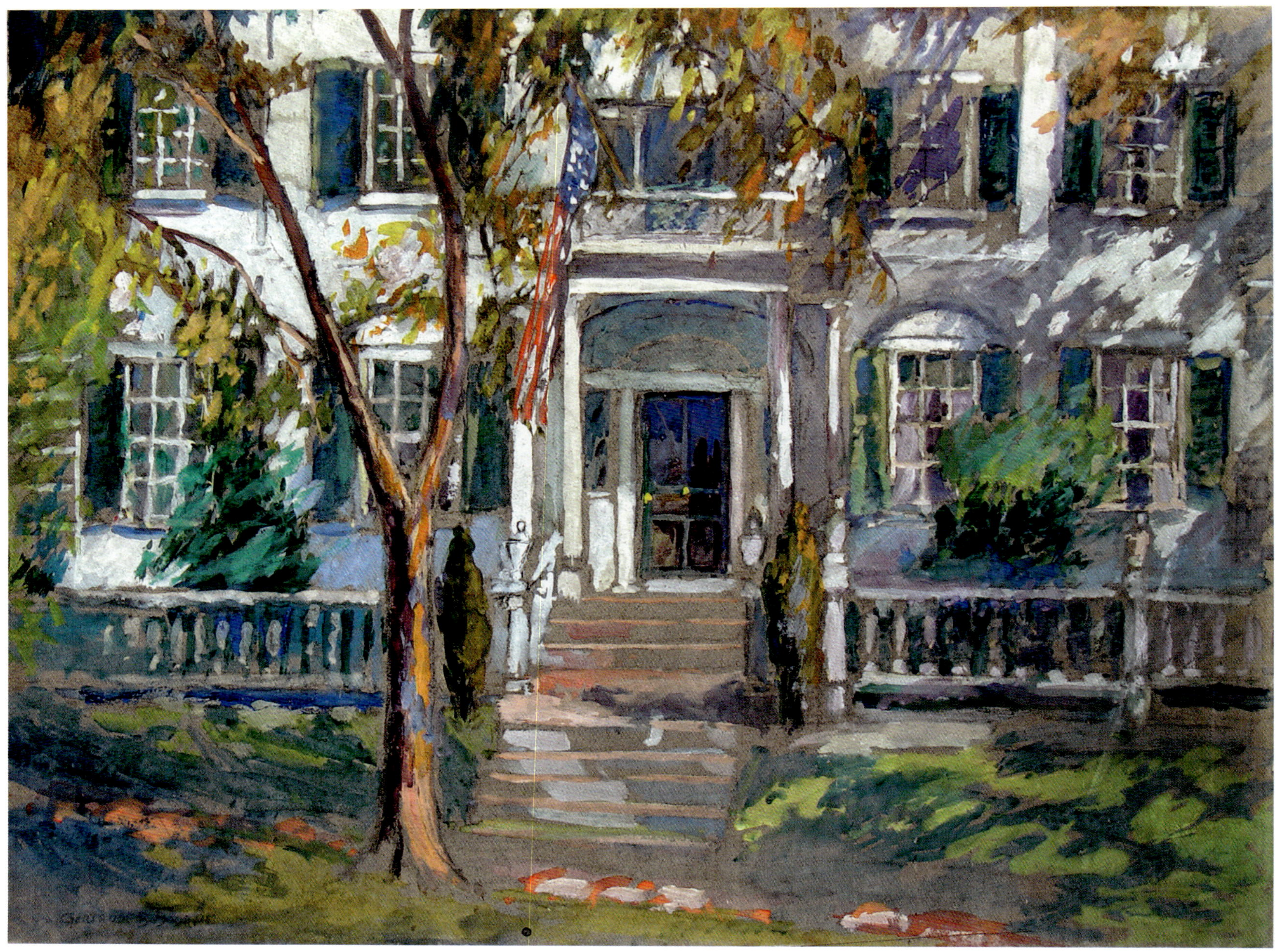

CHAPTER THREE

Marriage and Family

The emotions and upsets of courtship, so characteristic of certain undisciplined elements in other sections of the country, are, fortunately, no part of our best tradition... Mr. and Mrs. James Bosworth announced the engagement of George Apley to their daughter, Catherine—in every way an eminently suitable match, not only from the point of view of propriety but, more important still, from a community of healthy tastes and tradition. These two had played together in childhood and had trod the same paths of youth with a similarity of upbringing which could not but make them congenial.[1]

—John P. Marquand, *The Late George Apley*

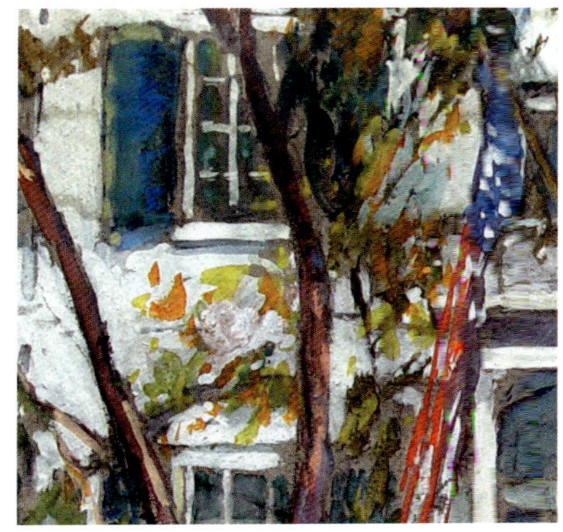

Miss S.'s House—Wiscasset (New England Colonial House), c. 1921.
Watercolor and gouache on gray paper, 20 x 26 inches.
Exhibited at the Art Club, Washington, D.C. 1923.
The façade of the Nickels-Sortwell House in Wiscasset, Maine which was owned by Frances Sortwell, one of the best-known women preservationists on the Maine coast and a leader in Colonial Revival architecture and gardens. Now an S.P.N.E.A. property.
Courtesy of Childs Gallery, Boston.

By the standards of her society, on her thirty-sixth birthday (May 21, 1904), Gertrude Beals was a confirmed spinster. She had settled on a career as an artist and was compiling a respectable exhibition record. She was living an outwardly comfortable life in the bosom of her family in their capacious Back Bay house which included a studio that would be the envy of many of her male counterparts. Her social peers may have been surprised, then, that she had been courting, became engaged to and, less than a month after her birthday, was married to Frank Augustus Bourne. It was a first marriage for each of them, and in the confusion of the moment there may have been a slip, because in her marriage record in Boston Vital Statistics, Gertrude listed her age as 35 (not 36).[2] Was she sensitive about her age at the time of her marriage, or was she sensitive about being nearly three years older than her husband?

Frank Bourne was born in Bangor, Maine on January 14, 1871 to Augustus L. and Maria Antoinette (Stevens) Bourne. He began his bachelor's degree at the University of Maine in 1889, but transferred after two years to the Massachusetts Institute of Technology in Boston where he studied architecture, received a bachelor's degree in 1895, and received a master's degree in 1896.

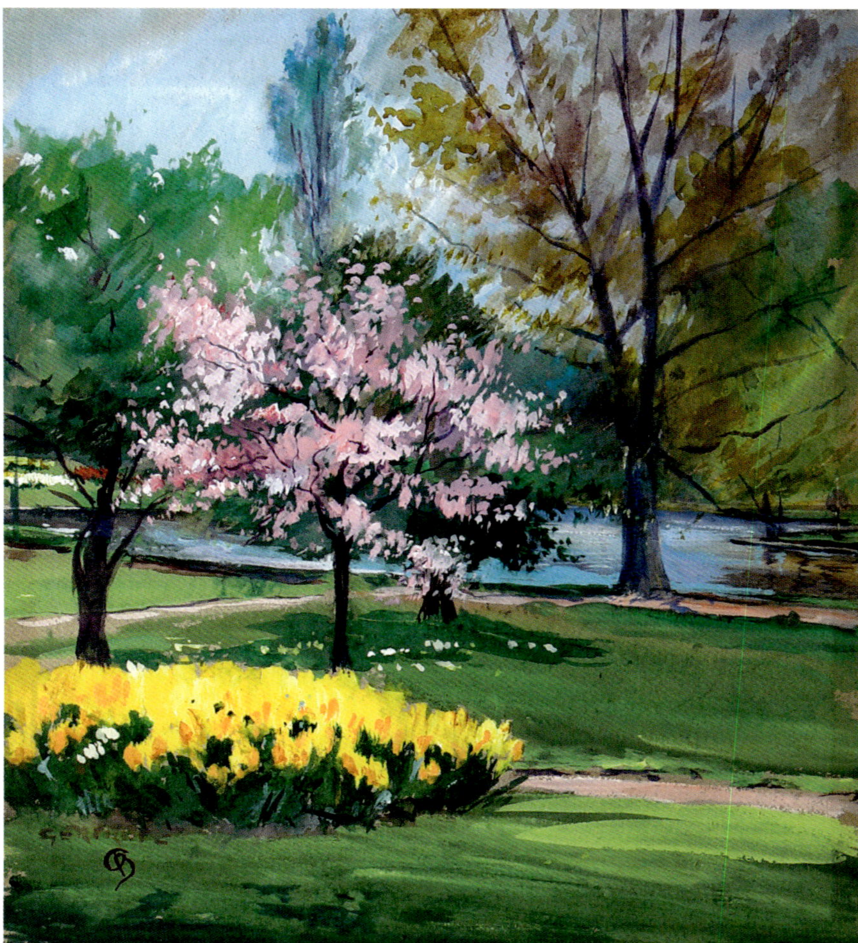

Judas-Tree in the Public Garden [Boston], c. 1909-10.
Watercolor and gouache on board, 16 x 14 inches.
Monogramed "GB" and signed indistinctly "Gertrude Beals Bourne."
Submitted to the Metropolitan Improvement League "Picturesque Boston" Exhibition c. 1910-11. Courtesy of the Bourne Art Trust.

At MIT, Bourne studied with the recently arrived French architect, C. Désiré Despradelle. Bourne later recalled, "I shall never forget the enthusiasm [he] created on his arrival at the Institute. Even in the junior class his visits were almost daily, and we all had the inspiration of his enthusiasm fresh from the ateliers of Paris."[3] Despradelle's courses at MIT thoroughly trained Bourne in the architectural history of Greece and Rome, the Classical landmarks, and, because much of Despradelle's inspiration was drawn from study of Gothic architecture, a thorough grounding in the latter.

While Bourne was studying architecture, McKim, Mead, and White's designs for the Columbian Exposition in Chicago (1892-93) set new standards for attention to details in Greek and Roman sources, correct proportion, and an understanding of ancient and modern precedents. The Exposition gave great impetus to the establishment of the American Beaux Arts. In this atmosphere, Frank Bourne learned the practice of architecture and its literature. Closer to home, Bourne could study McKim's Boston Public Library which continued, in the tradition of Renaissance craftsmanship, to be refined by the addition of sculpture and mural painting well into the 1920s.

After a stint as a draftsman in Bangor, Bourne found a position in 1896 as a draftsman and designer with what was perhaps the most prestigious architectural firm in New England—Shepley, Rutan and Coolidge. They were the successors to H. H. Richardson's architectural practice after his death in 1886, and they vied successfully for national commissions with such firms as McKim, Mead, and White, Richard Morris Hunt, Daniel Burnham, Henry Bacon, and John Russell Pope. From their two floors in the impressive Ames building skyscraper on State Street—which Shepley, Rutan, and Coolidge had designed—they continued the Richardson tradition of massive, ornately embellished stone structures. However, they rapidly added the new Beaux Arts style to their repertoire. While with Shepley, Rutan and Coolidge, Bourne helped to design picturesque bridges in stone in the Richardson style for the Boston and Brookline parks departments, which prepared him for later similar designs as an independent architect. It was perhaps while working on these commissions which were at least partly in Boston's "Emerald Necklace"—the elegant urban green belt designed by Frederick Law Olmsted—that Bourne may have first met America's greatest landscape architects. All of the Boston architectural world must have noted the easing out of Olmsted, Sr. in 1895 with the onset of dementia and his replacement at the firm by his talented son, Frederick Law Olmsted, Jr. (1870-1957). Bourne and Frederick Law Olmsted, Jr. would form a strong friendship.

During this period, Bourne also assisted the firm in the design and supervision of numerous Congregational churches in New England which helped to establish him as a specialist in ecclesiastical architecture. His most important project during his final period with Shepley, Rutan and Coolidge was assisting with the design of the dramatic new Beaux Arts South Station Railroad Terminal in Boston. The building was certainly a result of the influence of the new interest in Classicism at the Chicago Columbian Exposition, which was itself influenced by the Pantheon in Rome.

In his early years as a draftsman, Bourne had boarded at 364 Columbus Avenue in the South End, but in 1898 he moved to board at 17 Marlborough Street—just two blocks from the Beals' residence.[4] Bourne left Shepley, Rutan and Coolidge in the same year, when South Station was largely completed.

Perhaps it was at this point that he met Gertrude Beals. Not only did they live near each other, but the two had common interests. From her earliest exhibitions Gertrude had showed an interest in historic architecture as a subject. The increase in historical architectural subjects in Gertrude's work during the last years of the nineteenth century and the first years of the 20th may have been a result of meeting Frank Bourne and sharing his interests in older architecture and the Colonial Revival. Or, conversely, their meeting may have taken place as a result of his seeing her exhibition pictures of these subjects.

Frank Bourne availed himself, in 1898-99, of a year of advanced architectural study at Harvard and then established his own firm. He moved his residence to a room at 8 Huntington Avenue, then in 1900 he moved to 105 Mount Vernon Street, and about 1901 moved again to 20 St. Botolph Street. One of Bourne's first independent projects, a public library in his hometown of Bangor, Maine, showed the deep influence of the Beaux Arts design and motifs that he had assimilated on the South Station project. It was a grand design which was intended as a landmark to distinguish Bangor with the sophistication of the Classical traditions of Greece and Rome. The library's designs were published in *The American Architect and Building News*, *The Architectural Review*, and the *New England Master Builder*. Although the library was never built, by 1900 these publications had announced Bourne to a national audience as a sophisticated and accomplished architect.

In 1901 the First Congregational Church of Bangor commissioned Bourne to design a massive new church building. The prominence and success of the library design undoubtedly recommended Bourne as the architect for the project. His work for Shepley, Rutan and Coolidge was informed by the recent designs of Ralph Adams Cram for All Saints Church in the Ashmont section of Boston, Massachusetts (1892-94) and St. Stephen's Church in Cohasset, Massachusetts (begun 1899) as well as the precedents for design, materials and workmen set out in H. H. Richardson's Trinity Church in Boston. The Bangor church was recognized as a landmark after its completion in 1902, formed a precedent for many other Maine churches, and firmly established Bourne as an independent church architect. He was also a young architect with a taste for innovation, and when given the project for St. Luke's Church in Chelsea, Massachusetts in 1907, he chose to specify concrete block as an innovative new material in which to execute the Gothic design.

In anticipation of his impending marriage, in 1903 Bourne purchased the unique "Sunflower Castle" at 130 Mount Vernon Street on the flat of Beacon Hill. The building stands out as a bit of yellow "Elizabethan" cottage gothic in a resolutely Federal and Colonial Revival neighborhood. This delightfully eccentric structure was designed by Clarence S. Luce in 1878, remarkably early in the aesthetic movement in Boston. It incorporated authentic medieval features of half-timbering, stucco, fishscale shingles and prominent carvings of coats of arms, griffins, lions, and—most importantly—sunflowers. It had been dubbed "Sunflower Castle" by Oliver Wendell Holmes. Douglass Shand-Tucci said of it: "The best-known [of the finest Queen Anne houses in Boston], though it is usually described as a kind of eccentric old house, is the conspicuously yellow and red-tiled residence that challenges so charmingly the red-brick corner of River and Mount Vernon streets... In fact, the 'Sunflower Castle' is simply an excellent example in an unexpected place of Queen Anne design."[5] Gertrude's father may have aided in the purchase of the property,[6] which would have been in the Brahmin tradition. George Apley's father announced such help in a letter: "It happens that I was obliged only the other day to foreclose a mortgage on a small dwelling house in Gloucester Street. This was one of a parcel of three. As I have already turned the other two over at a profit, I have nearly cleared this one house on the transaction, and I shall turn it over to you as a wedding gift."[7]

Bourne immediately set to work to enlarge, renovate, and improve on the design for himself and Gertrude. He added a Japanese garden, small kitchen ell, and made interior changes, including redesigning the attic floor as a studio for Gertrude. She and Frank furnished it with an eclectic mixture of antiques and curiosities. The final effect was both picturesque and an antiquarian's delight. "Sunflower Castle" was to be Gertrude Bourne's principal residence for the rest of her life. In 1904, Bourne moved his office from Suite 849 in the Tremont Building to the Mason Building at 70 Kilby Street.

Frank Bourne seems to have been the perfect mate for Gertrude Beals. From all accounts he was a kind and gentle man, a hard worker who knew his profession as well as any in Boston, and despite his modest demeanor, was both respected and accomplished at the age of 33. He had already completed several major commissions, was a member of the Technology Club, had his designs published in the most widely read professional publications of his day, and had acquired and renovated a house for himself and his fiancée. Presumably the engaged couple were collecting and choosing furnishings as the renovations went forward. Frank Bourne remained a resident of 20 St. Botolph Street in Boston until after the marriage.

The choice of 130 Mount Vernon Street as an address may have suggested a mild rebellion against the constraints of Back Bay society. When, in 1906, Frank Bourne renovated a house on Acorn Street—now known as the most picturesque street on Beacon Hill—an article appeared with photographs of the renovation. Bourne had taken a very simple house and added a much more decorative Colonial Revival treatment to the windows and the door. The author of the article went beyond commenting on the design quality of the changes to discuss the social changes on Beacon Hill signified by the renovation. The Bournes had to be aware of these social changes and what they meant.

> When, a quarter of a century ago, the "made land" of the Back Bay district was ready for use many old families who had been content to live in houses on the streets crossing the north and west slopes of Beacon Hill deserted

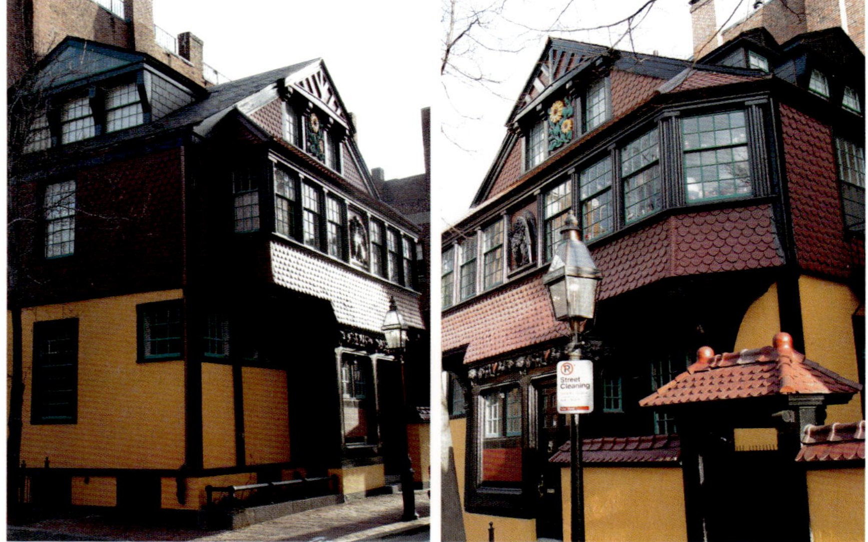

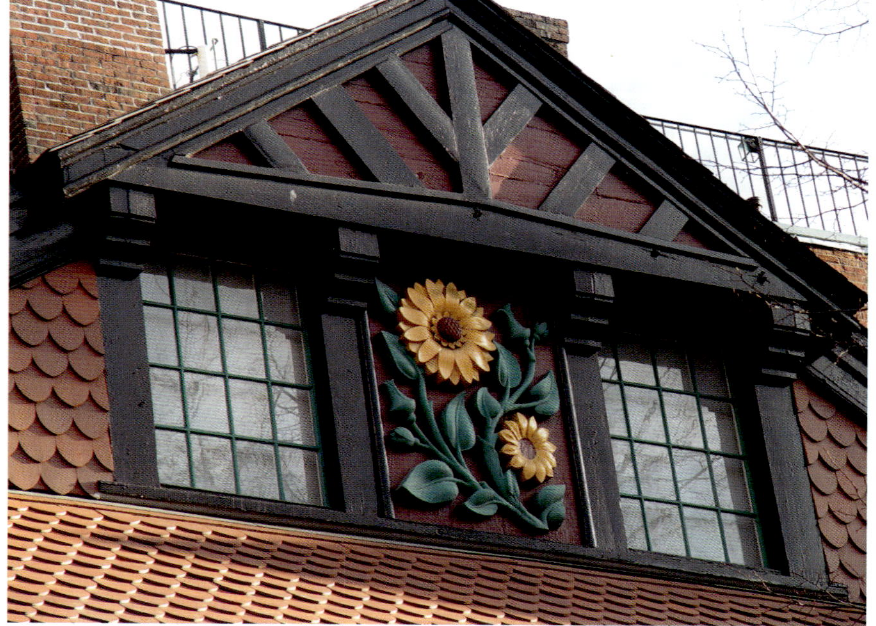

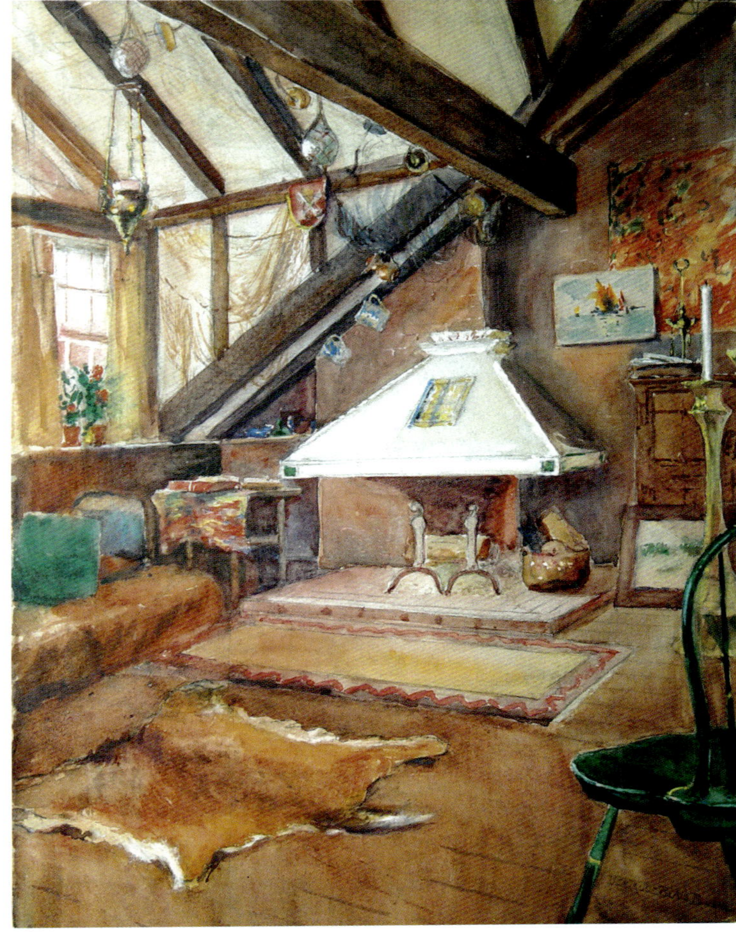

above: ***The Artist's Studio-Sunflower Castle***, c. 1910.
Watercolor on paper, 18 1/4 x 14 1/8 inches.
Frank Bourne transformed the third story of 130 Mount Vernon Street in Boston into a picturesque Arts and Crafts artist's studio for his new wife Gertrude.
Courtesy of the Bourne Art Trust.

left: ***Three Views of Sunflower Castle***, 2004.
Clarence S. Luce's 1878 Elizabethan Cottage Gothic House.

> their old houses for new ones built on the broader streets of the new territory. People of the same class shared their inclination and declined to fill up the houses left vacant and the owners had to seek tenants from less aristocratic classes. In this way the character of the population changed materially and a considerable portion of the territory was absorbed by Negros, while another portion was appropriated by stablemen and acquired the air of a series of London mews. Latterly, there has been a disposition to reclaim some of those streets, as bachelors found them very conveniently located with reference to the club-houses. Among others, Acorn street, one of the shortest and narrowest in the city, has been retenanted by lawyers, architects, artists, and others who appreciate quiet respectability more than the garishness of "all modern conveniences."[8]

Frank and Gertrude were to turn away, at least somewhat, from the rigid propriety of the Back Bay of turn-of-the-century Boston to the "quiet respectability" of the west side of Beacon Hill, among fellow artists and architects. Maurice (1859-1924) and Charles Prendergast (1868-1948) had taken a studio at 56 Mount Vernon Street in 1903; they would soon become a part of the Bourne's circle of friends and would remain friends even after their departure from the Hill for New York ten years later. Possibly Charles had a special relationship with Gertrude, since he had been born only six days after her. Laura Hills had a studio at 320 Boylston Street, but was boarding at 4 West Cedar Street on Beacon Hill and would soon move to 66 Chestnut Street. I. M. Gaugengigl and his patroness, Phoebe Jencks, had adjoining studios at 5 Otis Place, just around the corner from the Bournes' new home.

Sunflower Castle itself announced a separation from convention, for it was and is unique in the Back Bay and Beacon Hill for its eccentric aestheticism. Boston had, in its own self-assurance, at least, reigned supreme among artistic centers in America in the previous half-century, but knowledgeable critics expressed some doubts at this time, and one of the reasons was its lack of housing and studios. The *American Architect and Building News* opined that: "Naturally, Boston is peculiarly well adapted as a working centre for artists, and we believe that if landlords and real estate owners had found it profitable to cater to the needs of the class Boston would still be, as it once was, the chief artistic center of the country."[9] Within a dozen years even the most chauvinistic Bostonian would have had to agree that New York had eclipsed Boston as the center of the American art world for the advent of new ideas, and for the production and marketing of art. The Bournes as artist and architect had chosen the quiet respectability of Boston and Beacon Hill, but each would make a presence in New York and beyond.

Marriage as an alternative to remaining a single professional could not have been lightly undertaken by Gertrude Beals. There were models in Boston for successful women artists who had remained single, independent, and prosperous. She had not chosen earlier to leave her comfortable lifestyle indicating that she had been content with the situation of being a single woman in her thirties in her parents' household, with whatever restrictions that entailed. Or, alternatively, she may have been discontented with the eligible bachelors, or had been unwilling to give up the comforts of 328 Dartmouth Street to acquire an independence with reduced circumstances. Marriage to Frank Bourne seems to have given Gertrude both partnership and independence. They were like-minded in many things, including the idea that Gertrude would make major decisions. Frank seems never to have sought to dominate Gertrude, and they each seem to have cherished opportunities for independence as much as they seem to have enjoyed projects together.

Having settled the issue of where they would live, the couple were wed in a Unitarian ceremony which took place in the bride's home at 328 Dartmouth Street on Wednesday June 15, 1904. The Boston Globe recounted the affair:

> The ceremony was performed in the library by Rev. Paul Revere Frothingham of the Arlington St. church, the bride being given away by her father.
>
> She was gowned in white liberty satin, with applique lace yoke. Her tuile veil was fastened with a spray of orange blossoms and she carried lilies of the valley.
>
> The maid of honor, Miss Elsie Dalton, wore a gown of pale blue crepe de chine and a hat of white lace. She carried forgetmenots and sweetpeas.
>
> There were two bridesmaids, Miss Julia Little and the bridegroom's sister, Miss Anna Bourne. They wore white muslin gowns with sashes of light blue. Their hats and bouquets corresponded with the hat and bouquet of the maid of honor.
>
> The best man was Phillip Sharpless.[10] The ushers were Messrs Frederick Law Olmsted, Frederick Stone of New York, James De Wolfe Perry of New Haven, Henry Morse and the bride's two brothers, Gardner Beals and Sidney L. Beals.
>
> The floral and foliage decorations for the wedding comprised chiefly peonies and laurel, white blossoms being used in the halls and along the staircases, and crimson blooms adorning the room in which the ceremony took place.
>
> A reception followed the ceremony. Mr. and Mrs. Bourne will live at 130 Mt. Vernon St. and will be at home Wednesdays in November.[11]

The ushers included the distinguished landscape architect, Frederick Law Olmsted, Jr., who had recently, with his brother, John Charles, taken over the Olmsted firm after his father's retirement.[12] Frederick, Jr. had been a classmate at Harvard of Gardner Beals—who perhaps introduced him to both Gertrude and Frank. Another usher was James De Wolfe Perry (1871-1946), rector of Christ Church (Episcopal) in Fitchburg, Massachusetts. He would soon be made Bishop of Rhode Island (in 1908 he would marry Edith Dean Weir, the daughter of the painter John F. Weir and a successful painter in her own right).[13] Henry Grant Morse (1876-1934), was originally from Canton, Ohio, studied at the Massachusetts Institute of Technology and is known to have also studied painting and drawing in Boston while at M.I.T. He formed the architectural firm of Hale and Morse in 1897 with Herbert Hale, son of the famed Boston orator, Edward Everett Hale. Presumably Frank Bourne found Morse a kindred spirit as a young M.I.T.-trained architect who had just opened his own practice. Morse also practiced landscape architecture.[14]

Not finding the couple "at home" until November of 1904 may have been occasioned by the extended Italian trip of the summer of 1904. While it was certainly a honeymoon for the Bournes, with extended stays in Venice, Florence and Cortina, it was also a working trip for both of them. Frank was undoubtedly looking at architectural examples of correct proportion in preparation for a book he was writing on the orders of architecture, while Gertrude was using the Italian sites as subjects for her watercolors. The trip also represented Gertrude's first opportunity for travel completely independent of her parents presence or guidance. She now had the companionship of a mate who respected his wife's need to work at her calling as much as she understood his need to pursue his own. This first trip together set standards and programs for their extensive travels of the future. Upon their return to Boston, Mr. and Mrs. Frank Augustus Bourne settled into life on Mount Vernon Street.

The new Mrs. Gertrude Bourne also settled into an active exhibition schedule where she showed her work under her new name—first trying the signatures "Gertrude Bourne" and "Gertrude Beals Bourne" before deciding upon "Gertrude B. Bourne." From April 7 – 29, 1905 she exhibited one of the works from the honeymoon trip, *Palazzo Daris, Venice*, at the Boston Art Club. That year she placed her married name in *The Artists Year Book* with the Mount Vernon Street address.

Later in the year she made her first entry in the 15th Annual New York Water Color Club exhibition from November 11 – December 3; she showed *Golden Glow, Garden of Weld, Brookline* priced at $50. It may have been at this exhibition that Gertrude met Henry B. Snell who would soon become her second acknowledged teacher. Snell was a prominent member of the New York Water Color Club and had regularly exhibited at the Boston Art Club. Others exhibiting included New Englanders Lee Lufkin Kaula, William J. Kaula, Margaret Redmond, Charles Gruppe, Margaret Patterson, A. T. Bricher, Dodge Macknight, and S. P. Rolt Triscott.

The following year she exhibited *Summer Garden* and *Azalea Path—Arboretum* at the Rochester, New Hampshire Fair. While Gertrude Bourne had been interested in flowers from the beginning of her painting career, the two works shown at the Rochester Fair are among the first indications at a public exhibition of Bourne's interest in flowers, gardens, and natural settings. This would be one of the major subject interests for the rest of her career. She would often combine it with one of her other major subject interests—Colonial Revival architecture—to show a garden in front of a colonial house or doorway.

In 1906 she exhibited another of her "honeymoon paintings", *Villa d'Este*, at the Boston Art Club watercolor show alongside work by Henry Rice, Everett Shinn, Mary B. Titcomb, Charles H. Woodbury, and F. Luis Mora. At the 17th Annual New York Water Color Club exhibition November 10–December 2 Bourne showed *Lily Pond* for $75. She again exhibited a garden painting, *Rhododendrons*, at the Rochester Fair in summer 1907. And in the New York Water Color Club exhibition for November 2 –24 she offered *Rhododendrons in the Arboretum* for $125. At this point Gertrude had established herself in Boston and New York as a watercolor painter of flowers in natural settings at a price that commanded respect among her peers.

Colonial Revival

By the very last years of the nineteenth century, the art and architectural movement known as Colonial Revival was a major force in American design. It had its strongest roots, clients, and practitioners in New England, where the myths and facts of the founding fathers, their lifestyles, and their legacies were woven into culture, life, and education. John Hubbard Sturgis had made drawings of the 1737 Hancock House on Beacon Street (a short walk from Gertrude's birthplace and from her Simmons grandparents' house) shortly before it was torn down in 1863. Its destruction is often cited as the beginning of the preservation movement in America, but it could also be cited as the beginning of an interest in creating and building Colonial Revival architecture. The Centennial Exposition in Philadelphia in 1876 furthered the Colonial Revival and the already growing passion for collecting and studying American antiques.

By the 1880s copies of eighteenth and early nineteenth century furniture along with inherited and collected originals were finding their way into the fashionable interiors of newly built New England houses. The Massachusetts minister, Wallace Nutting, capitalized on this taste by selling reproductions of 'Pilgrim Century' furniture and hand-colored photographs of ancient houses, their interiors, and colonial gardens. Not surprisingly, artists found the subjects of old houses, pristine New England villages, and ancient New England interiors and their furnishings proper and popular subjects. The Boston architects Peabody and Stearns reproduced the Hancock House as the Massachusetts Building for the Worlds Columbian Exposition in Chicago 1892-93. The fair, which was supervised by McKim, Mead, and White, codified both a new Roman and

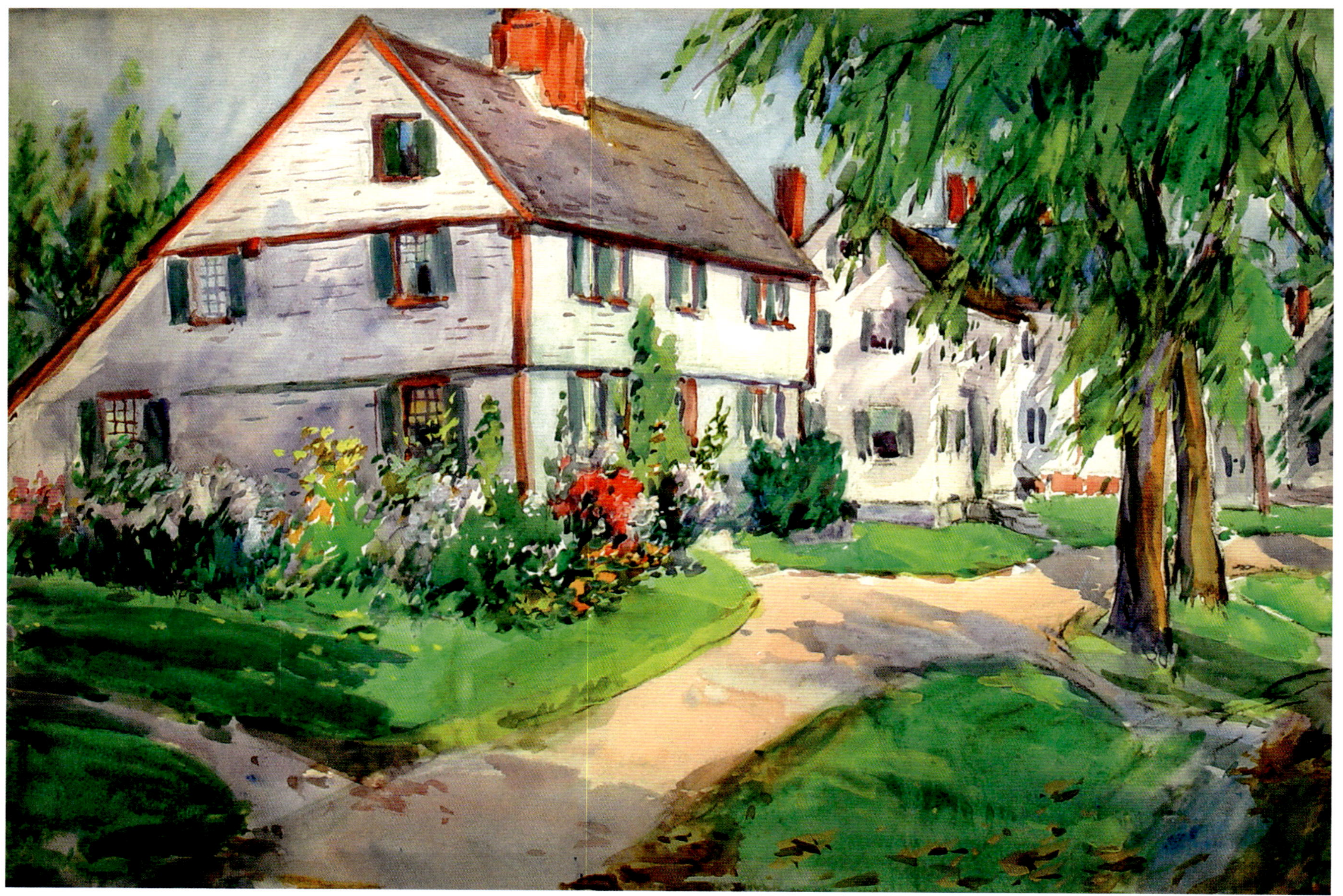

Colonial Revival that—as Beaux Arts architecture—would dominate American building and planning for several more decades.

Artists became, in some cases, equally passionate about explicating the images of the past glories of New England. Edwin Whitefield, an individual artist who saw the possibilities of benefiting from the growing interest in Colonial Revival subjects, began the illustrated publication *Homes of Our Forefathers* in 1879 with carefully lithographed drawings of early and picturesque buildings from across New England.

In December 1898 the Colonial Dames sponsored "An Exhibition and Competition of Colonial Pictures" at the Boston Art Club which included C. E. L. Green's *Old Barracks, Quebec*, Childe Hassam's *The Old Boston Post Road*, *Quincy Massachusetts*, and *The Cider Jugs*, Edward A. Page's *Old Boardman House, Saugus*, Charles H. Woodbury's *A Roadside Tavern* and *An Old Mansion Near York, Maine*, Theodore Wendell's *Witch Hollow* and *Old Newport*, and Ross Turner's *A Colonial Dame*. Included in the 56 paintings were works by eight women artists, including Ellen Day Hale.[15] This theme was repeated the following December with "A Second Exhibition and Competition of Colonial Pictures under the Auspices of the Colonial Dames of Massachusetts, " again with 56 paintings. Here Hassam showed *The Stairway: A Plot of the Revolution*; *Early Colonial Gravestones at Lexington*, and *Indian Summer in Colonial Days*. Carroll M. Bill (soon to become a close friend of Gertrude's) exhibited *Abigail Adams' Kitchen*, and Ross Turner again sent work. Ellen Day Hale participated along with six other women artists.[16] Bourne had undoubtedly seen both exhibitions since they took place on Dartmouth Street three blocks from her residence, and since she exhibited at the Boston Art Club during those years.

Perhaps the first exhibition of "Colonial Pictures" prompted her to paint *Old Nantucket*, her first datable Colonial Revival subject, which she showed at the Club in 1899. She was already interested in ancient architecture as was evidenced in her painting the old buildings of Dinan in 1892. Whenever Gertrude found architecture that seemed suitable for a subject to paint, it qualified as 'picturesque.' It had an ancient, often tumble-down quality that evoked history and romance. While other old architecture would continue to interest her, Colonial Revival subjects would form the greatest number of her most focused architectural watercolors. Unlike many other artists who pictured eighteenth or nineteenth century figures at work in interior or exterior subjects, Bourne's Colonial Revival works were always set in the present with the focus on the architecture of the past and not on the people of the present. (In most cases when people are the focus of a Bourne painting, as in *Kingston Market, Jamaica* (p. 98), the people are the picturesque subject instead of the architecture). William Ladd Taylor (1854-1925) of Jamaica Plain in Boston was one of the most successful of the Colonial Revival illustrators. His *The Hanging of the Crane* and *Home Keeping Hearts are Happiest* published as a supplements to the *Ladies Home Journal*, were framed and hung in large numbers of homes across America.

Matthew Perkins House, Ipswich, Massachusetts, c. 1917.
Watercolor, gouache, and charcoal, 14 1/2 x 21 inches.
Courtesy of Childs Gallery, Boston. Formerly known as the Norton/Corbett House, the building was built at the time of the wedding of Matthew Perkins in 1685. It was the birthplace of Arthur Wesley Dow and stands today at 6 East Street, Ipswich.

Although Gertrude Bourne had begun with *In Old Nantucket* (1899) and *Doorway Dedham* (1902), her exhibition offerings of Colonial Revival subjects increased rapidly after 1911 when she began to summer in Ipswich, Massachusetts amid a virtual museum of seventeenth, eighteenth, and nineteenth century buildings.

Motherhood

On November 30, 1907, Gertrude gave birth to her first and only child, Philip Walley Bourne.[17] The Bournes gave their son his first and middle names after Gertrude's good friend, Abigail Bromfield Phillips Walley (1845-1942). Walley, a descendent of some of the most eminent New Englanders, was a "gifted watercolorist," a prominent member of New Old South Church in Copley Square, and the treasurer and one of the first directors of the Boston Y. W. C. A.[18] She had joined the Copley Society in 1894. In 1907 she lived at 201 Clarendon Street, only about three blocks from the Dartmouth Street house

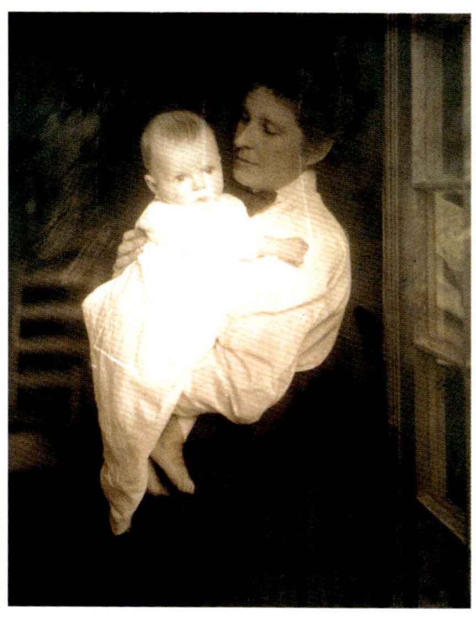

where Gertrude had grown up. This successful woman, close to the age of Gertrude's mother, must have acted as a role model and a mentor for a woman intent on having a career in the arts.

Gertrude was perceived later by her granddaughter as not really liking children and not easily relating to them, but that did not seem to be the case with Philip.[19] He was, however, expected to be on good behavior; Gertrude and Frank employed an early version of the "time out" with "the punishment chair" for his occasional transgressions. As a practical New Englander, Gertrude was not about to miss the opportunity of a seated model, willing or unwilling, and so may have significantly increased the punishment by painting the culprit. According to later reports, Gertrude was of a stiff-backed New England disposition, at least with any but close friends, while Frank was a much warmer person with an engaging disposition. Gertrude seems to have gotten on very well with like-minded people, whether they were interested in music, art, architecture, or gardening, but she was not interested in making small talk about subjects that were of no interest to her. Music was one of her passions. She was a regular attendee at performances at Boston's Symphony Hall. She maintained subscription seats in the balcony. Apparently, young Philip was able to bridge the divide between the worlds of adults and children. He embraced, or at least accommodated, his parents' interests. As a child, and later as an adult, he joined her in attending the symphony, and he maintained her seats as his own after her death.[20] Philip learned French—reportedly speaking it before he spoke English—played the piano, and later became an architect. He was also devoted to his mother. She was devoted to her son, with whom she maintained a close relationship for the rest of her life, but she did not let her duties as a mother prevent her from continuing to paint, travel, or exhibit. And young Philip did not get away with much under his mother's watchful eye.

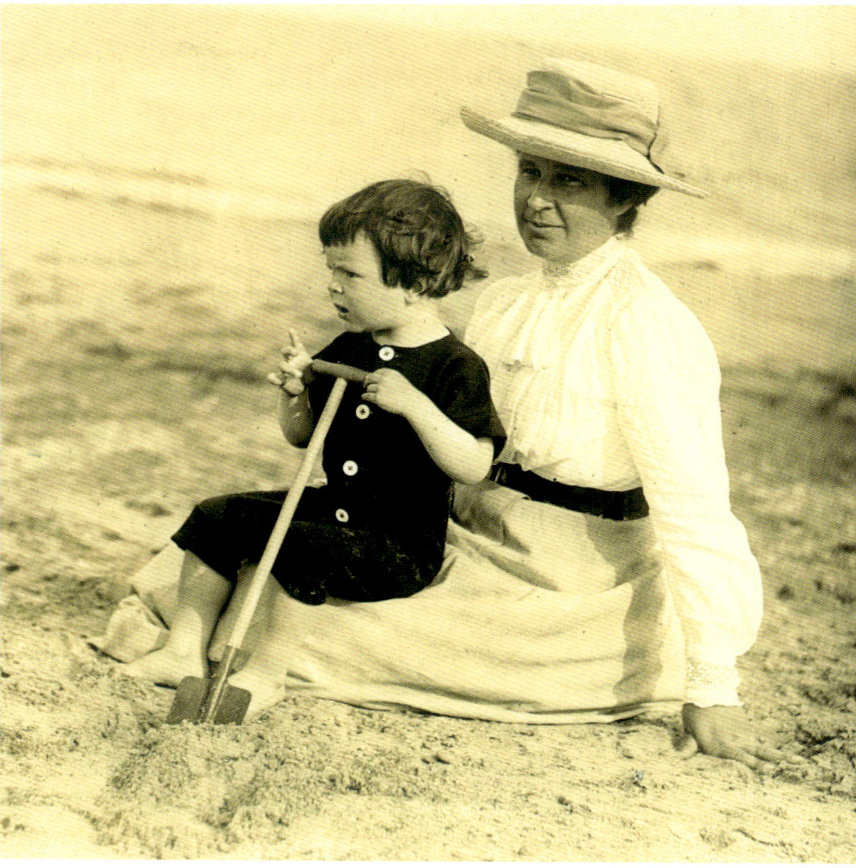

above: ***Gertrude Bourne with Philip Walley Bourne***, c. 1911. Gertrude and her son are shown at the beach, probably at Scituate, Massachusetts.

left: ***Gertrude Bourne and Philip Walley Bourne***, 1908.

Revivals, Restoration, and Adaptive Reuse

Frank Bourne's architectural practice brought him the commission to design, in 1909, Charles River Square, at the foot of Beacon Hill against the new Charles River embankment. The owner of the property, Beacon Hill Associates, was a partnership between William Coombs Codman and Gerald G. E. Street. Both of the partners had been concerned with the downward slide of Beacon Hill into rooming houses and tenements.[21] Their innovative development successfully reversed the trend, and Frank Bourne was to be one of their most trusted allies in the re-creation of Beacon Hill. Bourne, however, was viewed by some as even more than architect and ally. Walter Firey wrote in *Land Use in Central Boston*: "when the Hill had reached its lowest ebb…a noted architect, Frank A. Bourne by name, moved from his Back Bay home to a deteriorated one-time colonial dwelling on Mt. Vernon Street…in this way was begun the regeneration of Beacon Hill as a preferred residential district."[22] Firey and others viewed the Bournes' move to Beacon Hill as the catalyst for the turn-of-the-century revival of the neighborhood. Bourne would also build a project for Beacon Hill Associates on Brimmer Street between Chestnut and Lime Streets. Charles River Square—still today one of the most desirable residences in Boston—was emblematic of success in re-gentrifying Beacon Hill. The courtyard of townhouses emulates the Bulfinch models and other proper Federal period townhouses of the older sections of the hill—including Louisburg Square—rather than the more eclectic building of the Back Bay.

If Frank Bourne was in the forefront of the urban Colonial Revival, he was also in the vanguard of adaptive use. In 1909 the Bournes made the acquisition of another residence which was eccentric by the standards of proper Bostonians. By the end of the summer Frank and Gertrude had purchased and renovated a boat shop on the edge of Scituate Harbor into a house that could be used for the best six months of the year. They had visited the site the previous year, as is indicated by Gertrude's watercolor *Satuit Brook*, exhibited at the Philadelphia Water Color Club in November 1908 (along with *The Wide Spreading Pond*). The *Boston Globe* found the renovation process sufficiently unusual to publish an article which stated:

> To one unacquainted with architectural possibilities the weather-worn little building standing on the edge of Satuit Brook, at a point where it enters Scituate harbor, and built on posts directly over the water, which comes part way under it during high tide, seemed devoid of artistic qualities, but to the trained eye of Mr. Bourne it contained just the desired requisites for an attractive abode, and he accordingly purchased and remodeled it….
>
> The first floor [a single room] was left unchanged except for the portioning off of a space for the small kitchen and toilet beyond, the wall separation being contrived from a number of finely paneled doors, brought from the Wigglesworth house at Boston and stained gray to match the old weather-worn woodwork…

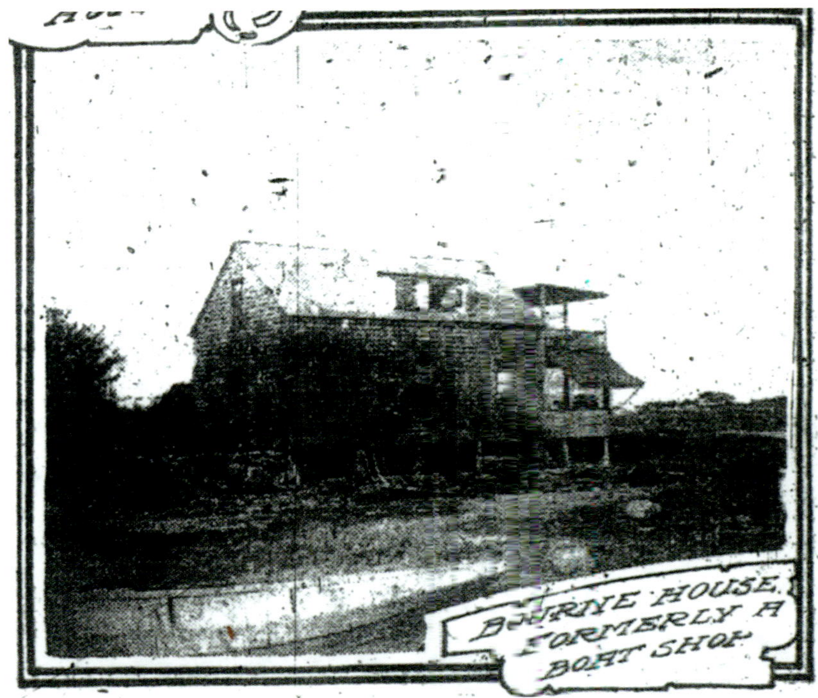

Bourne House—Formerly a Boat Shop, 1909.
As published in the Boston Globe, October 31, 1909

The dining table was contrived from two old wood sawhorses, with a drafting board laid across them, and the artistic lamp which graces the center was made from a pickle jar equipped with a shade painted by Mrs. Bourne, who is an artist of ability, while the old carpenter's bench that was in the shop at the time of its purchase was lowered to make a seat around two corners of the dining room portion of the apartment and boxed in underneath for storage purposes.

From the central beam depends the model of an old ship, emblematic of the building's original use, and from a rafter on the right hangs a candle fixture evolved by Mrs. Bourne from an old tin round. Lanterns of various types depend at intervals from other beams and furnish all the artificial light required.

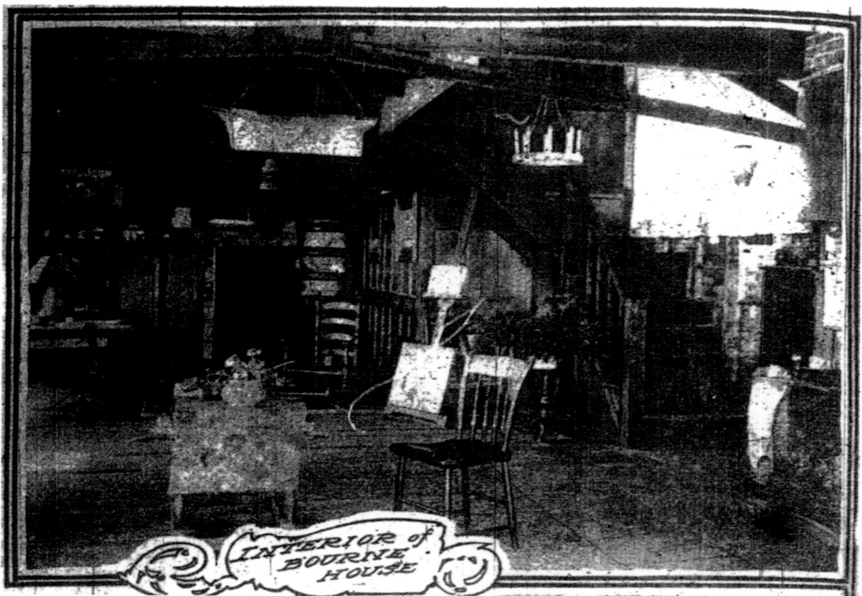

Interior of Bourne House [Scituate, Massachusetts], 1909.
As published in the Boston Globe, October 31, 1909.

The furniture is entirely colonial, picked up at odd times. Fitted into the chimney at one side is a queer old Franklin stove that relieves the chill of damp and stormy days....

The cost complete of purchase and alterations was but $500, and the result is an attractive and liveable home that serves as a residence for its owners six months of the year.[23]

The Scituate folly seems to have lasted only a few years. The only exhibition, aside from the Philadelphia Water Color Club at the Pennsylvania Academy, of Gertrude's Scituate works was in 1914 and may suggest that that was the last summer in the boat shop. But that they owned it at all is another example of the Bournes' choosing to be different and artistic as well as having a taste for the old, picturesque and "Colonial."

A New Teacher and New Exhibitions

A hiatus in Gertrude's exhibition schedule occurred after the Rochester [New Hampshire] Fair exhibition of late summer 1907 and the New York Water Color Club Exhibition which ended six days before Philip's birth. Bourne appears to have exhibited only three times from that date through 1914, showing the two aforementioned Philadelphia Water Color Club paintings in 1908, *A New England Porch* at the same venue in 1909, and the latter painting again at the Art Institute of Chicago's 24th Annual Exhibition of watercolors, May 7-June 5, 1912.[24]

In 1911, with a four-year-old son in tow, the Bournes set off for England and were in London in June when George V was crowned as the new King of England. Then, somewhat in emulation of her own parents, Gertrude and young Philip visited France, while Frank Bourne headed for Germany. In the following few years, no watercolors from this trip were exhibited, probably because she painted few watercolors during this period at all—the result of the exigencies of rearing a young son. Motherhood seems to have been Gertrude's consuming interest to the exclusion of her art for nearly seven years. There are, however, at least two watercolors of Boston subjects that bear the labels for the Metropolitan Improvement League Exhibition of 1910-11[25]. The League, led in part by Frederick Law Olmsted, Jr. and his brother, proposed, "to hold an exhibition of paintings, drawings, photographs, etc, in illustration of the picturesque aspects of Boston—a novelty in the way of exhibitions. The numerous responses received from intending exhibitors indicate a remarkable representation of picturesque charm of Boston streets, parks, the watercourses and the harbor." *Judas Tree in the Public Garden* (p. 52) was one of two labeled entries that Gertrude proposed. It is not certain that this exhibition was ever held, but the entries indicate that Gertrude was responsive both to a call from Olmsted and to an opportunity to present her vision of picturesque Boston.

Following the Metropolitan League watercolors, Bourne's style began to shift, probably as a result of instruction from her new teacher, Henry B. Snell (1858-1943). Snell, who was exactly a decade older than Gertrude Bourne, had been born in England and came to New York in his teens. He studied at the Art Students League and formed friendships with Charles Warren Eaton, Ben Foster, Leonard Ochtman, W. L. Lathrop, and Charles C. Curran. They all began to submit to the National Academy of Design (Snell's first painting was shown in 1896—the same year his wife, Florence Francis Snell first had a painting accepted). Soon Snell began to collect honors: he was made an associate of the National Academy in 1902 and an Academician in 1906. He won the gold medal of the Art Club of Philadelphia in 1896, first prize at the Tennessee Centennial in Nashville in 1897, honorable mention at the Paris Exposition in 1900, silver medal at the Pan-American Exposition, Buffalo in 1901, silver medal at the St. Louis Exposition in 1904, first prize at the Worcester Art Museum in 1905, and the Beal Prize at the New York Water Color Club in 1905. He was also a member, in 1911, of the New York Water Color Club, the American Watercolor Society and the Salmagundi Club. That year he had a one-man show of his paintings at the Worcester Art Museum. His interest in watercolors had become very serious by the early 1890s. He helped found the New York Water Color Club in 1890 and was its president for more than thirty years.

He was also a teacher of note, teaching at the Art Students League and privately. Among his students were Jane Peterson (1876-1965), Anna Fisher (1873-1942), and Felicie Waldo Howell (1897-1968). His willingness to take on women students and the woman-friendly New York Water Color Club, may have been attractive to Gertrude Bourne when she was seeking further instruction. His considerable success in taking prizes in national and international exhibitions would have been even more significant. But the most important reason for his selection was his reputation for encouragement in his teaching method. One writer noted:

> It is pleasant to hear Mr. Snell give a criticism. An earnest student tries to depict something which to him is beautiful but the result is only a meager and commonplace little rendering. One wonders if anything can be found in its favor. But not so Mr. Snell. He has the insight or intuition to see the loveliness of the vision of that student and he helps his pupil not only to develop an appreciation of beauty but an ability to express it. [26]

Snell was also noted as a helpful and patient judge who was often invited to be part of the jury for national exhibitions, museum exhibitions, and club shows. The writer concluded that "to be frequently chosen for jury service is a compliment, for it proves that the artist's colleagues have confidence in his judgement and honor."

Gertrude Bourne's most major exhibition to date came in 1914 with a two-man show at the Milton Public Library in Milton, Massachusetts from 9 - 30 September. Bourne's work in this show probably began to demonstrate the influence of Snell's teaching for the first time. The Milton Library show included eighteen of Bourne's watercolors together with seventeen watercolors by Abigail B. P. Walley. Walley seems to have made all of the arrangements for the exhibition in April 1914, including the decision that most of the watercolors would be shown matted, but not framed. She also made arrangements for publicity. Prior to the exhibition, she released this information to the *Boston Transcript*:

> The works shown are examples of straightforward, simple and conscientious watercolor work, of which one is not likely to tire. Boston, its park system, rhododendrons and other flowers, in private estates of Brookline, Cohasset, Cornish and South Carolina; many points of view of a Jerusalem road Italian formal garden, showing the picturesque possibilities of this kind of arrangement of paths and terraces, etc., which have grown up with daily use and care.

The passage may say what Bourne was thinking of her work at this point in time: "Straightforward, simple and conscientious … showing the picturesque possibilities."

F. W. Coburn of the *Boston Herald* wrote of the show:

> Both these painters handle watercolor cleverly. Both are ambitious and execute on pretty large sheets of Whatman paper compositions that are full of architecture, trees, flowers and other things. One criticism which might be made of much of their work is that the subjects of this complexity might be made with rather more emphasis upon a definite focus. This emphasis, of course, need not necessarily be accomplished, as the old masters worked it, through concentration of light. One may distribute the light equally, as in the modern spirits, but concentrate the attention by a greater lightness of handling in the focal than in the extra focal parts. These artists, like a good many other acquarellists, tend to work every part of the composition in about the same manner, that is neither very loose nor very tight. Many of the motives, and certainly those made in Scituate gardens, are so attractive and well chosen that one wishes they showed just a bit more artifice. It is quite legitimate not to be too naïve.
>
> The little two-woman show, for all that, is well worth seeing. It abounds in picturesque and beflowered old houses such as anybody who can draw at all would be keen to try a hand at. Of such part are Mrs. Bourne's *Blacksmith Shop, Egypt*, almost too floral for a real follower of Hephaistos to do business in; *Old House, Scituate*; *John Alden House, Duxbury*; and *Cohasset Garden*. The *Rear of the State House* makes a good motive, and this painter, too, has done the Cambridge bridge. In this last the limitation of her technique prevents complete justice being done to the essential charm of Mr. Wheelwright's creation: its graceful rigidity. *Scituate Light* memorializes a familiar landmark.[27]

Coburn continues by reviewing Walley's watercolors of gardens and mountains at Jaffrey, Cornish and Chocorua, N. H. making similar compliments and criticisms and, in his view, pointing the painters in the correct direction. From the similarity of the subjects and titles the two painters seem to have been going out and painting together. Both presented a Charles River Bridge, Ward's

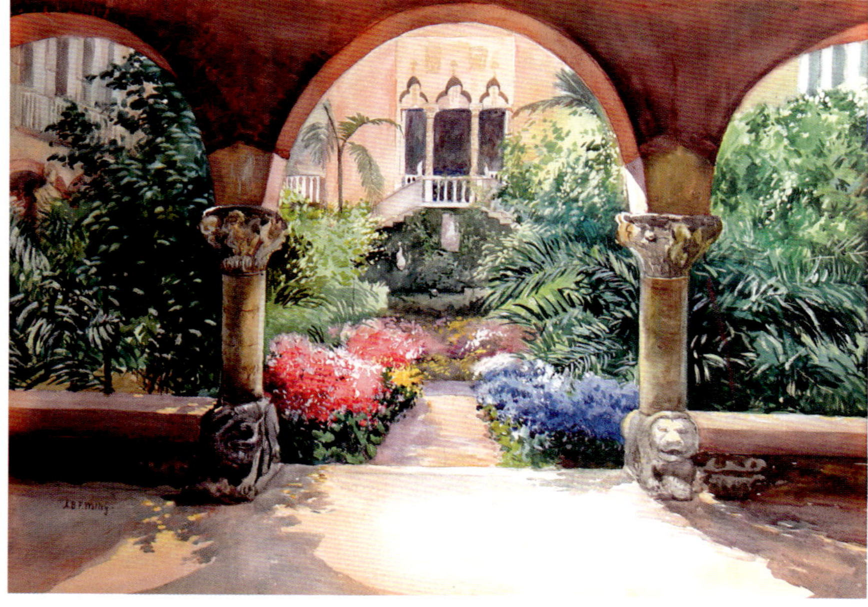

Abigail B. P. Walley (1845-1942)
Courtyard of Fenway Court—The Isabella Stewart Gardner Museum, c.1914.
Watercolor, 16 3/4 x 22 3/4 inches. Private Collection.

Pond, garden at Cohasset, and Scituate pictures. The latter may have been from visits by Walley to the Bourne's seaside summer house in Scituate. Bourne priced her unframed works in this exhibit a bit higher than Walley's—$40-$75 versus $25-$50—although in a letter to the library Walley stated: "We both … have had exhibitions in galleries—I have painted a good many gardens."[28] Coburn was correct in his identification of Bourne's technique at the time of the Milton exhibition. In the 1890s she had often focused the composition, particularly of flowers, in the center of the painting. By 1914, however, Bourne tended to compose the painting across the whole of the paper filling the composition to the edges. She never sharpened the focus of her later paintings by tightening the focal points or otherwise calling attention to particular parts through style or technique. Rather, in almost all of her later works, Bourne focused the paintings through forceful design.

On July 14, 1914, as Gertrude Bourne was preparing for her Milton Library exhibition, her father, Joshua, died of heart failure at his residence at 328 Dartmouth Street. He was a little more than a month shy of his 78th birthday. The forty-six-year-old Gertrude probably saw this, as most children do when they lose a parent, as a major passing and marker in their lives.

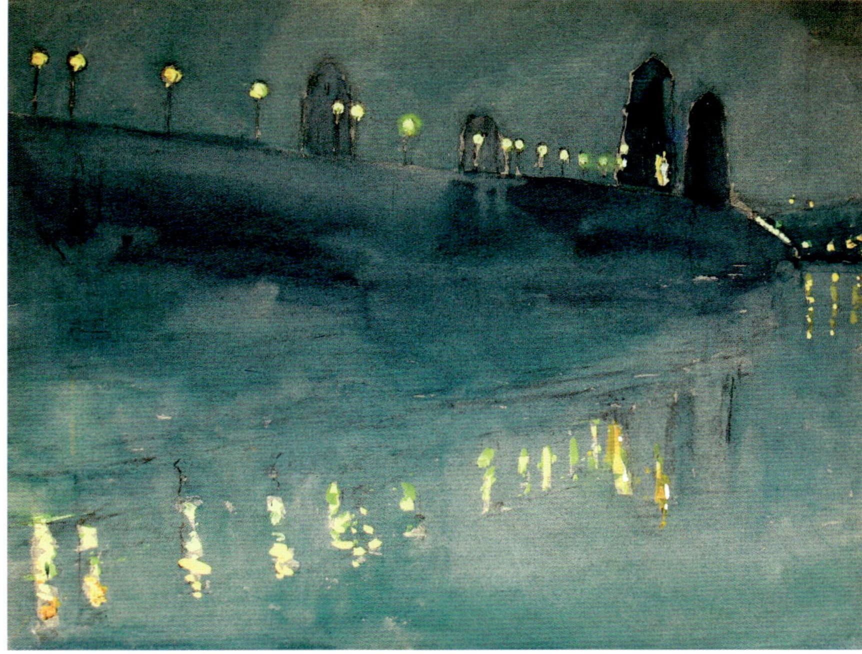

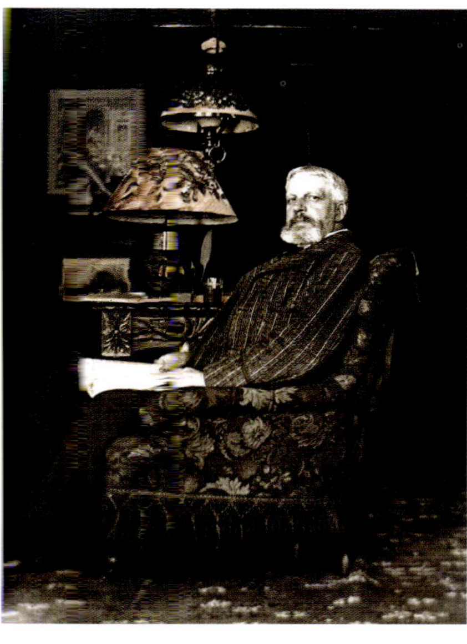

Would she have seen herself as the person to whom her mother would turn in this moment? Did she foresee the closing of the grand house on Dartmouth Street? For the rest of 1914, except for the Milton show and three entries at the Philadelphia Water Color Club, she apparently did not exhibit, perhaps because of time spent helping her mother settle the estate, or from the special trials of raising a seven-year-old boy. Joshua Beals left a considerable estate, by the standards of his time, to his wife.[29] Eventually a portion of the inheritance would devolve on Gertrude. By 1917, the large Dartmouth Street house of Gertrude's childhood had been sold, and her mother and her youngest brother, Sidney, had moved to nearby 41 Marlborough Street.

above: ***Longfellow Bridge on the Charles River***, c. 1915. Watercolor, gouache, and charcoal on gray paper, 20 x 26 inches. This shows the influence of Whistler and Tonalism on both Bourne and Boston artists in general. Courtesy of the Bourne Art Trust.

right: ***Joshua Gardner Beals at Home***, c. 1900.

More New Influences—Distinctly Professional

In 1912 The Museum of Fine Arts, Boston acquired a group of John Singer Sargent watercolors that had been painted only a few years earlier. Sometime shortly after their acquisition, Gertrude Bourne applied to the museum for permission to copy some of them. *La Biancheria (The Laundry)* and *Villa di Marlia: Lucca* were both painted by Sargent in 1910. Bourne's copies of both of these prove that she "studied" with Sargent as Sargent had "studied" with Velasquez—by making carefully observed copies of his work and internalizing the lessons in the detailed observance of technique, color, and composition.

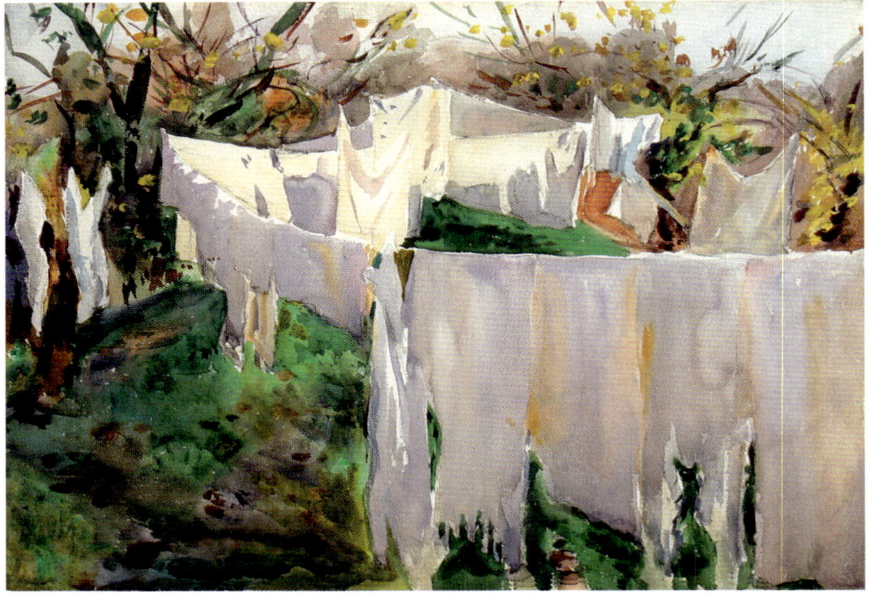

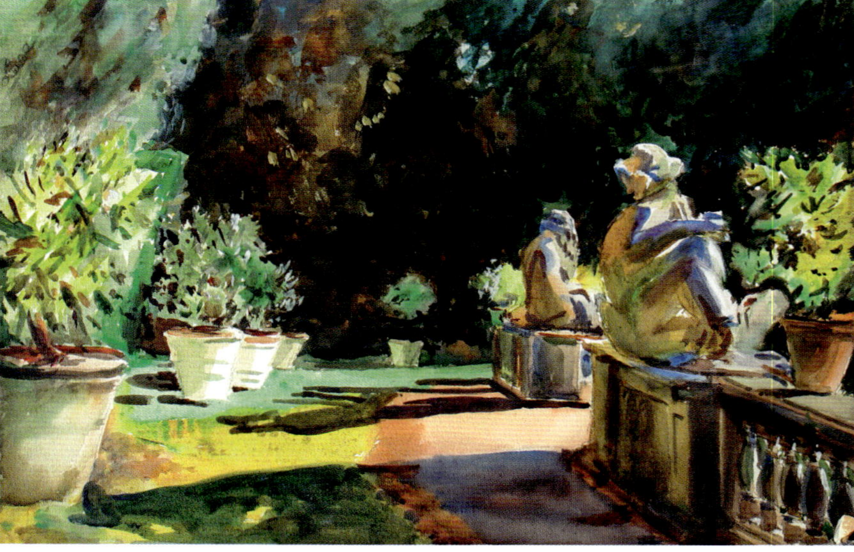

In 1915 she exhibited *Rhododendrons* at the Washington Water Color Club at the Corcoran Gallery from February 20-March 11. She did not, however, attend the show since she arrived at the Philbrook Farm in Shelburne, New Hampshire on February 18 for several weeks of winter painting. Dodge Macknight had arrived for his usual stint at Philbrook Farm on January 14 and was probably still in residence when Gertrude arrived.[30] The Philbrook Farm trip was clearly in preparation for Bourne's first solo exhibition at the Copley Gallery at 103 Newbury Street in Boston, to take place shortly before her forty-seventh birthday.

The Copley Gallery was one of Boston's most successful and prestigious commercial galleries in the 1910s and 1920s. The previous year it had hosted a solo exhibition for Jane Peterson and would shortly do the same for John Singer Sargent. It was also the gallery which represented one of New England's most successful women artists, Laura Coombs Hills, (1859-1952). Hills had been the most important New Englander in the small but popular movement for the revival of miniature painting starting in the 1890s, and her exquisite renderings of young women on ivory brought her both critical and financial success. She was also very interested in floral still-life and had begun to make a second career in pastels of floral arrangements. Hills' patrons were upper-class Bostonians and residents of Boston's North Shore, who would also have been in Bourne's circle of family and friends. According to Gertrude's son, the two artists collected each other's works.

From April 20 to May 1, Bourne exhibited 21 watercolors at the Copley Gallery. The works were heavily drawn from winter studies in the White Mountains of New Hampshire, but also included gardens from both New England and South Carolina, and architecture from Portsmouth, New Hampshire and Alexandria, Virginia. The titles of the works also suggest the

above left: ***La Biancheria [after John Singer Sargent]***, c. 1912-15. Watercolor on board, 15 x 21 1/4 inches. Verso bears title, "Copy of Sargent" and stamp: "Museum of Fine Arts/Boston/copied from painting/ in the Gallery." Courtesy of the Bourne Art Trust.
below left: ***Marlia Garden: Lucca, Italy [after John Singer Sargent]***, c. 1912-15.Watercolor on board, 14 1/4 x 21 5/8 inches. Courtesy of the Bourne Art Trust.

extent of her travels. The reviewers were complimentary, but also offered positive criticism. Most importantly, they recognized her as a maturing professional talent. The most important reviews came in the 1910s from the *Boston Transcript*, which reported:

> In the front room Mrs. Gertrude B. Bourne is exhibiting a collection of twenty-one of her watercolors, which are painted with much frankness, directness and crispness, with a good eye for color. The collection is divided into two sections, eight of the pictures depicting snow scenes and the rest garden motives. It is in the snow pictures, albeit this class of subjects no longer possesses any novelty, that Mrs. Bourne displays her greatest skill and facility. In such works as *The Ravine*, *Edge of the Woods*, and *Melting Snow* she manifests a good deal of that ready command of the medium which proves she has not mistaken her vocation. The now more than familiar blue shadows in such a work as *The Ravine* are put in with such justice of values as to give the picture great vitality and brilliancy. The garden pictures, too, give Mrs. Bourne many welcome opportunities to indulge her predilection for bright, pure and brilliant color. Excellent examples of this are the *New England Garden*, *A Southern Home*, *Hanging Moss and Azaleas* and *The Church in Alexandria*.[31]

The critic of the *Christian Science Monitor* was also positive, but with one negative, suggesting that her architectural subjects were of lesser quality:

> Miss Bourne is an artist who joys in the color of nature that she sees about her,—that much is plain to the most casual observer. The bright hues of sunlit gardens and flower bordered walks, of massed azaleas and rhododendrons and even of winter woods attract her eye and, are recorded on the canvas with an intensity of coloring that marks the artist's appreciation. Happiness must ever paint a gay world and by that sign we know Miss Bourne to be a very happy worker.
>
> Two of the best examples of her peculiar ability to emphasize the color notes of a composition and at the same time express a very certain sense of realism are *The Ravine* and *The Hillside*. Both are glimpses of snowy slopes broken by transparent blue shadows and decked with winter

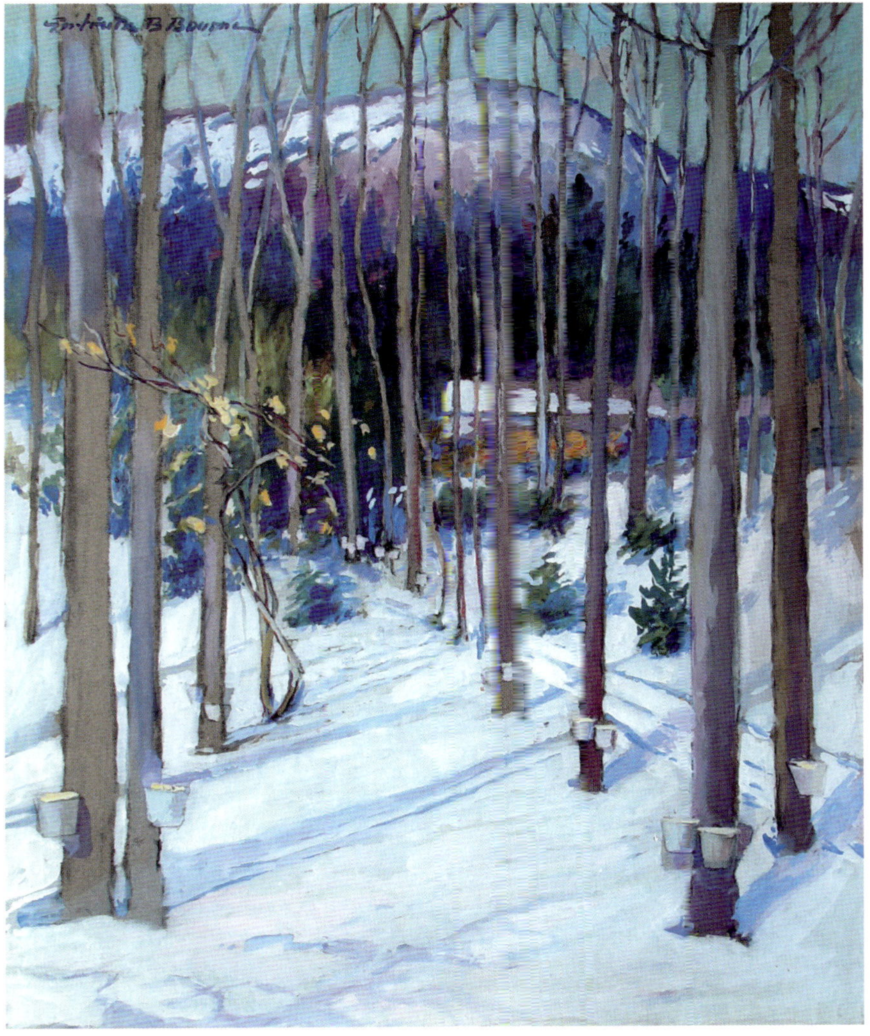

Mt. Monadnock and Maple Grove, c. 1925
Watercolor and gouache on gray paper, 24 [illegible]/4 x 1[illegible] 3/4 inches.
Courtesy of Childs Gallery, Boston.

> foliage—rich brown, red and dark blue shrubbery and trees. They are direct, almost sketchy in handling, yet full of sunshine and sparkles. A number of these snow scenes are shown, all attractive.
>
> Among Miss Bourne's summer scenes perhaps the best is *Old Fashioned Garden*, with its verdant hedge enclosing a riot of larkspur, peonies and roses, all aglow in the sunlight. Equally delightful is *Phlox*, showing a winding walk bordered with handsome clusters of these flowers, and *Rhododendrons*, with its placid pool almost hidden beneath great masses of the ruddy blossoms. There are in all some 20 paintings on exhibition, all full of their message of sun and color. Only the sketches of the buildings are faulty and uninteresting.[32]

F. W. Coburn, the art critic of the *Boston Herald*, had been following Bourne's career for some time. He noted:

> This aquarellist exhibited last summer at the Milton Public Library, and in a notice then written some of the characteristics of her work were described. Several of the works now shown were in that exhibit. Others have evidently been made during the past winter. Among these *Edge of the Woods* strikes one as a good example of what our friend Eben Cumins calls "area cutting." The line where the pasture leaves off and the pine woods begin follows a good diagonal course across the composition. While, indeed, one is still close to the word "edge" one might like to talk a little about the excessive crispness of the edges in this and other works. Yet, as that is to an extent the way of water color washes and as the opposite fault of fuzziness is much more detestable in an aquarelle, let it stand that Mrs. Bourne is learning fast to think a picture clear through and arrive at a finality that is distinctly professional.[33]

Finally, Marian P. Waitt wrote in the *Boston Journal*:

> These [paintings] are strong and framed like oils without a mat. Several snow scenes were painted in Shelburne, N.H. *The Ravine*, *Edge of the Woods*, *The Brook*, and *Birches* are smart little paintings with fresh, clear color "dropped in" in a smart and knowing way. *Edge of the Woods* is very handsome and a large expanse of white snow in the foreground is broken in a pleasing manner by a blue shadow cast by a tree partially out of the picture. In a group of gardens, No. 10, *Phlox*, No. 11, *Rhododendrons*, and No. 12, *The Fountain* are all painted with a knowledge of the limitations of the medium. She shows how the limitations of a water color can be made its chief charm, getting the full value of the transparency and the crispness possible only in water color.
>
> Two others worthy of special mention are *New England Farmhouse* and *Church in Alexandria*.[34]

The *Boston Transcript*, the *Christian Science Monitor*, and the *Boston Journal* all made either direct or oblique reference to the so-called "blue shadow school." For several years New England painters and especially New England watercolorists, were employing pure blues to represent shadow, most noticeably on snow where it was unadulterated by other colors. John Singer Sargent may have been the godfather of the blue shadow school, and his models were quickly adopted and heightened in New England by Dodge Macknight, Frank W. Benson, and others. Gertrude was now acknowledged by critics as a member of the school.

The *Boston Journal* review of the show noted that Bourne had set up in Shelburne, New Hampshire where the New England watercolorist Dodge Macknight went nearly every winter to paint. Macknight had had a special sledge constructed where he could be drawn out to a painting site by horses and left in a tiny mobile cabin with a picture window and a miniature stove, to paint the winter landscape in comfort. The winter views of New Hampshire suggest that Bourne may have availed herself the same device. She continued to exhibit the results of her New Hampshire painting later in the year with *Adams and Madison* at the Philadelphia Water Color Club.

The following year, 1916, Bourne arrived at Philbrook Farm on January 24 and Dodge Macknight checked in the following day.[35] It may be a leap to suggest that she was studying with Macknight, but she was certainly engaging him, studying his works as they were being created, and discussing watercolor technique with him. And it can be no accident that they arrived nearly simultaneously for a winter painting session. With her studies with Henry

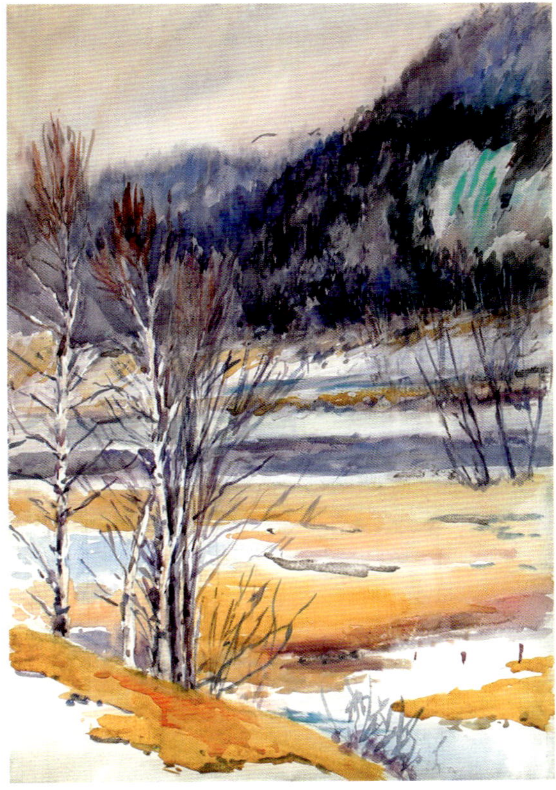

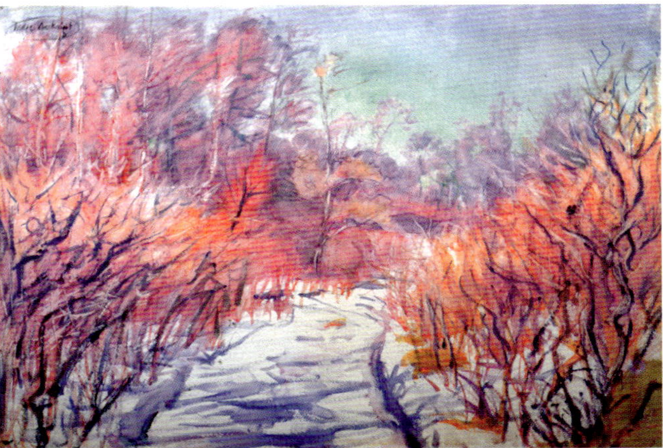

above: ***Dodge Macknight*** (1860-1950)
Winter Road, Shelburne, N.H., c. 1915.
Watercolor on paper, 15 x 22 inches. Courtesy of Childs Gallery, Boston.

left: ***Mt. Winthrop and Moses Ledge, Androscoggin River, Shelburne, N.H.***, January 27, 1916.
Watercolor and gouache on paper, 21 1/2 x 14 1/2 inches. Painted at Philbrook Farm while Macknight was also in residence. Courtesy of the Bourne Art Trust.

Snell, her carefully observed copies of Sargent's recent Italian watercolors, and her opportunity to observe Dodge Macknight at work in Shelburne, Gertrude transformed her watercolor technique of the 1890s and the first decade of the twentieth century into a new and much more forceful style. She was also making trips to the South. Perhaps she went to Washington to see her picture exhibited with the Washington Water Color Club earlier in the year and slipped across the Potomac to paint *Church in Alexandria*. It seems that the Bournes were in Charleston, South Carolina in April of 1914 so that she could paint *Hanging Moss and Azaleas (Charleston, S.C. in April)*(p.70).

F. W. Coburn of the *Boston Herald* equivocated between criticizing Bourne for "excessive crispness" and his relief that she had not fallen into the watercolor trap of "the opposite fault of fuzziness." Marion Waitt of the *Boston Journal* celebrated the "crispness possible only in watercolor," thus demonstrating the difficulty for an artist who might try to take direction from critics.

Waitt also noted that Bourne's works were presented "like oils without a mat" and could sustain that treatment because of their strength. This was a practice that Gertrude would use in presenting her work throughout her career. Bourne's increasing use of gouache and colored papers created many works which stood up well in their boldness against oil paintings. In the future critics would note that Gertrude and her near-contemporary (and fellow Snell student) Jane Peterson (1876-1965) were employing many of the same devices—colored papers, gouache, bold design—and achieving similar results. In their approach to watercolor and in their choices of exhibition venues, the careers of the two women followed parallel courses.

With swashbuckling strokes, George Luks (1867-1933) was increasingly turning to watercolor and gouache to create "paintings" on paper. Luks was one of the "The Eight" along with Maurice Prendergast, John Sloan, and Robert Henri—who encouraged a break with academic tradition and adopted Modernism. He was noted for his bold approach to oil painting as well as his embracing of "inappropriate" Lower East Side of Manhattan subjects. In watercolor, however, he adopted a brighter palette and usually selected country subjects of landscapes, seascapes, or gardens that were similar to those in Bourne's and Peterson's watercolors. All three artists often ended up in the same New York Water Color Club Exhibitions. Looking at the work of the three painters in the latter 1910s each had achieved a level of Modernism that was pretty advanced for the time, and each would sustain that level, for the most part, until their deaths.

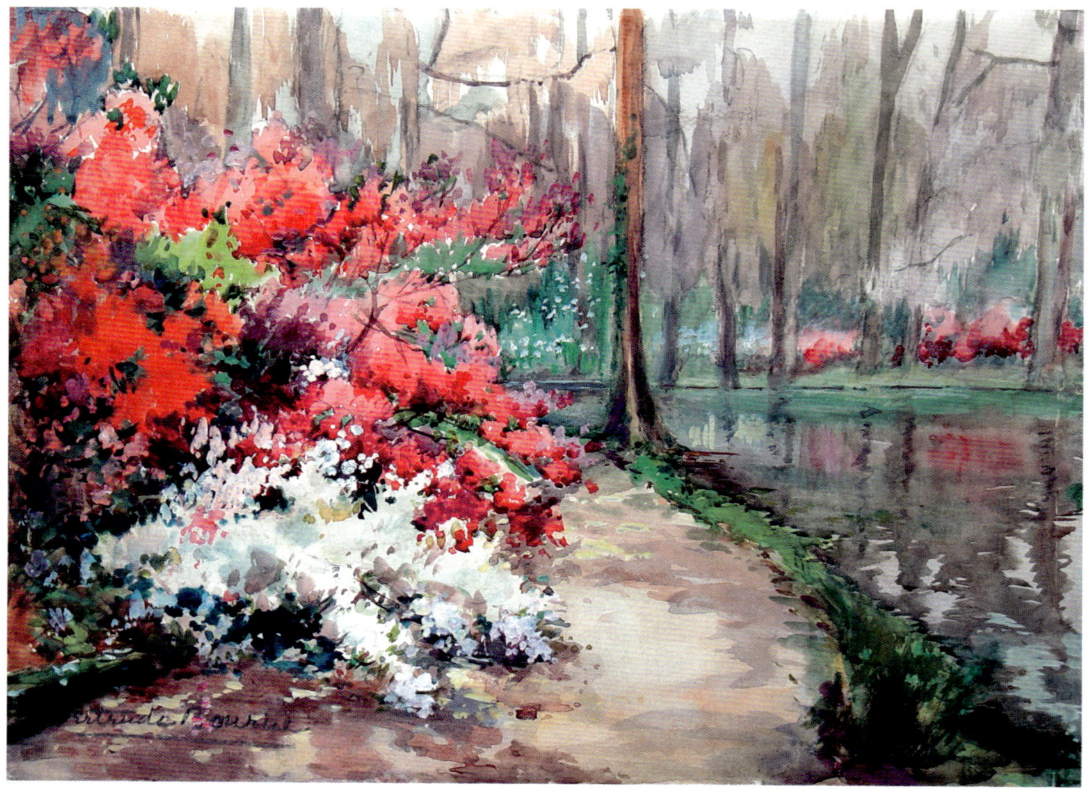

Hanging Moss and Azaleas (Charleston, South Carolina), 1914.
Watercolor on board, 15 x 20 inches.
Courtesy of Childs Gallery, Boston.

In 1916 Bourne submited her first work, *Birches in Winter*, to the Baltimore Water Color Club exhibitions. She also placed a work in the "Concord Annual Exhibit," *The Brook, January*. From December 31, 1915-January 20, she exhibited *Church of Alexandria* and *Birch Trees (Winter)* at the Washington Water Color Club's 20th annual exhibition at the Corcoran Gallery in Washington. That year Bourne returned after a hiatus of fourteen years to exhibit in the American Water Color Society Exhibitions in New York. She showed *A Newburyport Garden* and *A New England Garden* at the 49th annual exhibition from February 3-27. This was a major change of venue to an exhibition with a national audience. The Boston Art Club by contrast was highly respected at the time that Gertrude began to exhibit, but by the 1910s was dying. Membership had declined and the longstanding annual oil painting and watercolor exhibitions were suspended. The Washington Water Color Club was in the nation's capital, but did not reflect the national influence that its name might imply today. The American Water Color Society was in New York, the largest city in America and the undisputed financial and cultural capital. The same year she also joined the New York Water Color Club where she had been exhibiting since 1905.[36] In their annual exhibition from November 4 to November 26 she submitted *February, Cape Cod*; *Birch Trees, Winter*; *The Cove*. A large contingent of Boston painters was represented. The styles represented were a common broad-brush, modernized Impressionism, incorporating Japonism, Arts and Crafts, and European Post-Impressionism, as well as Ash Can. George Luks was represented by four watercolors—three of French subjects.

In February 1917 Bourne appropriately exhibited *February* at the 50th annual exhibition of the American Water Color Society and she again showed *February, Cape Cod* and *The Cove* at the 21st Annual Washington Water Color Club Exhibition. As a group of four pictures at the Philadelphia Water Color Club, Bourne exhibited *February, Cape Cod*; *Garden Sentinels*; and *Birch Trees in February*. Later that year the Washington club held its 22nd Annual Exhibition from November 17 to December 5 where Bourne submitted *Noonmark Mountain, Adirondacks* and *The Old Wharf*. Gertrude was establishing a pattern where recent works that were successfully submitted to one venue would be submitted as well to other upcoming exhibitions, as well as a pattern of being a regular contributor on a nearly annual basis to many of the most prominent watercolor annual exhibitions.

She continued to be included in all but three exhibitions of the Washington Water Color Club through 1931 (the 36th exhibition).

By the summer of 1917 the family began renting a summer house in Ipswich from the influential painter, Arthur Wesley Dow (1857-1922). This presumes the sale of the Scituate folly and may indicate some enhanced income from her father's estate. The first evidence of her painting an Ipswich subject was the exhibition of a painting at the New York Water Color Club in November 1917. Summers in Ipswich probably began in 1917 and continued at least through 1919, but seem to have ended before Dow's death in 1922. Bourne may have met Dow through Maurice Prendergast, who was a mutual friend, or they may have met earlier at one of his studios in Boston.

In the 1890s Dow maintained studio addresses just off Copley Square in the Back Bay.[37] Ipswich and Dow both would have been of interest to Frank and Gertrude Bourne. Dow was both a trained artist and a respected antiquarian who had dedicated himself to the preservation of seventeenth[th] and eighteenth[th] century architecture in Ipswich and had been co-founder of the Ipswich Historical Society. Gertrude Bourne had been painting Colonial Revival subjects since 1899 and Frank Bourne had been designing, preserving, and adapting colonial and federal American architecture for about the same length of time. The romantic and picturesque buildings and streets of Ipswich proved a mine of material for Gertrude Bourne during the next few years. The Bourne's seem to have rented the Emerson Howard House on Turkey Shore Road, which was not only owned by Dow, but had also been the site of his Ipswich Summer School of Art. While Bourne does not credit Dow as one of her 'teachers,' she almost certainly gained from criticism at some level from Dow and from her association with other artists in the Ipswich community. In addition to Dow, she would have been in the middle of a summer colony of artists that included Dow's good friend Henry R. Kenyon, the Impressionist Theodore Wendel, and F. H. Richardson. Bourne's summers in Ipswich narrowly missed the arrival of Jane Peterson and her new husband who established themselves in the mid-1920s in Ipswich at 'Rocky Hill.'

Her first titled Ipswich painting *South Green Church, Ipswich*, was exhibited later in 1917. She does not appear to have exhibited Ipswich paintings after 1919, so that may have been her last year renting from Dow. She also

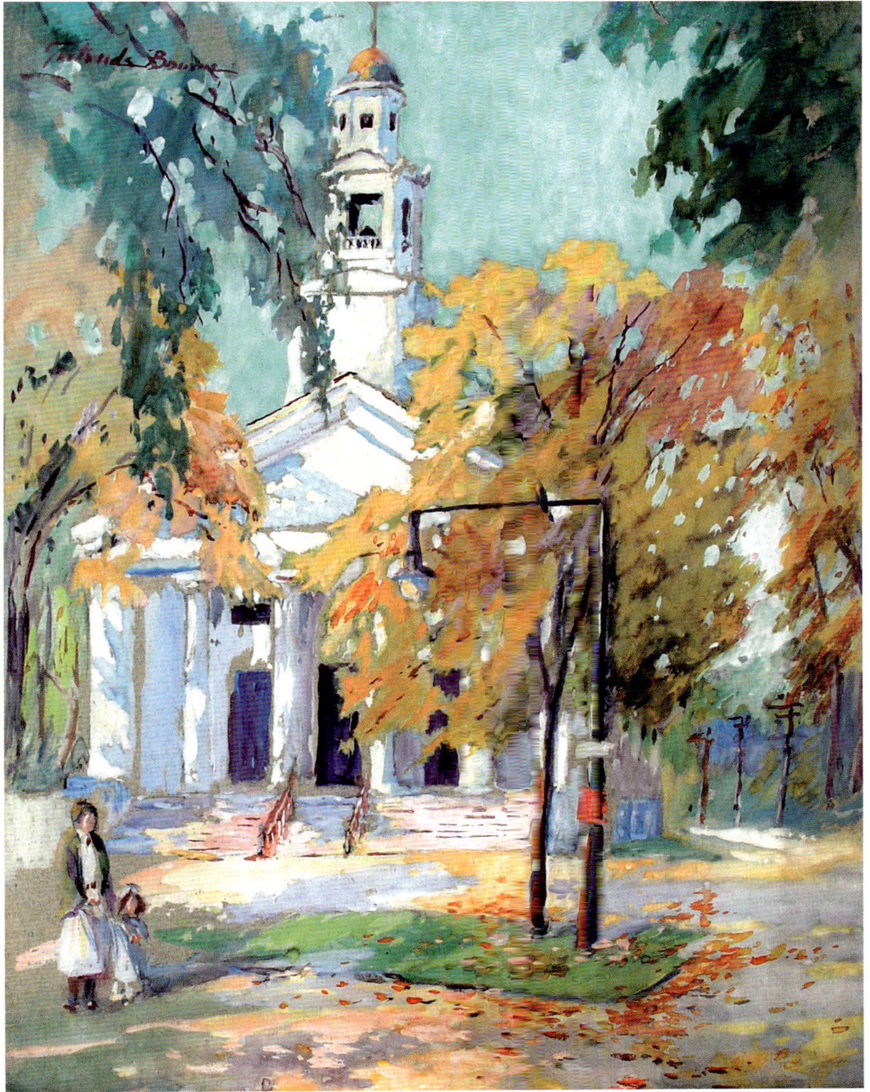

South Green Church, Ipswich, 1917.
Watercolor and gouache on gray paper, 24 1/2 x 1[illegible] inches.
Courtesy Childs Gallery, Boston.

began exhibiting in the nearby Gallery on the Moors exhibitions in Gloucester in the summer of 1917. Over the next several years Bourne's paintings began to reflect an interest in, an appreciation of, and an influence from Dow. She may have been honoring him when she painted Dow's birthplace in Ipswich, the Matthew Perkins House (formerly known as the Norton/Corbett House). Bourne was already working with broad Tonalist painting (as in the *Longfellow Bridge on the Charles River*)(p. 65) from the mid-1910s, but increasingly in the later 1910s and in the early 1920s her use of simplified compositions, her rejection of detail to compose large masses, and her increased interest in vibrant color parallel Dow's choices in his paintings and his theories in his writings.

From November 3-25, 1917 Bourne showed four works at the 28th Annnual Exhibition of the New York Water Color Club: *Green Street Bridge*, *The Deep Pool*, *A Cape Ann Garden*, and *South Green Church, Ipswich*, priced respectively at $125, $100, $80 and $100. Bourne, who had exhibited with the New York Water Color Club for a dozen years, was now a member as well as an exhibitor. The other exhibitors included some of the most respected American watercolorists: Gifford Beal, George Elmer Browne, Albert P. Button, John F. Carlson, Colin Campbell Cooper, John Costigan, Eugene Higgins, Tod Lindemuth, George Luks, F. Luis Mora, and Walter Launt Palmer. The women included Peggy Bacon and Jane Peterson. Most of the artists submitted one to three works. Of the artists mentioned above, only Beal, Button and Peterson submitted more than three works. Most of the other painters were Bourne's contemporaries or younger, and most were working in an Impressionist or Post-Impressionist style.

Bourne had chosen to put her work in New York alongside "modern" American painters, and she would choose to do so again. Although we may find Bourne's painting today less than radical, it would, in 1917 have been squarely within the growing movement of the "Moderns." New York and the New York Water Color Club allowed Bourne a venue with national exposure where she could be comfortably ensconced with artists that ran the gamut from quite conservative to nearly radical. On that scale in 1917, Bourne's work would have been in the middle (or just to the radical side) and reflective of the influences of her friends Prendergast and Dow. It would be easy to draw comparisons between Bourne's watercolors and those of Jane Peterson,

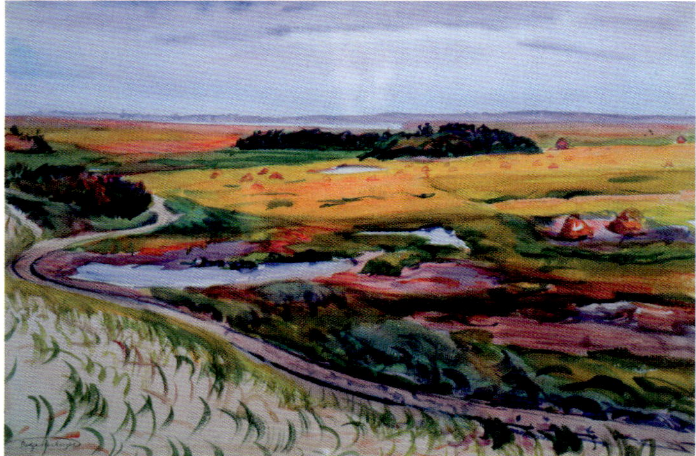

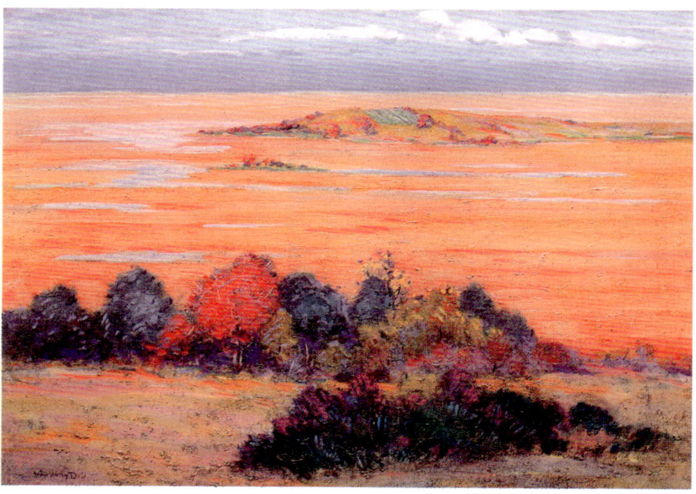

top: **Dodge Macknight (1860-1950), *The Barnstable Marshes***, c. 1902. Watercolor on paper, 15 3/8 x 22 1/4 inches. Courtesy of Childs Gallery, Boston.
bottom: **Arthur Wesley Dow (1857-1922), *From Bayberry Hill***, c. 1910. Oil on canvas, 26 x 36 inches. Courtesy of Ipswich Historical Society.

right: ***Marshland with House (Essex Marshes)***, c. 1917-19. Watercolor and gouache on paper, 20 x 26 inches. Gift of Philip W. Bourne. Courtesy, Museum of Fine Arts, Boston.

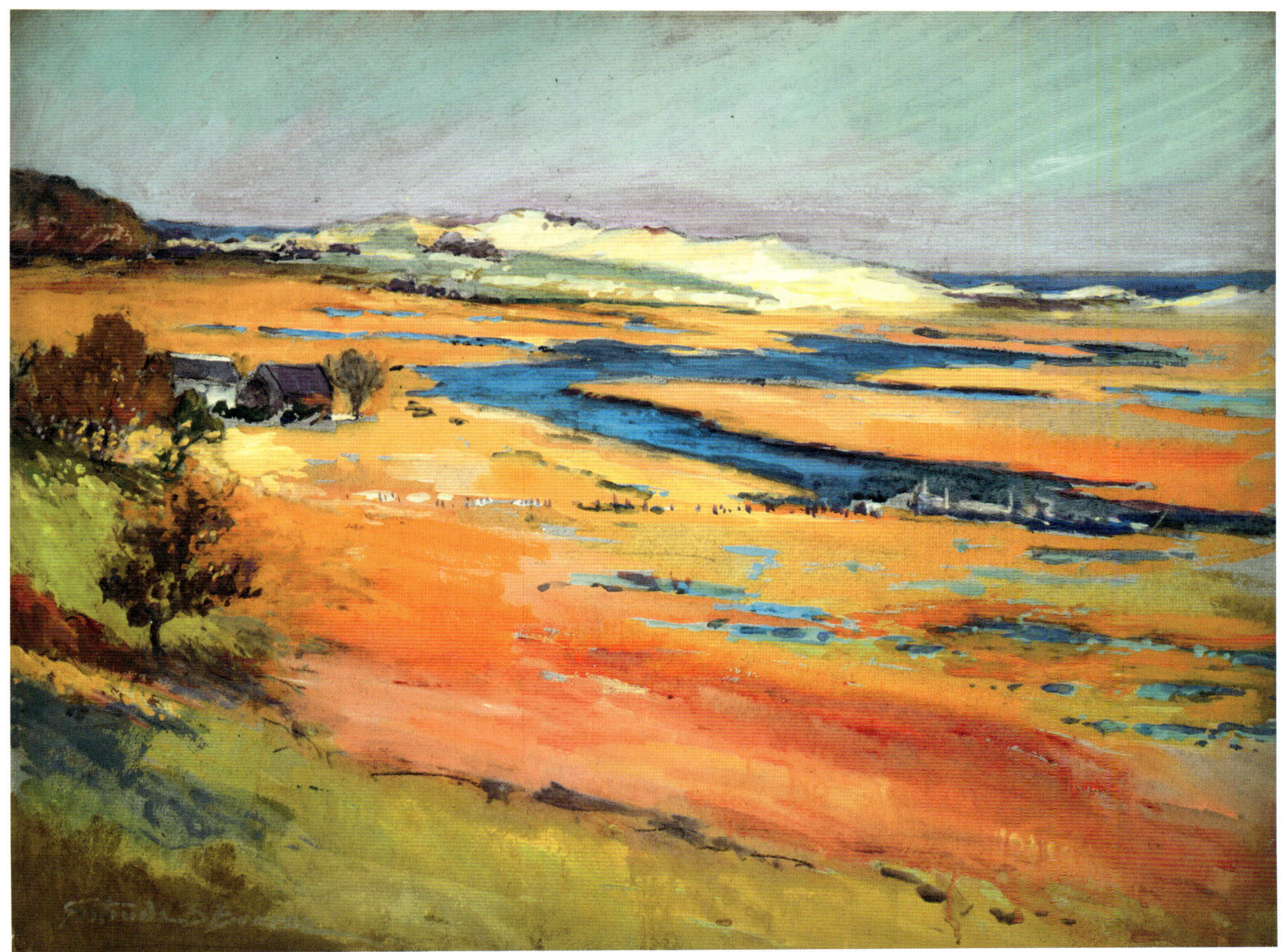

who was eight years Bourne's junior. Peterson's style in watercolor, her choice of subject, her use of tinted papers and gouache, and her compositions make for a strong visual comparison with Bourne's style. At the New York Water Color Club, they would have a chance to assess each other's work. Peterson exhibited six works, five of which were priced for sale: three at $100, one at $125 and one at $200. The nearly identical price structure would suggest that at least the artists themselves regarded the value of their works as comparable.

In 1918 Bourne submitted two works to the Gallery on the Moors in Gloucester, *The Brook and the Ravine*, and *Fitzwilliam Church*. And, she again showed at the New York Watercolor Club on November 2-12 *The Ravine*, *New Hampshire Village in Winter*, *Fitzwilliam Church*, *Ipswich River*, and *Salem Street Where the Italian Prince Came to Boston*. The latter painting recorded the celebration surrounding Prince Ferdinando di Savola di Udine's visit to Boston on June 25 following his addresses to the United States Congress. The U. S. entered World War I on April 6, 1917 to the relief of the European Allies. The Prince of Udine was on a mission of thanks and encouragement to the Americans who had entered the war. Nowhere was his reception greater than in Boston's North End where "Little Italy . . . made the occasion a holiday, and fairly bubbled with the exuberance of its welcome. Bands played martial airs at the principal street corners and young women in white dresses saluted the prince with a bombardment of flowers as his automobile passed."[38] This celebratory painting was especially appropriate for exhibition in New York at this time, for during the New York Water Color Club exhibition the Armistice was signed ending the war.

Jane Peterson was again represented, with four watercolors, as were many of those who exhibited the year before. In addition, William Meyerowitz (from Cape Ann and fellow Gloucester exhibitor), Maurice Prendergast (now living in New York—but summering in Gloucester), and Jan Matulka added to the "Modernists" in the exhibition. In addition to the watercolorists, some of the most distinguished young American sculptors exhibited their work: Mahonri Young, Paul Manship, Malvina Hoffman, Cecil Howard, Edward McCartan, Albin Polasek, Herbert Adams, Hunt Diedrich and Gaston Lachaise. All of them would have been considered among the new generation of American

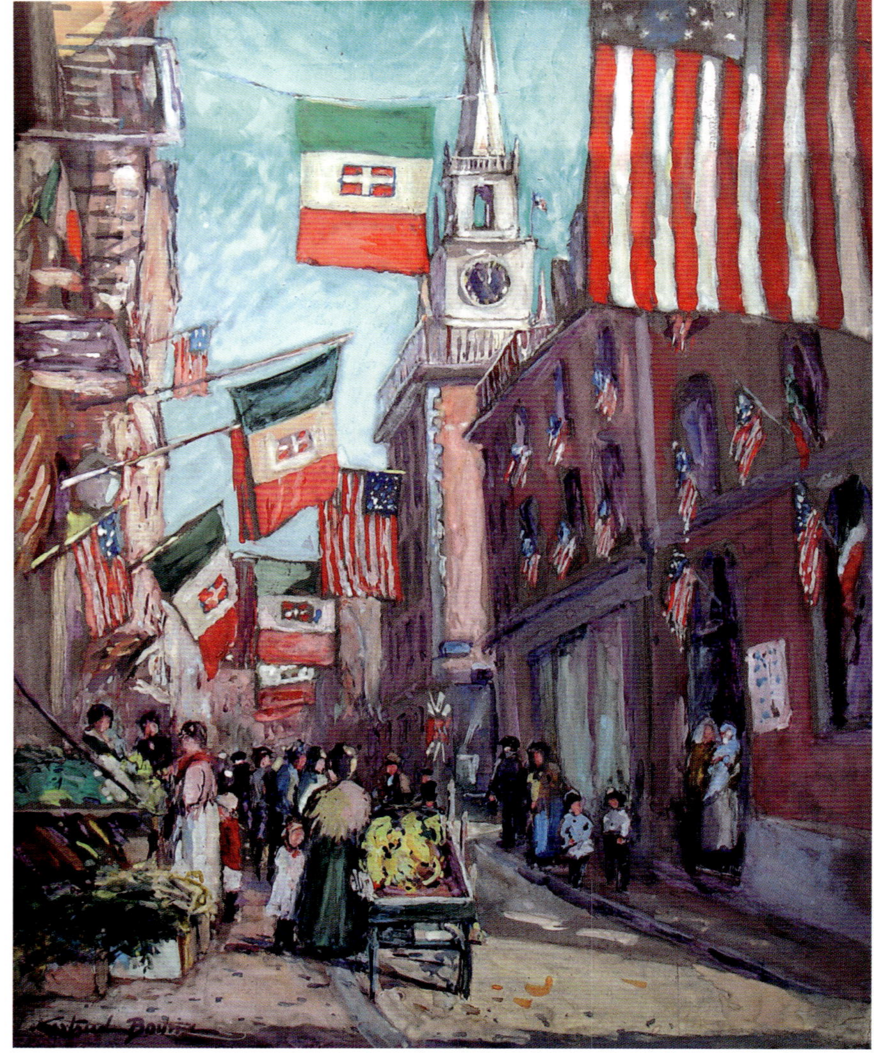

Where the Italian Prince Came to Boston, 1917.
Watercolor and gouache on paper, 24 3/4 x 20 1/8 inches.
Commemorating the visit of the Prince of Udine to Boston's North End on June 25, 1917. Courtesy of the Bourne Art Trust.

sculptors and Diedrich and Lachaise would have been viewed as distinctly "modern."

The year 1919 was Bourne's most active exhibition year to date. In her first time exhibiting in this venue, the National Association of Women Painters and Sculptors, in their 28th Annual Exhibition from February 15–March 3 at the Fine Arts Building, 215 West 57th Street in New York, Bourne showed *A Garden*, *The Cobbler's Shop*, *The House at the end of the Bridge*, *The Garden Gate*, and *A Holiday*. Perhaps she was introduced to the Association through Florence Francis Snell (1850-1946), the wife of Bourne's teacher, Henry B. Snell. Florence Snell had been chairman of the Association's membership committee in 1913-14, on the committee of awards in 1918, and was, in Gertrude's first year of exhibiting, the second vice-president. This was Bourne's first exhibition of her work in a venue that allowed only women exhibitors. She had been exhibiting in New York at the American Water Color Society and the New York Water Color Club since 1902 and 1905 respectively, so she did not choose the venue just to be able to show in New York; she made a conscious choice to exhibit with women artists. Each of those prior venues may have been entered at the urging of Henry Snell, and so her membership in the National Association of Women Painters and Sculptors may also have been undertaken at the Snells' suggestion and encouragement. She was one of five exhibitors from Boston.[39] Again she could compare her work with two paintings and two "sketches" by Jane Peterson. Bourne would continue to exhibit with the National Association of Women Painters and Sculptors through 1928, and she would help initiate a Boston chapter.

As one of the fourteen initial members, she may have helped to organize the Boston exhibition of the Massachusetts chapter of the American Association of Women Painters and Sculptors at the Copley Gallery from April 14-26 where she showed *Winter Wanes* and *February 24, 1919* (p. 4).
The *Boston Evening Transcript* reported:

> A Massachusetts chapter of the National Association of Women Painters and Sculptors having been formed, the first Boston exhibition held under the auspices of the organization was opened at the Copley Gallery 106 Newbury Street… Twelve members of the newly organized chapter contribute pictures and two members exhibit sculpture. In addition to the Massachusetts group fourteen of the New York members are represented by paintings...
> Mrs. Bourne's *Winter Wanes* is a well-painted little landscape of a happy Yankee valley with a cozy village nestling in it, a real and attractive portrait of a picturesque locality.[40]

Bourne's other entry *February 24, 1919* was her first showing of one of her most-exhibited paintings and the frontispiece of this book—the picture was exhibited under several variant titles. The image depicts the moment just before the triumphal passage of President Woodrow Wilson past Beacon Street as he motored from the harbor to the Copley Square Hotel in Boston. Wilson had just landed in Boston after his visit to France to negotiate details after the November armistice. The *Boston Evening Transcript* reported:

> Through a double line of guards—soldiers, sailors, marines, State guard and the city police—President Wilson progressed through Boston's streets…All down Beacon street, at the Somerset Club and at private houses there was a rolling cheer as the car containing the President passed along.[41]

From May 15 to June 15 she sent *The Bridge*; *New England Church*; and *The Lavender Door* to the 31st annual exhibition of watercolors at the Art Institute of Chicago. And on July 12 the Art Association of Newport opened the Eighth Annual Exhibition of Pictures by American Painters with five of Bourne's watercolors, including *Marines, February 24, 1919* (p. 4). The Bournes spent the summer on Turkey Shore Road in Ipswich, Massachusetts. The Washington Water Color Club, because of scheduling changes had a second exhibition from October 31 – November 23 in 1919 (and none in 1920) where Bourne exhibited *The End of the Day*; *The Bridge, Low Tide, Cos Cob*; and *Hillside in March*. She received a good review in the Washington press: "Strong work has been contributed by Gertrude B. Bourne of Boston, who sends [three works], landscapes, very different in character, but each broadly handled and impressive."[42]

Bourne exhibited *Marine's Beacon Street Boston, February 24, 1919* at the Duxbury Art Association in August and again along with *Boston's Welcome to the Return of the 26th Division* at the Art Association of Newport

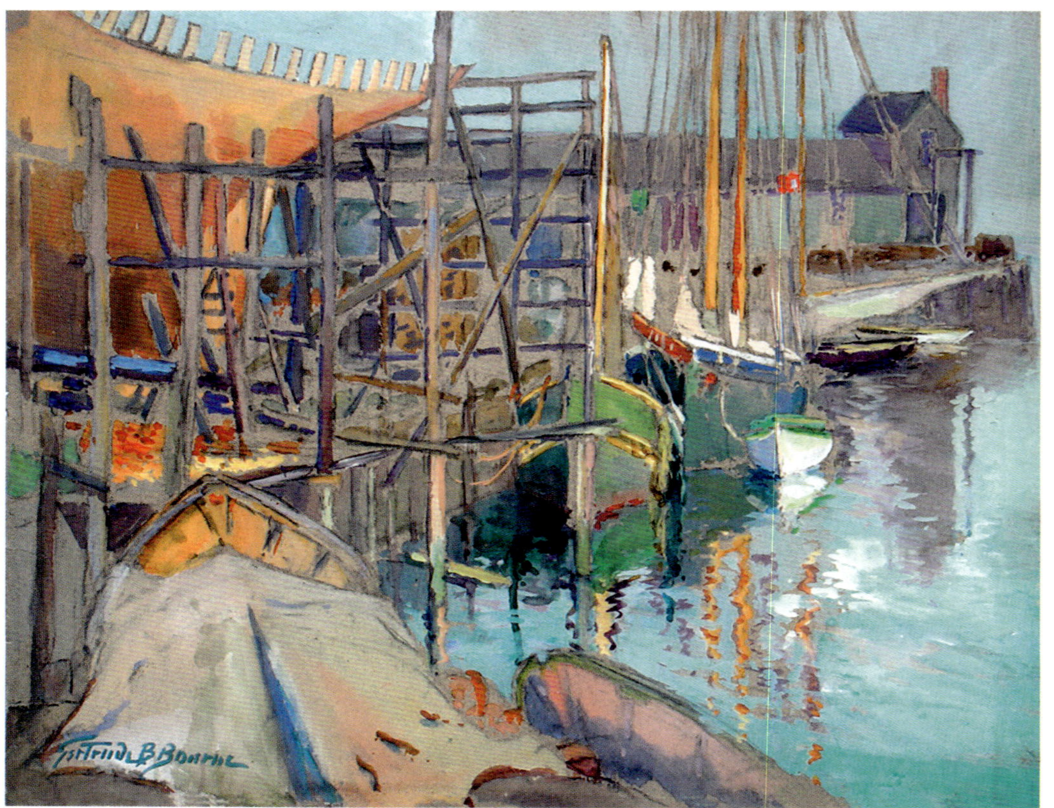

The Wharf or ***Boatbuilding, Rockport***, c. 1919.
Watercolor, gouache, and charcoal 19 3/4 x 25 3/4 inches.
Exhibited Essex Institute, Salem, 1988. Probably exhibited NY Water Color Club, 1919. Private Collection.

and the Pennsylvania Academy of Fine Arts-Philadelphia Water Color Club 17th annual exhibition all in 1919. The former painting is notable for its use of a crowd of figures as the prime decorative element. Rather as Prendergast used figures decoratively and blocked color in clothing and faces, Bourne has used the repeated figures, colors, and uniforms to build a compositional rhythm.

The exhibition of two paintings that celebrate the end of World War I came in the middle of a notable lack of travel to Europe. From a London trip of 1911 to another London trip of 1923 there is no evidence of European travel—the longest period without such a trip in the Bournes' married life. After war broke out in 1914 there would have been great danger in such travel, and even after the Armistice in November 1918 there would have been great discomfort and privation, if not danger, associated with European travel for some time.

Shortly after the October 1919 Washington exhibition opened, the New York Water Color Club opened its annual exhibition at the American Fine Arts Building in New York where Bourne placed *Guinea Boats*; *Boston's Welcome to the Return of the 26th Division*; *Boatbuilding Rockport*; *Drying Sails*; and *A Cincinnati Market*. During this year she had the opportunity to see her work placed beside hundreds of paintings by her colleagues. In the women's exhibitions she could be compared to Cecilia Beaux, Mary Bradish Titcomb, Marion Boyd Allen, Margaret Patterson and Gertrude Fiske. At the New York Water Color Club her watercolors could again be seen beside six of Jane Peterson's, and Bourne's prices (four at $150 and one at $100) were similar to Peterson's (five at $150 and one at $200). She could also be compared to Lester Stevens, William Meyerowitz, Alfred Hutty, Birge Harrison, John Costigan and Reynolds Beal. All of these men were interested in coastal subjects similar to three of Bourne's watercolors in this exhibition. Most had worked on Cape Ann or on the Massachusetts coast. Again the colleagues that she exhibited with were solidly within the Impressionist and Post-Impressionist norms of the day. As with Bourne, the other exhibitors were neither especially conservative nor especially radical.

With Gertrude Beals Bourne's return to a serious exhibition schedule in 1914, she had moved beyond a two-man show at the Milton Public Library, five years before, to a solo show at the Copley Gallery in Boston and major national venues. Bourne placed works in shows organized by the American Federation of Arts, Washington Water Color Club, Art Institute of Chicago, Baltimore Water Color Club, American Water Color Society, New York Water

Color Club, and the National Association of Women Painters and Sculptors. She had, by the opening of the decade of the 1920s, asserted herself to be a serious watercolor painter whose work was accepted by juries at major national venues, where she was placed beside, and could be judged against, the most established American watercolor painters of her time.

The 1920s—A Decade of Travel and Exhibition

1920 began with another exhibition of the National Association of Women Painters at the recently opened Grace Horne Gallery in Boston, February 3 – 14. She submitted two works including *The Stone Bridge, Ipswich*. The review in the *Boston Post* was very favorable, which must have been gratifying, coming from the paper owned by her family nearly a half-century before.

> Yesterday the whole main gallery was hung anew with a selection of paintings by the Massachusetts section of the National Association of Women Painters and Sculptors. In addition there are shown 10 canvases by the members of the New York branch. It is an interesting exhibition throughout, being unusually even in the high quality of the work shown, and reflects credit on this fine and enterprising body of women artists.

The lead of the story was an illustration of Bourne's *The Stone Bridge, Ipswich*, with the caption: "The house shown in the painting was built in 1640 by ancestors of Ralph Waldo Emerson." The author, Sidney Woodward, continued: "Two watercolors by Mrs. Gertrude Bourne are particularly fine in their spontaneous treatment. *A Summer Day* by Jane Peterson, is the artist at her best, which, in the view of her already established reputation, both here and abroad, is saying much."[43] The juxtaposition of Bourne and Peterson would continue as they exhibited, similar works in similar styles in the same venues. Bourne was pleased enough with the Woodward review to write to him on February 10: "I was much pleased to see the reproduction in the *Post* last Wednesday, and think it came out very well indeed."[44]

The New York show of the National Association of Women Painters and Sculptors, April 10–May 1, at the Fine Arts Building saw Bourne again with *Nocturne* and *A Blue Garden*. The number of Boston exhibitors had increased to eight—and two of them were her near neighbors, Ruth Anderson (53 Charles Street) and Amy Cabot (72 Chestnut Street). We may suppose that Bourne led the way for or encouraged her Beacon Hill women artist friends. From May 11 – June 6 she was included in the 32nd annual watercolor exhibition of the Art Institute of Chicago with *Rockport Drying Sails*. She also exhibited *White Sulphur Springs Porches* at the Duxbury Art Association and *The Ravine* at the Baltimore Water Color Club. As with so many of her exhibited works, titles serve as documents for her recent whereabouts, and show that she had recently visited White Sulphur Springs and the Greenbrier in West Virginia. Titles show that she also spent time in the early 1920s in Rockport, Massachusetts. This may have developed from her proximity to Rockport when she was renting in Ipswich and exhibiting at Gallery on the Moors, but developed further when she became a member of the North Shore Arts Association in neighboring Gloucester.

In the following year, 1921, Bourne was back exhibiting at the Washington Water Color Club, February 4 – 28, with *Nocturne* and *The Lavender Door*. She continued to submit successful works to more than one venue and would do so with works as much as two years old. *Nocturne* was probably the same painting shown at the National Association of Women Painters and Sculptors in New York in 1920, and *The Lavender Door* was probably the same as shown at the Art Institute of Chicago in 1919. She seems to have found certain work that caught judges and juror's eyes. Bourne returned repeatedly to nocturne subjects, and she certainly knew the nocturne works of both Whistler and Monet, each of whom had had extensive exhibitions in Boston and who had works in public and private collections there. At this time Monet was well along on his dramatic final series of Nymphea or waterlilies which formed the subject of his "Grandes Décorations"; he was already well-known for his earlier waterlilies which he had begun to paint in his water garden at Giverny in the late 1890s. From 1903 to 1908, Monet had painted his series "Les Nymphéas" which were exhibited at Durand-Ruel in Paris in the latter year. Gertrude exhibited her *Waterlilies* (p. 105) at the Baltimore Water Color

Club and *Mt. Adams and Mt. Madison* at the Gallery on the Moors. At the end of the year Bourne showed *House at Boothbay Harbor*; *Mt. Adams and Mt. Madison*; and a *Wiscasset Garden* at the first combined exhibition of the New York Water Color Club and the American Water Color Society from December 31, 1921 to January 15, 1922. The artist's peripatetic life can be viewed through the lens of her work and in this period it shows that she was painting in rural New Hampshire in the winter and painting in coastal Maine in the summer. In addition, she made at least one winter painting trip to view New York from across the East River. In 1922 Bourne joined the American Water Color Society and remained a member until 1957. From February 11 to March 5 she exhibited *Waterlilies* (p. 108) at the Washington Water Color Club. She was back exhibiting with the National Association of Women Painters and Sculptors again in their 31st Annual Exhibition at the Anderson Galleries in New York, April 4-15, 1922. Her entries were *Peck Slip* and *Skyscrapers*. Bourne returned again to the Art Association of Newport for the Eleventh Annual Exhibition with two paintings: *Cornish Garden* and *Golden Screen*.

During the 1922-1923 exhibition season, Bourne was back at the National Association of Women Painters and Sculptors again in New York from October 18-30 at the Fine Arts Building in New York where she showed *Pond Lilies*. At the end of the year she submitted two works, #265 *East River*, and #437 *New Year's Day, Boston* (priced at $200 and $250), to the New York Water Color Club and American Water Color Society combined exhibition in New York from December 22, 1922 through January 9, 1923. While the New York show was on, the Washington Water Color Club opened its annual exhibition which ran from January 6 – 28 and included Bourne's *Monhegan Harbor*, *Spring Garden*, and *Trinity After Snowstorm*. This was followed with a solo exhibition of Bourne's watercolors at the Arts Club in Washington in March and April. The following month the *American Magazine of Art* published a small article with three illustrations reviewing the show:

> Mrs. Bourne has for some years been contributing to the leading watercolor exhibitions, and her work has been steadily increasing in strength and interest. The comprehensive showing therefore only conclusively confirmed the growing conviction that here was one of real power and insight, an original talent of exceptional power.

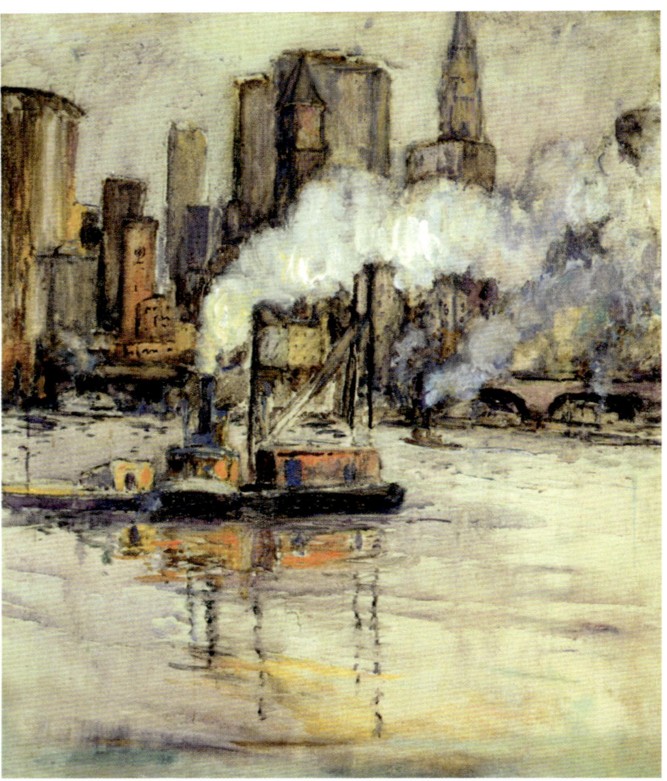

> The majority of Mrs. Bourne's paintings are of subjects found in the vicinity of Boston, old houses bedabbled with sunlight, glimpses of village streets, typical New England themes so rendered as to have new significance. Her compositions are carefully selected and arranged, and her colors are pure and put on simply and directly with a full brush. Occasionally she uses body color on gray paper or canvas. Some of her paintings in gouache have been exhibited with oil paintings instead of watercolors because of their strength and carrying quality. She has studied under the direction of Henry B. Snell and the late Henry W. Rice, but her work has distinct individuality. She commands her medium and her work has that painter-like quality which lifts it far above the average.[45]

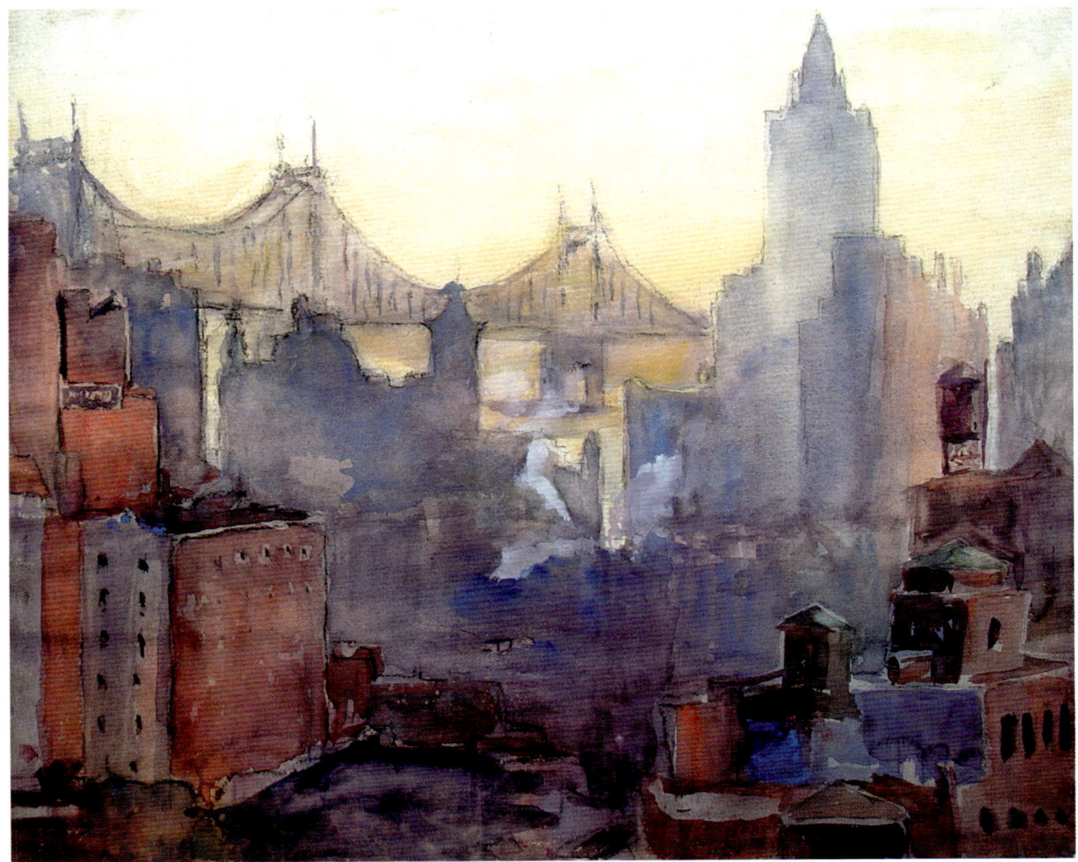

above: ***Buildings and Bridges, New York [Queensboro Bridge]***, c.1922. Watercolor, gouache, and charcoal on paper, 20 x 24 inches. Courtesy of Childs Gallery, Boston.
left: **Skyscrapers**, c. 1922. Watercolor and gouache on paper, 30 x 25 inches. Illustrated *American Magazine of Art*, May 1923. Private Collection.

The *American Magazine of Art* selected *Skyscrapers*, *New England Colonial House* (p.50), and *Sunlight and Shadow, New England Village* for reproduction. *Skyscrapers* gives a gritty and powerful Ash Can view of the New York harbor with a tug puffing smoke in front of an ominous skyline, which could come out of the work of Luks or any other of "The Eight."[46] The other two works could hardly be more different as they represent the Colonial Revival sensibilities of an elegant—perhaps mythical—and carefully crafted antique past. A past from which New England, and ultimately the country, had sprung. The reviewer singled them out as "typical New England themes," but continued that they had been "rendered as to have a new significance." He also noted "their strength and carrying quality" and "that painter-like quality." The point that was made in the review was that this was no 'lady painter.' The work had, in his eyes, "strength and interest." The author made all the right points in analyzing Gertrude Bourne's maturing style. Hers are strong, painterly works with pure color and clear evidence of the brush across the paper. Bourne now painted with a boldness that allowed her watercolors to stand up in visual force with oil paintings.

Gertrude Bourne must have been pleased with the review, for it set her out in a national magazine as having "insight," "exceptional power," "command of her medium," and as being "far above average." The commentary about her work in gouache was especially telling, for it was only a few years earlier that Bourne had begun to regularly employ opaque watercolor, as china white, or gouache in her works, and only shortly before her solo exhibition at the Arts Club that she had used it for a complete work. She had absorbed Snell's training as had Jane Peterson, but others were also moving in the same direction. Since her exhibition at the New York Water Color Club in 1916, Gertrude might have been paying close attention to the extraordinarily powerful watercolors of George Luks who employed 'full brush,' gouache, and bold colors. Luks had regular watercolor exhibitions in New York in the late 1910s and 1920s, and Bourne may have seen them. Luks had visited Boston in 1922 to recuperate from an illness and to paint. He lived with the socialite-artist Margarett Sargent McKean (Mrs. Quincy Adams Shaw

McKean) who kept a studio at 30 Saint Botolph Street as well as a large country house at Pride's Crossing, Massachusetts.

At a time when many of the purists in the watercolor establishment were calling for transparent watercolor to be used alone, Bourne set a course for breaking whatever rules got in her way to achieve a better solution for her subjects and her temperament.

Although she began with transparent watercolors, adopting the "blue shadow" aesthetic, and working generally in Impressionist and Post-Impressionist modes (that related to her Boston contemporaries), Bourne was also able to break out as required by her personal aesthetic to bolder work that she achieved by increasing use of gouache, bold color palette, and dramatic modern compositions. Consciously or subconsciously, Bourne was navigating between delicate and insipid styles that were expected of the 'lady painter' and an abstracted deconstruction of art that Gertrude would find rude, meaningless, or both. These works in watercolor were acknowledged by the critics as "paintings" that could and should be shown with oils. And they noted that she framed them "close-up" as with oil paintings. Prints, drawings, and most watercolors are presumed to require the 'relief' of a mat surrounding the work so that it is not visually pressed upon by the frame. With more powerful works on paper, however, there is no need for a mat to protect the work from the surround of the frame, and this was the case with Bourne's watercolors of the 1910s and later.

The Beacon Hill Association

Many changes were coming to Beacon Hill in the 1920s; some were supported by residents like the Bournes and others began to be resisted. Boston had no zoning and developers were beginning to see possibilities of profit in rebuilding sections. William C. Codman, one of the developers, had a plan for widening of Charles Street. In the previous few years he and partners had succeeded in buying up most of the buildings on the west side of Charles Street. As the widening began in 1920 by the tearing down of the façades of the buildings and the removal of several yards of the east side of each building the Charles Street Meeting House, designed by Asher Benjamin, remained as a conspicuous, architecturally significant monument. Frank Bourne seems to have agreed that the widening of Charles Street was a beneficial project, but the Meeting House posed a problem. It was also nearly opposite his house on Mount Vernon Street. He undertook moving the church the requisite number of feet to the west, and he gave his services to the impoverished congregation and helped to raise the funds for the project. The restoration of the Meeting House would remain a continuing project for the rest of Frank Bourne's life.

A contretemps arose on Beacon Hill in the fall of 1920, at the same time as the moving of the Meeting House. The City of Boston, through its public works department, proposed re-paving Mount Vernon Street with red shale blocks. A number of residents of the Hill organized to oppose the plan. They claimed that the new pavement would be noisy, garish, and slippery for man and beast. Among the organizers were Frank Bourne, William C. Codman, and Marion C. Nichols (the younger sister of Rose Standish Nichols whose house is preserved on Mount Vernon Street).[47] These three residents of Beacon Hill continued after the successful defeat of the shale to collaborate on organizing to defend and shape the character of Beacon Hill. By April 1922 the three had promoted an organizational meeting of the Beacon Hill Association at which the first members enrolled and paid dues. On December 5 the first general meeting of the Association was held at the assembly room of the Twentieth Century Club at 3 Joy Street where about seventy members and guests were present. By the second meeting in April 1923 Arthur D. Hill (partner of the law firm Hill, Barlow and Homans) had been elected president, March C. Bennett, vice president, and Marion C. Nichols, secretary. Alan Forbes (president of State Street Bank) was soon appointed treasurer. Frank A. Bourne and William C. Codman were the first two members of the Board of Directors, but were soon joined by law professor Felix Frankfurter (later to be appointed a justice of the United States Supreme Court) and Bernard J. Rothwell (former president of the Boston Chamber of Commerce). From the beginning Bourne chaired the all-important zoning committee. By December 1 the zoning committee had issued *The Manifesto*, a document that summarized the zoning regulations that the Association would strive to enact over the next few years. The major principles were "to have Beacon Hill preserved as a place of residence, with dwellings of the character prevailing today, free from additional businesses." They recommended instituting zoning for Beacon Hill to encourage the residential character of the Hill, making Charles Street the only commercial center, limiting the height of buildings to 65 feet, and considering light and air as essential qualities in approving density in any new project.[48]

The following year Boston adopted its first zoning law, and almost all of *The Manifesto* was incorporated. An omission of Beacon and Joy Streets from the 65 foot zoning opened a hole into which the Diocesan Council of the Episcopal Church of Massachusetts dropped an 80 foot building at 1 Joy Street. Despite much protest the Association suffered defeat in its efforts to prevent the building from being built according to the original plan. In his apologia Bourne reported to the annual meeting:

> It is hardly necessary to report what has happened, as you know that only too well: the successes and failures—although, of course, the Beacon Hill Association never makes any failures. We have heard this question, however: 'Why did not the Beacon Hill Association have Joy Street put into the 65-foot district before any one attempted to put up an 80-foot building?' Perhaps I could tell you why, but I won't. From our experience of the past year let us see what can be done to prevent similar encroachments in the future.[49]

Shortly thereafter most of Joy Street and Beacon Street from the State House to Charles Street was incorporated in the 65 foot district. By the committee biding their time—Bourne stated "when the opportune moment arrives…we are ready to petition with a reasonable hope of success"—Beacon Street opposite the Public Garden was also added to the 65 foot district in 1933. Bourne set the pattern for vigilance and incremental victories that have characterized the Beacon Hill Association (now the Beacon Hill Civic Association) from its inception until the present. His manifesto is still the guidepost for the zoning of the Hill, and his vision of an architecturally harmonious neighborhood free from willy-nilly incursions of non-residential uses has been realized. At the Fiftieth Anniversary celebration of the Beacon Hill Civic Association John Codman, the son of William C. Codman, praised eight of the founders, saying of Bourne that he "crystallized the image of what Beacon Hill was and should remain, and never let us forget it… [He was] devoted to preserving the Charles Street Meeting House."[50]

In April 1923, Frank Bourne moved his architecture firm from Kilby Street to 177 State Street, Room 700 where he would maintain his office for the rest of his life. Immediately following his move and the return of Gertrude's exhibition from the Arts Club in Washington, Frank and Gertrude began preparations for an extended summer in Europe. Meanwhile, Gertrude selected and arranged for shipment of two watercolors for the fall exhibition of the Washington Watercolor Club before their departure.

By June they were in London and then visited Oxford and Wroxham before leaving England for France. Perhaps this was the occasion where Gertrude arranged for an exhibition at the James Newman Gallery, 24 Soho Square, London. Among the dozen or more watercolors were: *Wet Pavements—Washington [Square] Arch*; *Waterlilies* (p. 108); *Morning Sunlight, East River*. In Paris, as in 1892, Gertrude, now with Frank, went to the Salon to see the current official exhibition of painting. They also saw one of the legendary exhibitions of American painting in Paris—and one which should have been of very special interest to Gertrude. Frank Bourne recorded his impressions in his sketch book: "Just before [the Salon] I had seen the remarkable exhibition in Paris of the work of four Americans: Sargent, Dodge Macknight, Winslow Homer and Paul Manship. There were fresh and interesting motives in the American work that seemed wholly lacking in the long corridors of the Salon."[51] This exhibition of three American watercolor painters, plus the young American sculptor, Paul Manship, is mentioned in nearly every history of American watercolor. The Bournes would have already been very familiar with the work of all three and may have even known them all (even though Homer had died in 1910). Sargent was spending a great deal of his time in Boston in the early 1920s completing mural commissions at the Boston Public Library and the Museum of Fine Arts. He was living at the Copley Plaza Hotel in Copley Square just a block or so away from the Copley Gallery, the Boston Art Club, and the Grace Horne Gallery. Bourne studied Sargent watercolors at the Museum of Fine Arts, Boston by copying them, learning them stroke by stroke. Dodge Macknight, who had spent time with Bourne in Shelburne, New Hampshire in 1915 and 1916, had nearly annual, highly successful

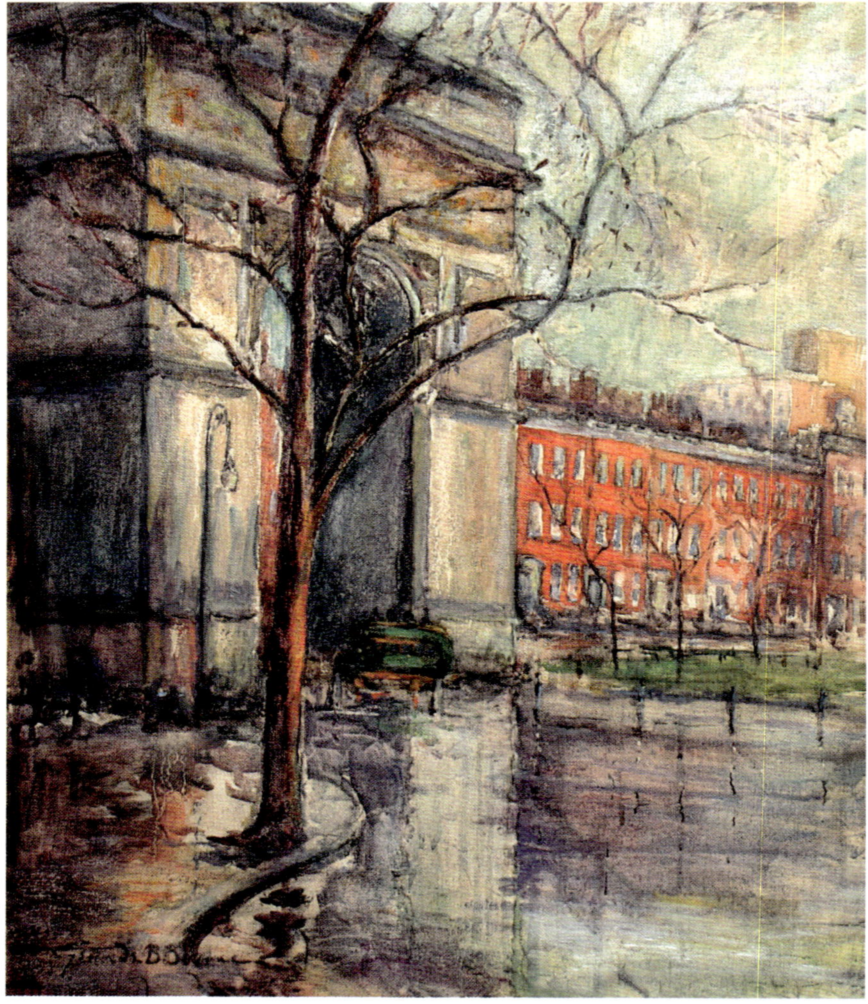

Wet Pavements—Washington [Square] Arch, c. 1922
Watercolor and gouache on canvas, 30 x 25 inches.
This is one of the rare instances of Bourne using primed canvas as a support for her art. Private Collection.

exhibitions at Doll and Richards Gallery on Newbury Street until the early 1930s. This exhibition would have appeared to Gertrude Bourne as a showing of three 'hometown' American watercolorists whom she, as a New England watercolorist, very much admired.

In later June, the Bournes went to Concarneau where they stayed at least through July 10. On August 4, they were in Stockholm and in September were on the Rhone on the 4th in Moret of the 6th and visited Vevey, Montreaux, Chillon, Mt. Blanc, and Geneva, Switzerland, and Nantua, France before returning to Paris by September 23rd. They then returned to the United States and Boston.

By the early 1920s, both Gertrude and Frank began to help found organizations to promote the arts and civic preservation. The North Shore Arts Association was founded in 1922 in Gloucester, Massachusetts, close to the Bourne's summering spot in Ipswich. The association was principally active summers, and so conveniently provided a venue where both Bournes could exhibit with prominent North Shore women artists as well as male colleagues. Although Frank made his living as an architect, all architects of his generation were thoroughly trained in drawing and rendering architectural elevations in watercolor. Frank and Gertrude Bourne were practically founding members of the North Shore Arts Association since they both joined in 1923 during the first year of the group. That summer Gertrude exhibited *Waterlilies* and Frank sent the drawings, *House at Rockport* and *Charles Street Meeting House*.

The Washington Water Color Club exhibited Bourne's *The Brook in February* and *Thorn Mountain* from October 27 – November 7, 1923. The selection of works suggests that she did not have the opportunity to ready her new European work for the show. She put together three-quarters of her submissions to the New York Water Color Club and American Water Color Society combined exhibition (December 28, 1923 – January 15, 1924) out of her European trip. Bourne offered *London Bridge* (p. 6); *St. Paul's from Tower Bridge*; and *Flower Vendor, Paris*. She also submitted *Morning Light East River* from her previous work.

Other than this initial exhibition at the start of 1924, Bourne participated in no exhibitions during the year. It was, however, an exciting and productive year, including a trip that began in July in France with a stay in Paris and in the

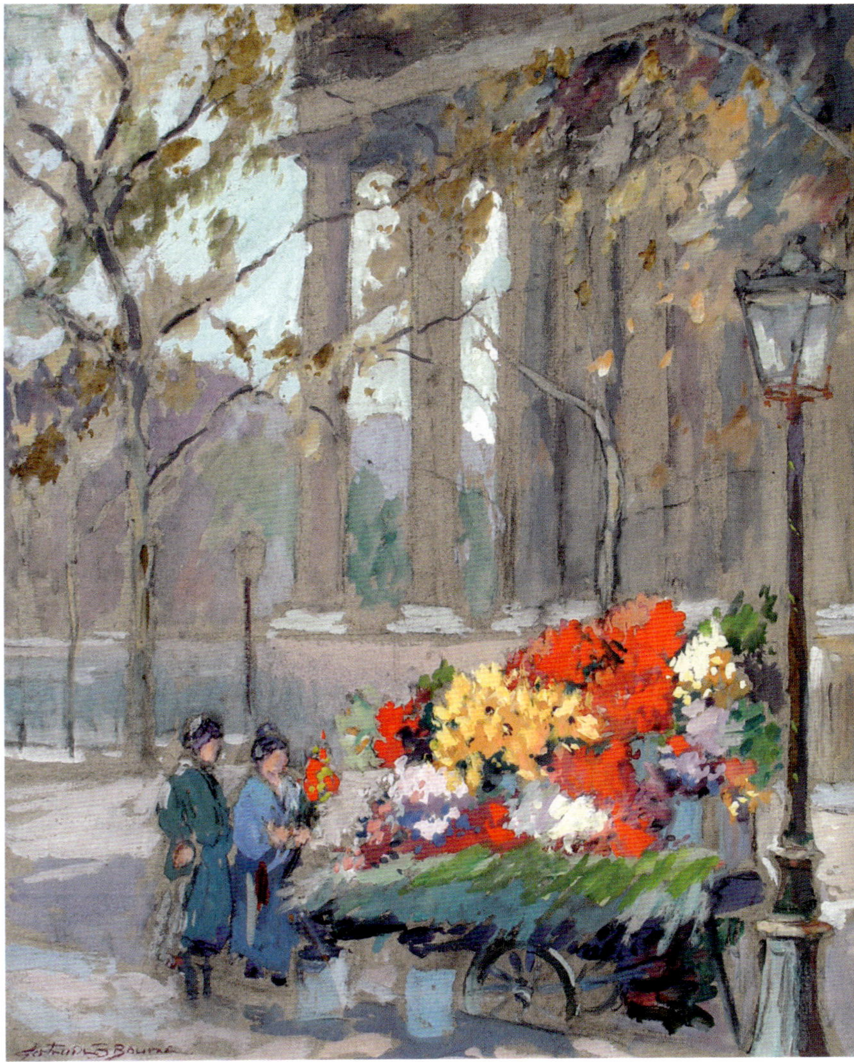

***Flower Vendor, Paris*, 1923.**
Watercolor on gray paper, 24 x 19 inches.
Private Collection.

South of France, before traveling to Venice and Trieste and spending a good part of August on the Dalmatian coast including Ragusa, Mostar, and Sarajevo. Frank Bourne's sketchbooks indicate that he, at least, was also at Ravello in Italy on the Almafi coast. The Dalmatian watercolors would provide exhibition material for nearly half of Gertrude's exhibition submissions through 1927.

Boston and Ipswich provided stable points in the early 1920s as the Bournes traveled extensively. While at home she could arrange her submissions to juried exhibitions, but the pace was so great that she must sometimes have felt that she always had her hat on. The summer of 1925 provided another painting trip in Europe to London, Chelsea, Oxford, Skipton, and Wraxton. Before she left for the trip she sent *Ragusa, Dalmatia* and *Winter in Vermont* to the North Shore Arts Association for exhibition during the summer.

Bourne began the year 1926 by sending *Between Voyages* to the Washington Water Color Club's exhibition at the National Gallery of Art from February 5 – 28. [52] The title was particularly appropriate, since she may have felt in this period that she was perpetually "between voyages." From February 16 – March 21 Bourne participated in the Baltimore Water Color Club's 30th Annual Exhibition held at the Baltimore Museum of Art by sending *Winter in Vermont* and *Winter—Vermont*, each priced at $200. She also sent *The Flower Show 1926* and *Wine Boats, Ragusa, Dalmatia* to the North Shore Arts Association exhibition. Gertrude's interest in the Massachusetts Horticultural Society's Flower Show would soon prove to be a new venue for the display of her talents.

Their son, Philip Bourne, an eighteen-year-old freshman at MIT, went to Europe with two of his classmates for the summer of 1926. One of the classmates contracted typhoid fever, causing Philip to join his parents. When Frank and Gertrude arrived in Europe with a Model T Ford which they used to tour, the three Bournes traveled for the summer and then sold the car when they returned to America.

In 1927 Bourne sent a Dalmatian work, *Market, Ragusa, Dalmatia* to the Baltimore Water Color Club's annual exhibition. She and Frank took off in late February or early March on another voyage, this time to the Azores (which they reached by March 5), Morocco and Spain; followed by Italy in April (Ravello, Rome, Pisa, Florence), Switzerland; and Britain (Winchester,

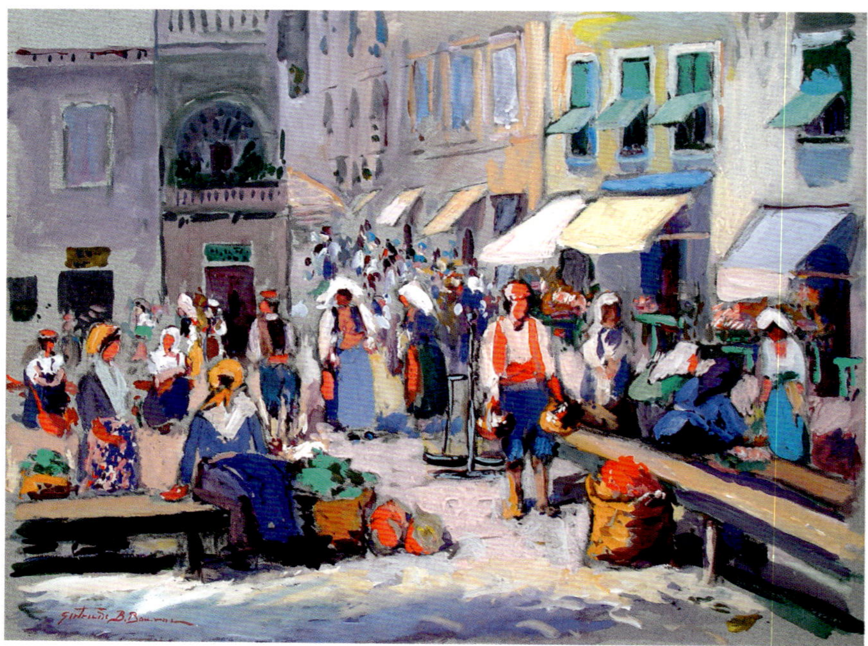

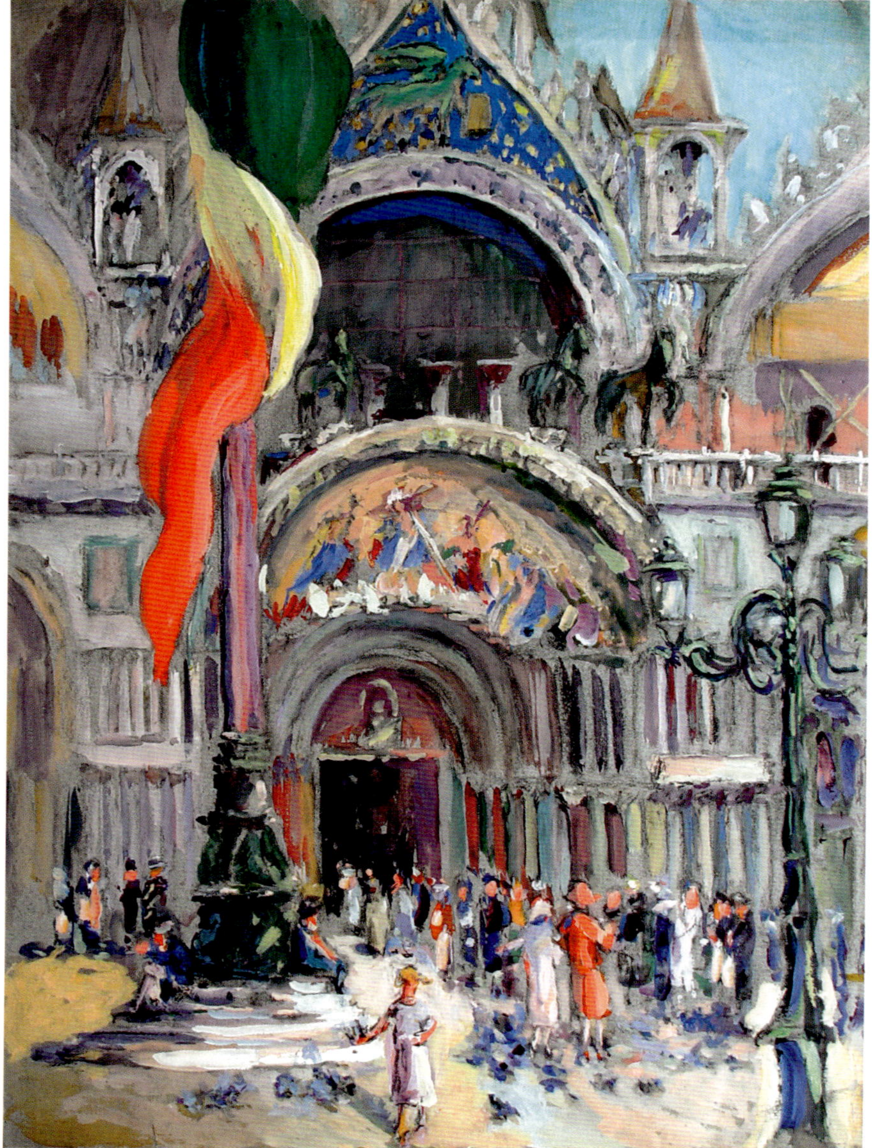

above: ***Market, Ragusa, Dalmatia***, 1924.
Watercolor on gray paper, 19 1/2 x 25 5/8 inches.
Courtesy of Childs Gallery, Boston.

right: ***Piazza San Marco, Venice***, 1924.
Watercolor, gouache, and charcoal on gray paper, 25 1/2 x 19 1/4 inches. This work, made the year of Prendergast's death, is an homage to his bright, free, modernized late work and to his subject matter of the 1890s. Private Collection.

Penshurst, Burrswood, Polperro) departing Southampton June 8 to LeHavre and arriving in New York on the 16th. It seems that Gertrude and Frank split up according to their interests. Frank studied architecture in Spain at Ronda, Alameda, and Granada, and after a while, it seems, Gertrude went to Morocco and painted the street life and markets of Marakesh and Fez. Frank continued his studies in Italy. He was at Ravello in early April, in Rome on April 26, Pisa May 1, and in Winchester, England on May 29. Meanwhile, it appears that after leaving Morocco, Gertrude went to England where she spent most of her time painting at Polperro.

Soon after their return, on August 9, Gertrude's mother, Edith Ware Beals, died at her residence at 65 Mount Vernon Street. After the death of her husband she had finally elected a smaller residence only a few short blocks from her daughter and an even shorter distance from the house on Walnut Street where she had grown up.[53] Her estate went to her three children (presumably divided evenly), which changed Gertrude's financial status to that of a reasonably wealthly woman.[54] With both of her parents dead and her son nearly grown, Gertrude must have thought of Frank as more important in her life than ever.

In January of 1928 the fruits of Bourne's English seaside stay of early 1927 were first shown at the combined exhibition of the New York Watercolor Club and the American Water Color Society from the 4th to the 17th—*Polperro Harbor No. 1* and *Polperro Harbor #2*. She followed that with #149 *New England Church* and #196 *Some Pumpkins* (p. 86) which were shown at the 32nd annual exhibition of the Baltimore Water Color Club at the Baltimore Museum of Art from March 6 – April 1; each was priced at $200. On April 9th the National Association of Women Painters and Sculptors opened their exhibition (which continued through May 7th) at the Brooklyn Museum, and Bourne showed *Spring in Spain*, *Back Yards*, and *Heel Mountain*. Both Bournes exhibited at the North Shore Arts Association in Gloucester: Gertrude with *Some Pumpkins*, *A New England Church*, and *The Wayside Inn*; and Frank with *Fairlawn – the Survival* and *Puit Cluny*. With the subject of Longfellow's *Tales of a Wayside Inn* as the ultimate sentimental favorite of Colonial Revival painters, Gertrude punctuated her career as a Colonial Revial artist by exhibiting *The Wayside Inn*. It was her final exhibited Colonial Revival painting—excepting only the interior painting *The Ancestor* (p. 115), shown in 1936. After this point, the role of architecture in her paintings was to complement garden scenes or to identify exotic non-New England locations, New Hampshire, or other wild landscapes.

From March 14-24 Goodspeed's Print Shop held an exhibition of Etchings and Lithographs by Frank Bourne. The *Boston Evening Transcript* reported:

Frank A. Bourne, the architect, of this city, has found diversion from the making of formal building plans in etching and lithography and is now exhibiting a group of his prints, his first show of the kind, at Goodspeed's Printshop on Ashburton place. Architectural motives prevail: an etching sketchily shows the Charles Street Church after having been moved back, an enterprise in which Mr. Bourne was professionally interested.

The greatest clarity of style prevails in the lithographs which consequently became the more readily appreciated. The delineation of Bodiam Castle and moat, its towers reflected in smooth waters, is accomplished in telling lines and in the lithographs of the fine old structures at Ightham, Groombridge, and Penhurst the stone has retained somewhat the qualities of the pencil handled in a telling manner.[55]

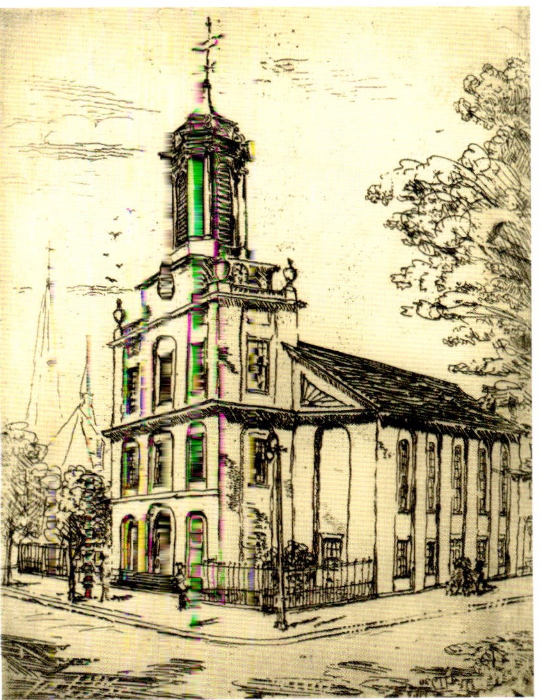

Frank Augustus Bourne, (1871-1936)
Charles Street Meeting House, 1920.
Etching, 9 1/8 x 7 inches.
This work, part of Frank Bourne's Goodspeed's Print Shop Exhibition, had been made about the time he had begun the move of the Meeting House. The Church is nearly opposite Sunflower Castle.
Courtesy of the Bourne Art Trust.

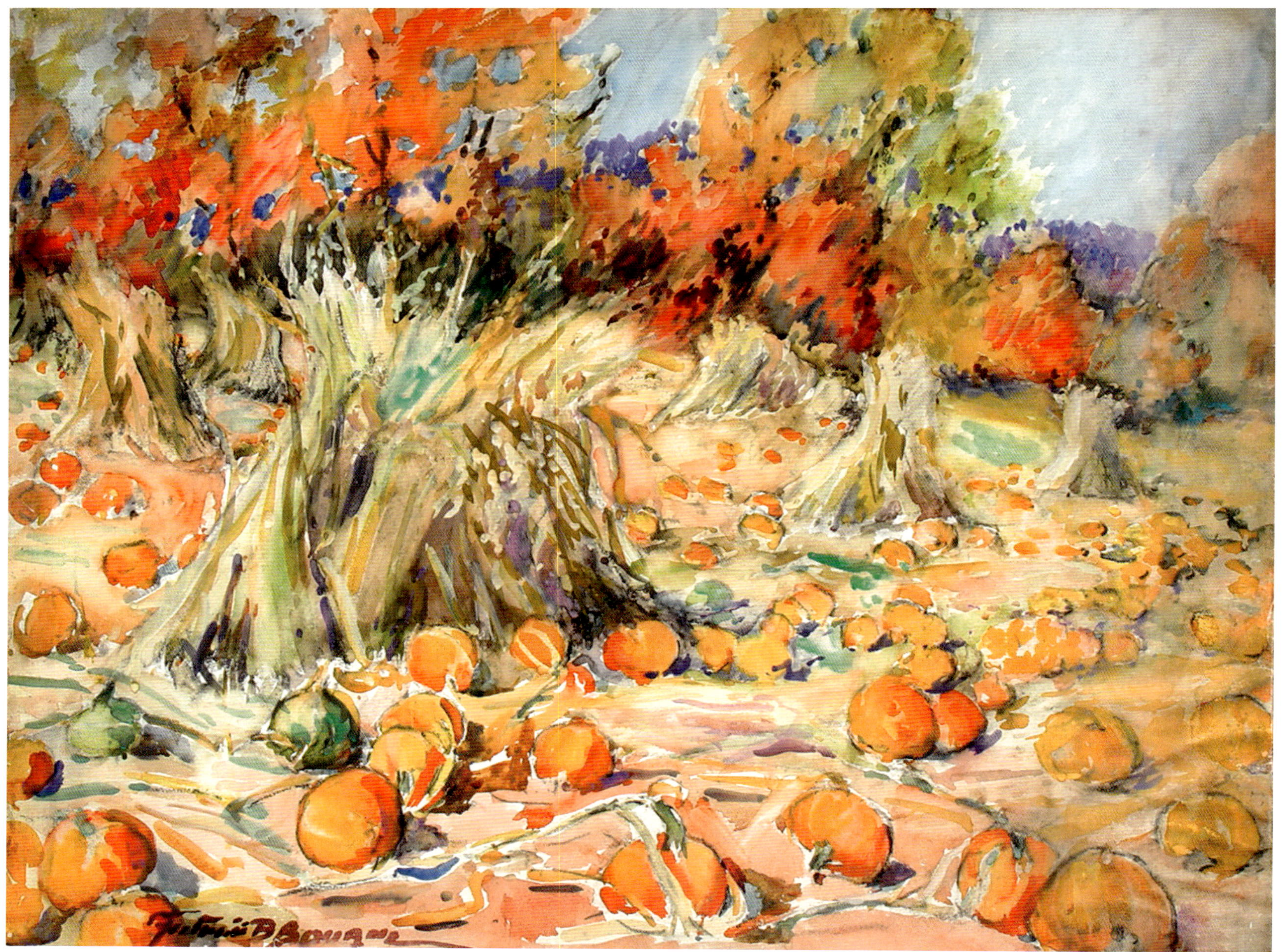

This single print exhibition by Frank Bourne received an encouraging review, and was shown at Goodspeed's, which, in the latter 1920s was one of the premiere commercial galleries in Boston exhibiting contemporary as well as old master prints. Frank Bourne is noted as having received instruction from George T. Plowman and Aimé Edmond Dallemagne in Paris. He acquired the etching press of the late Robert S. Peabody and his etchings were made directly on the copper. The lithographs were made on zinc plates drawn directly on the spot and printed in Paris.[56] The review also highlights, by contrast, the single-minded approach of Gertrude Bourne in choice of medium. Surprisingly, in an era when black and white printmaking of the sort that Frank exhibited was being extravagantly praised and even more extravagantly collected, Gertrude seems to have not even attempted printmaking, even though there was an etching press available in her own home. Almost without exception, she exhibited work in transparent watercolor and in gouache. Reviews almost always commented favorably on Gertrude Bourne's use of color—"her predilection for bright, pure and brilliant color" and "fresh, clear color 'dropped in' in a smart and knowing way." And color was not admired in printmaking in the 1910s and 1920s. Color printmaking in those years was often thought of as commercial or less serious. If Gertrude thought of herself as a "colorist" and a serious artist, the result may have been a reluctance to venture into printmaking at all.

The Bournes were graduating, by the late 1920s, to a position of senior resident artist and architect. To suggest that they had established a salon for the young artists on and about Beacon Hill would be excessive, but they engaged and encouraged younger painters.

Frank Bourne, in the role of critic of critics, shared his opinion of some of his fellow-artists. In February of 1927 he wrote an "appreciation" to the *Boston Evening Transcript* of the Aiden L. Ripley exhibition at the Guild of Boston Artists in which Frank wrote that the watercolor exhibition "deserves more than the passing comment in Saturday night's Transcript."[57] Frank and Gertrude noted and admired the mastery of the difficult medium by a young artist. By the late 1920s, the Bournes had added to their circle of friends many of the younger Boston artists including the Ripleys. Aiden Lassell Ripley (1896-1969) and his wife Doris had recently returned from Europe with paintings and watercolors from his extended stay in 1923-25; Ripley was the recipient of the Paige Travelling Scholarship (the highest award for a graduating senior at the School of the Museum of Fine Arts, Boston). In his first watercolor exhibitions his works were compared to, and indeed had, the control, life, and dash of Sargent's work. And the Ripleys were part of the arts community of Beacon Hill, living at 98 Chestnut Street, only about two blocks from the Bournes. By 1928 Ripley was an instructor at the School of the Museum of Fine Arts. Artists and architects were much in evidence in the life of the Bournes. In addition to the Ripleys, the Bournes had made friends with Beacon Hill artists Ruth A. Anderson (1891-1957) and Ellen Watson Cushing, and the well-known portrait painters Lydia Field Emmett and Marie Danforth Page. Bourne and Emmett were fellow exhibitors at the New York Water Color Club.

Some Pumpkins, c. 1927.
Watercolor on paper, 20 x 26 inches.
Exhibited: Baltimore Water Color Club, Baltimore Museum of Art, 1928; North Shore Art Association, 1928; Corcoran Gallery, Washington, D.C., 1929. Courtesy of Childs Gallery, Boston.

Beacon Hill Garden Club

In the 1920s Gertrude Bourne demonstrated her interest in flowers and gardens with her selections of watercolors to show in national venues. In the fall of 1928, at the age of sixty, Bourne took on a new challenge which would result in an enduring legacy. The founding of a club to increase and enhance tiny green spaces in the city of Boston and to invite visitors to share the "Hidden Gardens of Beacon Hill" was very much in line with the sentiments of Dr. Oliver Wendell Holmes who extolled bits of city greenery in 1858.

> —My idea was, in the first place, to search out the picturesque spots which the city affords a sight of, to those who have eyes. ... There were shrubs and flowers in the Franklin-Place front yards or borders: Commerce is just putting his granite foot upon them. Then there are certain small seraglio-gardens, into which one can get a peep through the crevasses of high

fences, —one in Myrtle Street, or at the back of it, —here and there one at the North and South ends. ... I don't know anything sweeter than this leaking in of Nature through all the cracks in the walls and floors of cities.[58]

Bourne's seraglio-garden had been the subject of an article in August 1928 before the founding of the club and both a harbinger and an impetus to the club's creation. In the beginning of the article, "High, Low and Hidden Gardens as They Bloom on Beacon Hill," the author, Katherine Crosby noted:

> On the afternoon of last Tuesday week I went up on Beacon Hill to look for gardens. That sounds simple, except that I didn't know one single solitary garden-owner on the whole territory, and from the sidewalks you can't tell whether a house has a garden or not. There is nothing so perfectly uncommunicative—on the subject of gardens—as the front of a dignified, high-shouldered old Beacon Hill residence. It maintains a reserve that makes the British article seem like Will Rogers by contrast. To look at an ordinary Hill house—if any Hill house is ordinary, which I myself would be willing to question—you would never guess a garden in it anywhere.
>
> But the trouble raised over the shadows cast on Walnut Street gardens by the Diocesan House extensions indicated that there were—there must be—gardens there that didn't show from the sidewalk.
>
> Now of course mid-summer is not a time to go calling anywhere in the politer reaches of this town. Everybody is away. Houses are closed and blanketed in gloom. They look less than ever as if they had gardens. Nobody comes to the door when you ring. Doorbells echo through empty halls.
>
> I had just decided it would be a happy thought to do an article about deserted gardens—a tale that would make absentee owners fly home to console their forsaken birdbaths—when it occurred to me that I had yet to find even a deserted garden. But it long ago became a habit for anyone who wants to know anything about the Hill to call up that Original Settler—of the

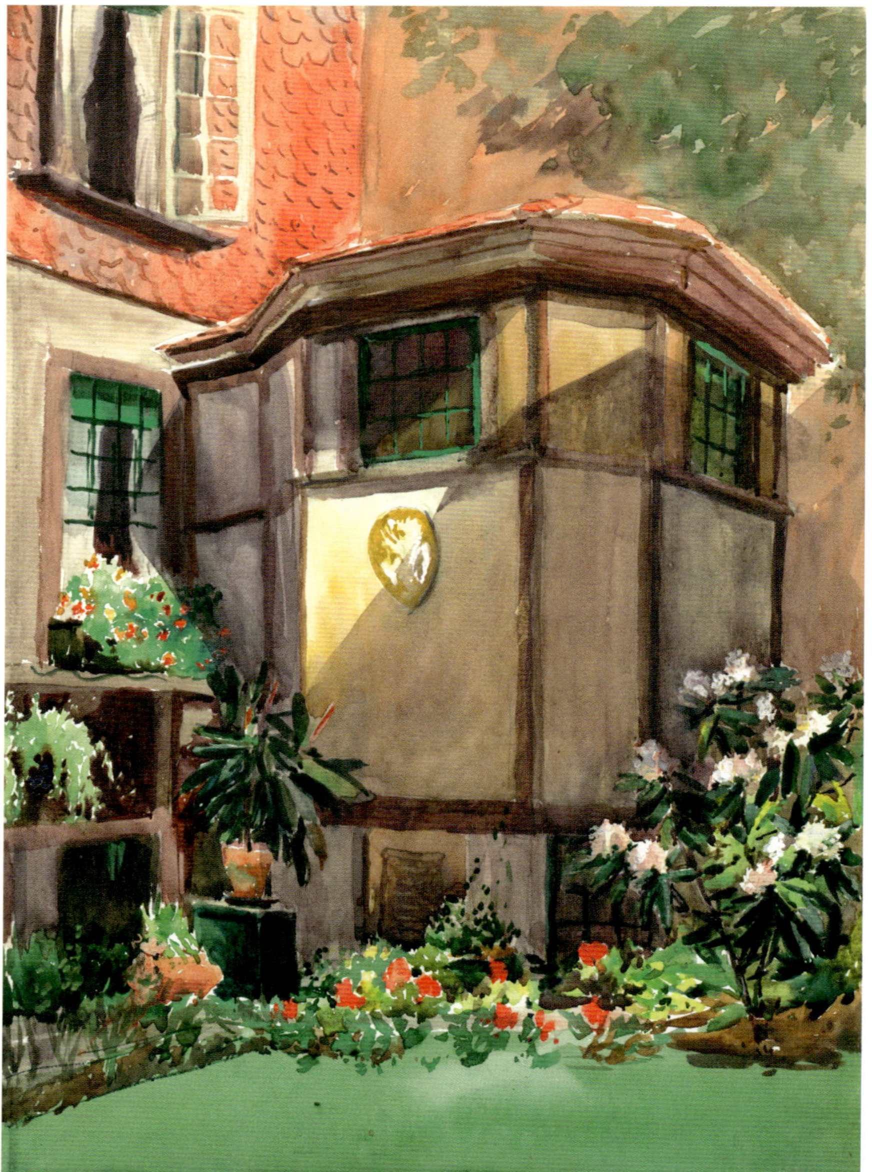

***"Yard Garden" 130 Mt. Vernon St. Showing China closet and one of the dining room windows with boxes of nasturtiums*, c.1910.**
Watercolor on paper, 14 3/8 x 10 inches. View of Gertrude's garden before she founded the Beacon Hill Garden Club, showing the future site of the iron staircase. Courtesy of the Bourne Art Trust.

New Hill—Robert Chase and ask him… I found more than I knew what to do with—backyard gardens and side-yard gardens that were deserted and gardens that were very much not deserted, gardens that were the pets and playthings of their owners, and gardens that were looked after by hirelings, gardens that women planned and tended, but even more gardens that were the outdoor sport of men.

Then Ms. Crosby threw down the gauntlet:

> Right here is the timely place to mention the need of a garden club for West End gardeners. Several of them jumped at the idea when I suggested it. They longed for a chance, they said, to pool their experience and to profit from each other's successes and failures. The bits of information I was able to carry from one to another about vines that would grow on shaded walls, and perennials that could stand city soil were received with an almost pathetic eagerness.
>
> For these gardens are becoming simply epidemic on the Hill. From one roof garden you can see half a dozen or more, and most of them new ones. There have always been trees-of-heaven—always, that is since before the exodus—but with few exceptions these and a bit of turf have contented the house owner. Now business and professional men are discovering that a round of work in the garden after a day in a State Street office gives one a satisfaction quite comparable to a good golf score, and more productive. Most of the gardens I saw had been started this year or last.

Under the sub-heading of "A Twenty-Year-Old Garden" Crosby, in the *Boston Evening Transcript,* continued:

> Another side garden belongs to the house numbered 130 on Mt. Vernon street. That is nearly opposite the Church of the Advent, down near the river. Anyone at all familiar with that part of town will remember the house, because it stands out from its surroundings, with some half-timbering above the brick.
>
> This belongs to Frank A. Bourne, who remodeled the house some forty-odd years ago. "Sunflower Castle" Oliver Wendell Holmes called it, from the sunflowers in the frieze along the front. Mrs. Bourne started the garden about twenty years ago.
>
> In spite of the years that have gone to its making, this is a "flower-pot" garden. It has its vines and its tree box hedges, strongly footed in the soil. But its auratum lilies that flank the oval fountain; its oleanders and other flowering plants, are all in pots.
>
> Two wall fountains drip into their basins on opposite walls. Turquoise blue lines the larger basin and covers the cushions of the big lounging chair. A bright awning shelters the table where the family has its meals through warm weather. (The kitchen has its own private entrance to the garden, up a few stair steps.) Vines and shrubs mark the front wall. On the wall near the lilies, hangs the cage of Harry, the big white cockatoo. He flaunts his yellow crest and is like a great big lily himself. Only there is nothing lily-ish about his voice. That has considerable range and power and leaves little to the imagination. But, he is a lovely thing, especially when not eating the lilies.
>
> Mrs. Bourne finds that Dutchman's pipe makes a good vine for city yards. But she specializes in tulips. Last fall she set out hundreds of bulbs and made the place a blaze of glory this spring. It was so successful that she is planning to repeat it this coming year.
>
> One must not forget one of the features of this garden—the Japanese bird house, quite as convincing as if it had not been made from an inverted butter firkin thatched with straw from pre-war champagne bottles.[59]

Gertrude Bourne, took up Crosby's challenge. On September 26, only a little more than a month after Crosby's article, Bourne gathered 24 residents of Beacon Hill together at "Sunflower Castle" "for the purpose of forming a Beacon Hill Garden Club with the object of interesting persons living on the hill in beautifying their yards and roofs into gardens."[60] At the second meeting of the club, on October 10th at the home of Mrs. Robert Cushman at 98 Mount Vernon Street, and with Mrs. Cushman chairman of the nominating committee, Mrs. Frank A. Bourne was nominated president. Additional nominations were: 1st Vice President Mr. Robert N. Cram, 2nd Vice President Mrs. Ellery Sedgewick, Secretary Mrs. Bryan S. Permer, and Treasurer Miss Eleanor Raymond. The slate having been unanimously elected, Mrs. Bourne "took the chair and read the articles and by-laws of the proposed constitution, which were then voted on separately and adopted."

For the next two years Bourne dedicated herself to the advancement of the fledgling club. Her bold projects and initiatives that were to become the most cherished and profitable traditions of the Beacon Hill Garden Club occupied much of her time. At the November 1 executive committee meeting Mrs. Sedgwick presented tentative plans for the club to exhibit in the March 1929 Spring Flower Show of the Massachusetts Horticultural Society to be held at Mechanics Hall in Boston. At the regular meeting that followed, the members voted to go ahead with the exhibition as long as the necessary funds were raised by voluntary contribution and that plans be left fully with the executive committee. The meeting concluded with the first of the regular informative talks on gardens with Mrs. Permer speaking on "Spring Bulbs."

By January 6, 1929 plans had been developed to such an extent by Robert Cram for a display titled "Back Yard Garden" for the Flower Show that Gertrude Bourne was appointed temporary chairman of its committee and empowered to spend up to $500. But by February 7 only half the money had been raised—a problem that was solved by March 5 when the secretary recorded that the new club would exhibit at the Centennial Exhibition of the Massachusetts Horticultural Society on March 19th as planned. To help defray expenses the club sold in advance many of the plants that were to be used at the exhibition. Gertrude purchased eight rhododendrons for $28.50. In addition she and Frank purchased the iron staircase that was to be the centerpiece of the display for later use in the garden of 130 Mount Vernon Street. The club members signed up for rotating duty at the flower show so two members would always be present at the exhibition.

The carefully considered entry did not prove to be in vain. The Beacon Hill Garden Club, not quite six months old, won the Mrs. Gardiner M. Lane Silver Cup, and—all bills having been paid—had $50 in the treasury. Not to rest on laurels, the members decided at that meeting on April 4, 1929 to open some of their gardens to the public on May 20 and June 3, 1929, charging $1 "for the series." The Bourne garden at 130 Mount Vernon Street would be opened to the public for each of the days of the Beacon Hill Garden Club Tour. On May 6 Gertrude gave a report to the club of her visit to Virginia gardens. The newly won cup was displayed to the members. Later the eminent Miss Rose Nichols "gave a delightful talk on Spanish and Portuguese gardens."[61] By the next meeting, June 5, Mrs. Bourne reported that the club had received over $1,000 from the opening of members' gardens for the recent tour. Gertrude was thinking of both publicity and income when for the next tour she suggested that postcards be printed of some of the gardens for sale at the time of the garden club tours with the profit going to the club's treasury.

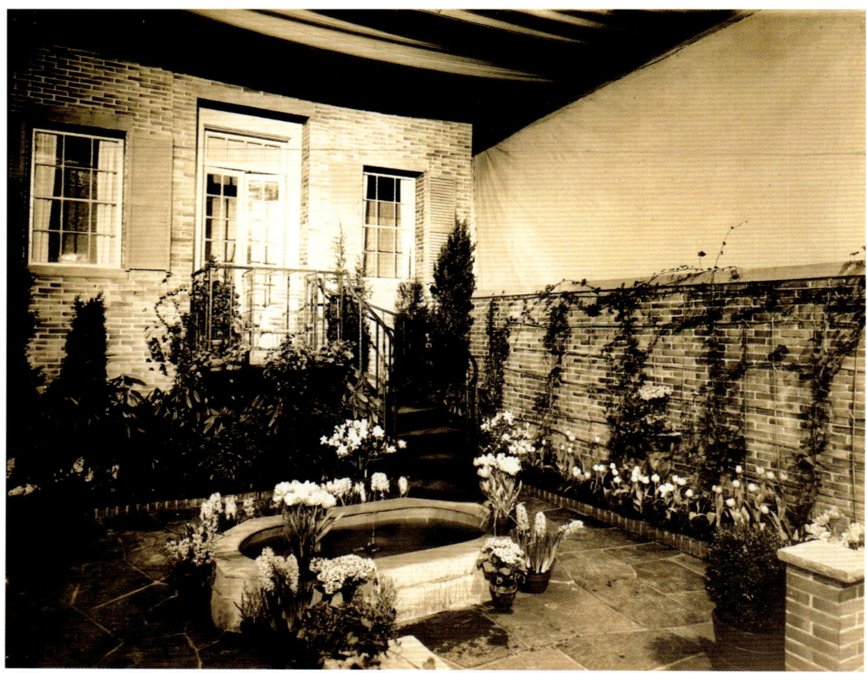

Back Yard Garden—Beacon Hill Garden Club, March 1929. The club's first entry for the Spring Flower Show of the Massachusetts Horticultural Society. Note the staircase that later appears in the garden at Sunflower Castle. Courtesy of the Beacon Hill Garden Club.

The annual meeting on October 17 was a celebration of the first year of the club. There were now 47 members and $1,095.51 in the treasury. Mrs. Bourne was duly re-elected as president. Miss Hetzer of the Lowthorpe School had already given a talk on "garden problems" at the May meeting. At the next meeting, November 7, the executive committee granted the Lowthorpe School $100, gave the North Bennett Street School summer camp $100, and allocated $50 for prizes for a competition of "children's window boxes" to take place on Beacon Hill the following summer. At the regular meeting Mrs. Seymore spoke of the work at the Lowthorpe School and noted how the girls raised funds for the school by raising flowering plants from seed and selling them during the summer and fall. The Lowthorpe School in Groton, Massachusetts had been founded in 1901 as the first school of landscape architecture for women in the United States.

On May 18, 1929 Katherine Crosby had delighted in announcing the founding of the Beacon Hill Garden Club, which, she stated, had been formed in the fall of 1928. And she continued proudly that the club had come about as "the seed was sown for its later activities in an article which appeared last August." She further stated:

> The Beacon Hill Garden Club, organized last fall with Mrs. Frank A. Bourne as president, is concluding its first season with an "open house." …Those who attended the Horticultural show at Mechanics hall this year will remember with delight the backyard garden which the club exhibited —although not competing, it nevertheless drew a prize almost in spite of itself. Its charm is repeated with endless variations all over the hill, for householders are discovering that this waste space at the rear of their homes can be used as an outdoor living room and gardens are appearing everywhere. Although the club has a limited membership, made necessary by the fact that it meets in the homes of its members, it is doing much by its activity to show the possibility for beauty and enjoyment in the city backyard. There is no reason why this movement should be confined to any special part of the town—one hopes another year to hear of the formation of a South End Garden Club, for instance, for plenty of backyards are there, ready for improvement…

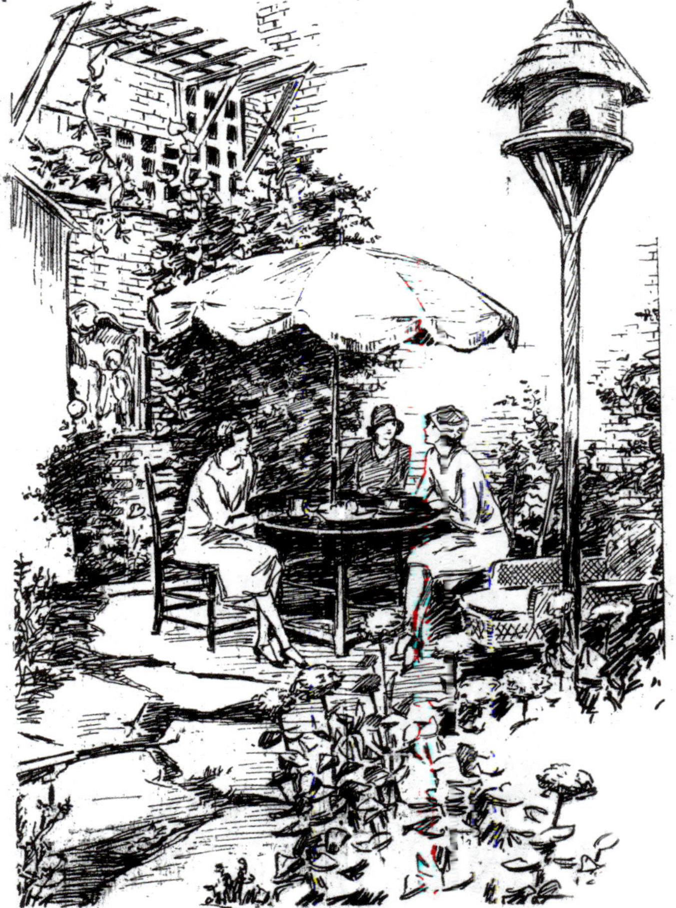

Sky and Umbrella Are Dining-Room Roof at the Bourne's

Sky and Umbrella Are Dining-Room Roof at the Bourne's, May 1929. As published in the *Boston Evening Transcript* May 18, 1929.

After acknowledging the gardens of Mrs. C. L. Norton, Mrs. H. F. Lesh, and Miss Eleanor Raymond, Crosby turned her attention to the Bourne garden.

> The curving iron stairway shown at the club's Horticultural Show garden has been set up in the garden of Mrs. Frank A. Bourne, 130 Mt. Vernon street, on the corner of River street. A dining table under a gay umbrella does duty through all the warm weather for the family meals, while a long chair with waterproofed cushions makes a restful spot among the flowers.[62]

Crosby's glowing review in *The Transcript* constituted a solid endorsement by the establishment publication—for it was then the newspaper of Boston Society—for the new organization.

The club began to organize its priorities. They included an exhibit at the Spring Flower Show, support for student and youth education about flowers and gardens, beautification of Beacon Hill and support of many of the measures promoted by the Beacon Hill Association. At the December 1929 regular meeting the club voted to again enter an exhibit for the Spring Flower Show of the Massachusetts Horticultural Society. The second year was again a success. At the April meeting the club reported that the Beacon Hill Garden Club had been awarded first prize at the spring flower show in Class B Border Planting and that two members, Mrs. Cushman and Mrs. Warren, had taken prizes in flower arrangement. Soon after, at the May 1st meeting of the club a letter from the Massachusetts Horticultural Society invited the Beacon Hill Garden Club to exhibit at the 1931 Spring Flower Show, "A Colonial House and Garden of the period of 1750. The house to be architecturally correct, and the garden to have plants available for that time. The exhibit to cover not more than 500 square feet."[63]

The January 1930 meeting of the club began a tradition of activism by the club. The executive committee heard a report from Mrs. Reed, chairman of the conservation committee, on her investigation into "signboard and smoke nuisances." After the report the executive committee voted to give $100 to the Massachusetts Bill Board Law Defense Committee. Later at the regular meeting, all members "were strongly urged ... to report to the Smoke Commission, all cases of black smoke issuing from chimneys with address of building and time of day noted." Letters were read from the Garden Club of America, Garden Club Federation of Massachusetts, the North Bennett Street School and the Lowthorpe School. The Beacon Hill Garden Club was now notable not only in Boston, but in Massachusetts, across America, and in England. The following month the secretary of the club was instructed to write a letter of endorsement from the club of House Bill 926 which sought to suppress smoke nuisance, an issue of burning interest to the Beacon Hill Association.

Educating Beacon Hill children and residents and keeping the club's membership well informed were two of the principal activities that Bourne instituted. On March 6, the executive committee approved $10 at the request of Mrs. Snow for 500 pins to be distributed to the children entering the window box competition. The club began a tradition of encouraging children to learn skills through gardening projects with the children's window box contest in the summer of 1929 that continues to the present as a window box contest for residents. At the regular meeting that followed, the well-known landscape architect, Fletcher Steele, spoke on "Town Gardens Abroad."[64] Although the club had already enlisted several speakers, Steele became the first of a large number of well-known experts in their particular areas of plants, flowers, and gardens to speak before them. In May of 1930 Bourne assigned the members the task of each writing "a short paper on some interesting garden subject."

Garden Club activities reflected a few indications of the depression plaguing most of society. A sad announcement was made in April 1930 noting the death of Mr. Robert Cram, the first vice president of the club; the general presumption among members was that Cram's death was a suicide due to financial reverses which had resulted from the stock market crash the previous year. Robert Cram had had very ambitious plans for his Roman garden on Beacon Hill and his lifestyle in general. The notice of his death, the omission of the June meeting out of respect for his widow, and Mrs. Cram's thanks for the garden club's flowers are some of the few indicators that the onset of the Great Depression was affecting the members of the club or Gertrude Beals Bourne. Caution, however, had the club instruct the treasurer in October 1932 "to change the savings account from...the Shawmut Bank to some old and well-established savings bank."[65] Later, in November of 1932 the executive committee would unanimously "assent that teas should be simplified."[66] And, on November 1, 1934 "on account of the depression it was voted to waive the payment of the initiation fees from new members." A least one grant was made to the city for the relief of workmen and the club voted *not* to reduce dues because of the depression. Neither Frank nor Gertrude Bourne traveled less frequently or made any other outward change in life style that would indicate that the Great Depression was affecting them.

On June 4, 1930 the regular meeting of the club was omitted in favor of a social evening of dancing at the invitation of Mr. and Mrs. Amos Little at 13 T Wharf. A light supper was served with chowder made by Mrs. Little, followed by a magician and dancing which ended with a Virginia Reel. This extended bit of socializing indicated that—in addition to its purposes of educating the members about city gardens, promoting landscape and gardens on Beacon Hill, encouraging student gardening, organizing as a political lobby with the Beacon Hill Association—the Beacon Hill Garden Club had become a center for Beacon Hill society. The teas, excursions, and dances became every bit as important to many of the members as new information on spring bulbs.

The Annual Report of the Beacon Hill Garden Club for 1930 gave a picture of an organization that had grown in numbers and in strength. A full complement of the fifty members allowed by the by-laws had been elected and there was a waiting list. Nine regular meetings were held with lectures in the homes of members. The garden tour had netted $1508 from the sale of tickets and postcards. On June 13, six members had accepted the invitation of Mrs. Franklin McElwain for a luncheon and tour of some of the gardens of Cohasset. That was followed by a June 16 visit to the Ipswich gardens of Mrs. Shurcliff followed by a tour of the gardens of the Crane Estate. In addition to the schools and causes supported, Mrs. William B. Snow, with the cooperation of the school teachers of Beacon Hill, helped some 100 school children to plant and to care for window boxes during the summer.

On Gertrude Bourne's last day as president, on October 10, the executive committee voted to hire a professional (at not more than $150) to look at members' gardens and advise on their planting and care. At the annual meeting, which followed, Mrs. Bourne retired after two years as president of the club, as required by the by-laws. She reiterated the history of the club, Mrs. Snow reported on the window boxes and presented three children to receive prizes, Mrs. Campbell reported on the proceedings for the flower show in the spring, and Mrs. Bourne reported for the treasurer (Miss Raymond) that the treasury stood at $2020.26.

The nominating committee proposed Mrs. Ellery Sedgwick president, Mrs. Frank A. Bourne 1st vice president, Mrs. Howard Brown 2nd vice president, Miss Eleanor Raymond treasurer, and Mrs. Charles L. Norton secretary. The slate was elected. Mrs. Sedgwick, as president then "asked for a rising vote of thanks to Mrs. Bourne for her faithful and efficient management of the club for two years, which was unanimously given."[67] On May 2, 1931 a new slate of officers was elected without Gertrude Bourne's name included. However, she remained an active and outspoken member of the executive committee who took on many tasks at the request of the new officers and who was among the most active in the club in proposing new members.

Gertrude Bourne had founded and set on its way an institution in every way as important to the life of Beacon Hill as Frank's Beacon Hill Association. The two organizations had—and still maintain in many cases—cross-membership and belong to a tight-knit group of Beacon Hill dwellers. The Garden Club members could be counted upon to rally to the Beacon Hill Association zoning issues. The Beacon Hill Association concluded in early 1932 that something had to be done to beautify the site of the demolished Old Ladies Home with its 56,000 square foot lot on the flat of Beacon Hill. Frank Bourne and the zoning committee had been involved in the fight to keep the lot from being developed outside of zoning restrictions. The Association referred the problem to the Beacon Hill Garden Club. Gertrude Bourne was appointed by the Garden Club to look into the matter. She enlisted the help of the president of the Women's Municipal League who agreed to help as long as the owners' permission was granted. Gertrude applied to the Beacon Hill Association for help in getting the owners' approval for a temporary use of the site for children's gardens. Frank Bourne, wearing his Beacon Hill Association hat, then wrote to his friend, Dana Somes, the architect chosen by the developers to put forth a larger project than the zoning would permit. Although Bourne requested permission for plantings, he did not give any quarter where the letter of the law was concerned. He said: "I do not want you to get away with the idea that I am condoning any infraction in the zoning law…I got into this by giving the names of the representatives of the owners to whom the ladies could apply. They wanted to have the vacant lot kept clean and presentable and used temporarily for children's gardens, and asked me how it could be done."[68] In April of 1933 Gertrude read a letter to the club from Mrs. Henry Tudor asking them to contribute to "school gardens to be planted at the vacant lot of the Old Ladies Home." The practice of contributing to the children's gardens continued through at least May 1941.[69]

Similarly, when Frank Bourne continued with his labor of love restoring the Charles Street Meeting House on the corner of Charles and Mount Vernon Streets, the Garden Club responded with financial support. In 1933 "it was decided that it would be appropriate for the club to give towards the expenses of repairing the steeple of the Charles Street Church as soon as such a fund is started." They ratified a grant of $100 for the cause.[70] On November 14, 1935 Gertrude again called on the club to support "the needs of the Mt. Vernon St. Church."[71]

As president, executive committee member, and as an individual, Gertrude Bourne visited and engaged other garden clubs across New England, America, and the world. As early as December 5, 1929 the club invited Mrs. John Harwood of the Chestnut Hill Garden Club to speak on her trip to the gardens of England as a delegate of the Garden Club of America. Harwood announced that American garden club members were "cordially welcomed by representatives of the English Clubs and most royally entertained. They were given the opportunity to visit many gardens rarely opened to visitors."[72] This certainly had appeal for the members of the Beacon Hill Garden Club and especially for an inveterate traveler like Gertrude. By May of 1929, Gertrude had visited gardens in Virginia as the president of the club. By 1930, the club was affiliated with the Federated Garden Clubs of Massachusetts and was being asked to propose nominations for officers. In 1931 Gertrude arranged to send slides of Beacon Hill gardens to the Federated Garden Clubs of

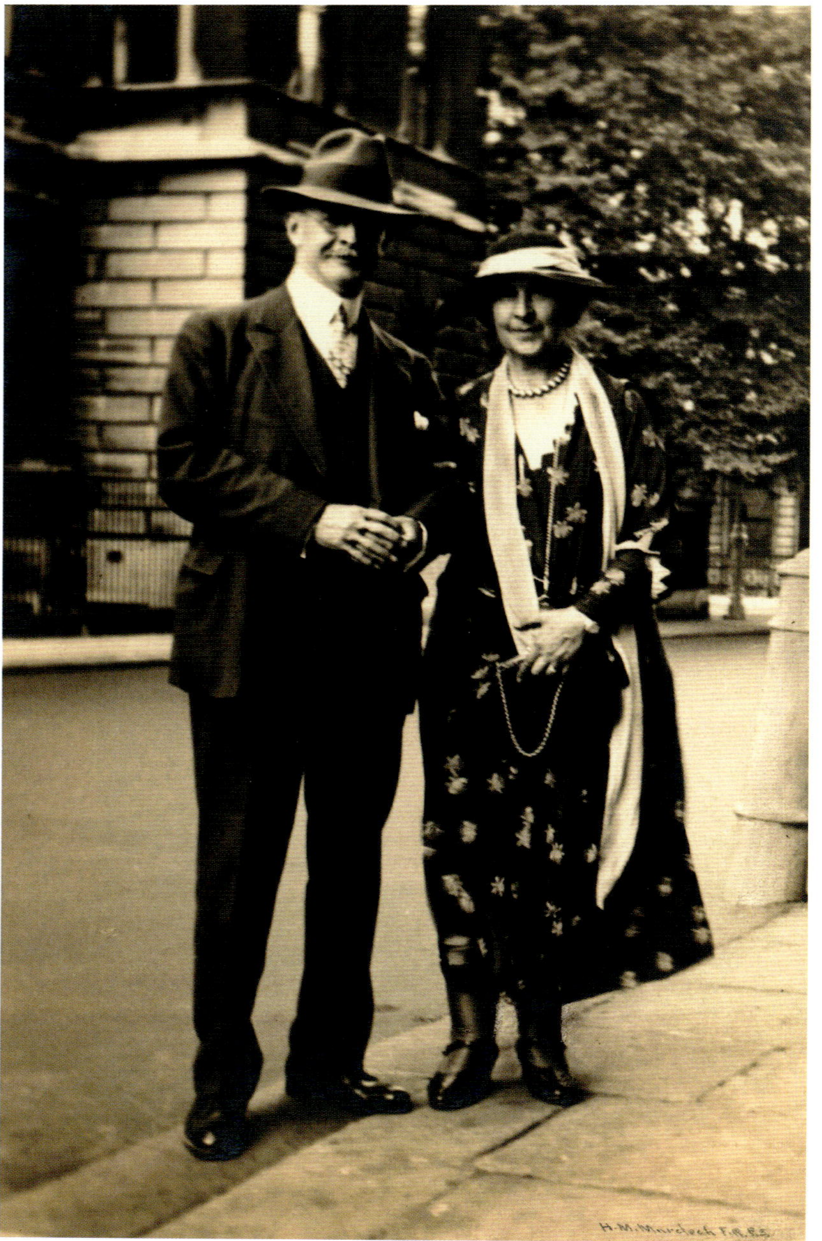

Frank A. Bourne and Gertrude B. Bourne at London Garden Club in the summer of 1932 in front of the clubhouse at 9 Chesterfield Gardens.
Photo by H. M. Murdock F. R. P. S.
Courtesy of the Beacon Hill Garden Club.

Massachusetts so that the federation might show them "in different parts of the country." In 1931, Bourne again traveled as a member of the executive committee to visit and report on Mexican gardens. In April 1932, photographs of six Beacon Hill Gardens were sent to the New York City Garden Club to be shown with pictures of other garden clubs from around the country.[73] A high point of this web of interconnected clubs and their interests was when Gertrude and Frank Bourne made a visit to the London Garden Club in the summer of 1932 and were photographed in front of the clubhouse at 9 Chesterfield Gardens. They were presumably met by and entertained royally by Miss Marion Crane of the London club. We may also suppose that the Bournes gained access to London and English gardens through the London club. The relationship continued when in October 1932: "Mrs. Bourne read from *Gardens in America* by Marion Crane, a director of the London Garden Club. Mrs. Bourne had introduced Miss Crane to some of the gardens on Beacon Hill."[74] In 1937 Gertrude and Mrs. Cushman sent pictures and wrote a brief history of the club at the request of Miss Margaret McKenny, secretary of the City Gardens Club of N. Y. McKenny was writing a book on city gardens that she was about to publish.[75] By the end of the year the book, *Your City Garden* by Margaret McKenny and E. L. D. Seymour, had been received with a short history of the club and illustrations of Mrs. Cushman's and Mrs. Warren's gardens.[76] Bourne and other members allowed their "names to be given to the Federated Garden Clubs of Massachusetts in order that their members may visit those gardens at any time by telephoning for permission."[77] Through her own travel, her correspondence, her diligence in arranging for photographs, and her generosity in opening her own garden, Gertrude Bourne fostered the positive image and reputation of the Beacon Hill Garden Club among the correspondent garden clubs everywhere.

Gertrude and Frank included their circle of friends into the activities of the Beacon Hill Association and the Beacon Hill Garden Club, but the new membership of both groups also provided new acquaintances for the couple. It is difficult to distinguish which of the participants in the Beacon Hill Garden Club that Gertrude knew well before it was organized, but it is clear who were regular contributors to the success of the club that would become increasingly important to her. Some like Felix Frankfurter of the Association and Christian Herter (Mrs. Herter was a member of the Garden Club) were of local prominence in the late 1920s, but each would grow to national stature. Frankfurter later became justice of the United States Supreme Court, and Herter was elected state representative in 1931, later to become governor of Massachusetts and United States secretary of state. Bremer Pond, chairman of the Department of Landscape Architecture at Harvard, was probably known to both of them before he lectured to the club.[78] Pond became a patron of the Bourne's young friend, Aiden Lassell Ripley. Laura Hills, the eminent and successful floral pastellist in the 1920s-1940s lived on Beacon Hill and accepted the task of acting as a judge for Garden Club flower arrangement competitions.[79] Morris Carter, the first director of Fenway Court, the Isabella Stewart Gardner Museum in Boston, became a lecturer for the Garden Club. If he was not a friend of the Bournes before he became associated with the club, he became one shortly thereafter. On April 25, 1935 the club members gathered in the garden courtyard of the museum where Morris Carter gave "an interesting talk on 'The Experiences of a Museum Director with Flowers', calling attention to the many problems and trials as well as the great joy. In his company [the members] wandered through the Museum, stopping in the large hall to hear from selections beautifully rendered on the harpischord."[80] Carter returned to speak on November 10, 1938 on "Some Gardens Around the World."[81] Part of the success of the club was the powerful and hardworking people that Gertrude enlisted to found and nurture it. And part of its personal value to her was the support that members could give to her and Frank's projects and causes. Members and their extended circles of acquaintances provided the source of friendships that would last for Gertrude for many years.

In addition to occasionally showing her watercolors of gardens to fellow club members, Gertrude successfully developed another art form for exhibition. Presumably her interest in gardens was accompanied from the start with floral arrangement; she was almost certainly responsible for the bouquets of flowers that she painted in the 1890s. On February 4, 1931, during her final month as an officer of the club, Gertrude competed in a club arrangement contest. With twenty-one members and guests present each member was supplied with an identical container and flowers and given a half-hour to complete an arrangement. The completed works were judged by Miss Laura Hills, Mrs. Gordon Allen, and Mrs. E. L. Oliver while the club's business meeting was held. Mrs. Frank A. Bourne was the first-prize winner, followed by Mrs. Howard Brown and Mrs. Robert Osgood. This appears to have been Gertrude's first public exhibition of her flower arranging skills and it was a signal success in front of her most valued peers. On November 16, 1933 a similar contest was held for wreaths and winter bouquets made prior to the meeting. The judges who made their decisions during the business meeting were Mrs. Langdon Warner (whose husband was professor and curator of oriental art at Harvard in 1933), Mrs. Romney Spring, and Mrs. Lawrence Oliver. Miss Eleanor Raymond, presiding in the president's absence announced that the winning wreath would be sent to the New England Wildflower Preservation Society contest, which would be held at Horticultural Hall November 23-26. The wreaths had been solicited by the Wildflower Preservation Society from each New England garden club—one per club, selected in a competition—the wreaths not to include laurel, ground pine, or holly. A few minutes later the Beacon Hill judges awarded first prize to Mrs. Bourne for a wreath of Japanese lanterns. A second round where club members voted, ranked Bourne's wreath second. While the judges did not acknowledge Bourne's winter bouquet, the club members voted her bouquet of yellow Mexican straw flowers as the second best. The wreath of Japanese lanterns was sent on to the Wildflower Preservation Society as the club's entry where it won the first prize of $25.00. The club then voted to use the prize money as a donation to the work of the Wildflower Preservation Society. The following year the same wreath contest was held with the formidable Mrs. Fiske Warren as one of the Beacon Hill Club's judges, together with Mrs. Gordon Allen and Miss Mary Barnes. Of the seventeen wreaths presented, Bourne's, of magnolia leaves and buds, was judged second. As part of the ongoing efforts to provide instruction to members "helpful criticisms on which the judges had based their decisions were given."[82] In May of 1935 Gertrude won a prize for "Altar Arrangement" at the Cohasset Flower show. At the Massachusetts Horticultural Society's Spring Flower Show in 1939 Gertrude, together with Miss Louise Condit, received a "yellow award for their vase of flowers in shades of one color."[83] Again, in 1940, Gertrude took an "award of C, or third place" for flower arrangement at the Spring Flower Show. In contrast to her exhibition career in watercolor, where in most cases the primary competition was to be judged worthy to place a work in the show at all, the flower shows were fiercely competitive—and in these contests Gertrude Bourne acquitted herself well.

Established and Disestablished Artists of Beacon Hill

Gertrude Beals Bourne's garden was a symbol of how well settled she and Frank were on Beacon Hill. Gertrude was in her early sixties and both of her parents were dead. She had inherited a substantial legacy from them by 1929. They had moved onto the "flat" of the hill in 1904 when Beacon Hill was Boston's Bohemia. By the late 1920s, however, Beacon Hill had begun to gentrify to such an extent that a 1927 newspaper article—again by Katherine Crosby—discussed the plight of artists not so well established as the Bournes:

> Bohemia on the move—the exodus of the artists has begun. Once Beacon Hill was theirs, its basements and attics and its old lodging houses. Their studios filled all the old picturesque odd corners for which the genteel white collar jobbers had no eye. The Hill was theirs because they alone appreciated its beauty. Then the women discovered that the old houses could be made over into kitchenette apartments, and that was the beginning of the end. Rents flew up over night, and the artists had to go studio hunting. A few of them discovered the possibilities of the then decrepit Fayette Quarter, and moved over there. But still the women followed, buying up the houses on which Art had set its seal of approval, and making them into kitchenette apartments.
>
> The third chapter in this long exodus is opening. The man who was perhaps the first artist to discover the possibilities of the Hill as a Latin Quarter was Robert S. Chase. That was eleven years ago. For years his studio in the old wooden house at the farther end of Bellingham Place was center for information about the neighborhood. He knew the streets and alleys intimately and loved them. But now he has left the Hill and set out to find a new Quarter, pioneering once again. He has bought a house and built himself a studio on the top of another hill—once called Snow, now known to every school child as Copps.

> Beacon Hill had reverted to a former deadly dull respectability. The old picturesque characters who had helped make its charm were gone, the artists had either disappeared or become prosperous.[84]

Crosby apparently did not know that a considerable number of artists were established on Beacon Hill well before Mr. Chase arrived in 1916, but she seems to have correctly assessed that by 1927 an artist needed to be "prosperous" or relocate. A comparison of the Boston City Directories in the period when the Bournes moved to Beacon Hill and in 1928 may be misleading. A similar number of artists seem to have residences on Beacon Hill in each instance. However, Gertrude Bourne did not list herself (perhaps from propriety) in either case. In addition, some of the artists who needed the cheap rents of Beacon Hill in the earlier period were also the artists who would not have been willing to pay to be listed in the city directory at all. There remained a few established "old comers" such as Laura Coombs Hills at 66 Chestnut Street and I. M. Gaugengigl at 5 Otis Place. The Aiden Lassell Ripleys had moved to the Hill after their return from Europe in 1925. Gertrude's friends, the artists Ruth A. Anderson (Mrs. Samuel Temple) and Ellen Watson Cushing were living respectively at 51 Charles Street and 2 West Cedar Street and each would be members of the Beacon Hill Garden Club (Anderson 1946-57 and Cushing 1931-35). But, Gertrude's friends, the Prendergast brothers, who in 1906 had lived at 56 Mount Vernon Street, had moved to New York where Maurice died in 1924. The picturesque in her own environment (Sunflower Castle) and that of her community as described by Crosby, is also reflected in Bourne's taste for the picturesque in her paintings. From her earliest works that included architecture, she painted the old, picturesque, tumble-down, and historical. By 1928, in an odd, interesting, and subtle—but inevitable—shift, the picturesque of old Beacon Hill was replacing the genteel brownstone modernity of the Back Bay of Gertrude's youth as the desirable dwelling-place for the fashionable. Suddenly the robber baron piles of the Back Bay seemed oppressive and tasteless when compared with the neat, Federal and Colonial style architecture of the Hill. Crosby even had a hand in the gentrification of the Hill that she decried. In her call for a "a garden club for West End gardeners" in 1928 she set in motion the Beacon Hill Garden Club (Gertrude's club), one of the most successful engines of that gentrification.

Exhibitions and Travels 1929-36

In 1929 Bourne's exhibition schedule began with the combined annual exhibition of the New York Water Color Club and the American Water Color Society in New York from January 3 – 20 with *The Brook, Wilton; Afternoon, February*, and *A New England Church*. From January 6 to February 3 she exhibited *Some Pumpkins* (p. 86), *A City Yard Garden*, and *A Cohasset Garden* at the Corcoran Gallery in Washington as part of the annual Washington Water Color Club exhibition. Bourne's showing of *A City Garden* and *My Yard Garden* followed her founding the Beacon Hill Garden Club and showed her continuing commitment to gardens and flowers and her increasing interest in her own "hidden" city garden and those of her fellow garden club members. *City Yard Garden* would be her final entry for exhibition at the North Shore Arts Association from July 6– September 2.

The summer of 1929 again saw the Bournes in Europe. On August 19th they were in Paris and by the 29th in Zurich and may have also visited England. From December 8 – 29 Bourne showed *The Farm in Winter* and *My Yard Garden* at the Corcoran Gallery exhibition of the Washington Water Color Club.

In August of 1930 the Bournes traveled through the Gaspé Penninsula and Grande Vallée and returned to Boston via the coast of Maine, stopping in Wiscasset. In the fall they were closer to home sketching in Newport, Litchfield, Connecticut, Marblehead, and Salem where Frank noted Gertrude's sketch of the House of the Seven Gables. From October 23 – November 16 Bourne showed *Cockatoo's Garden* at the combined annual exhibitions of the New York Water Color Club and the American Water Color Society at the Fine Arts Building in New York. One writer said of the event, "American artists today are probably at the top of the heap when it comes to watercolor."[85] It seems to have been her only exhibition during the year.

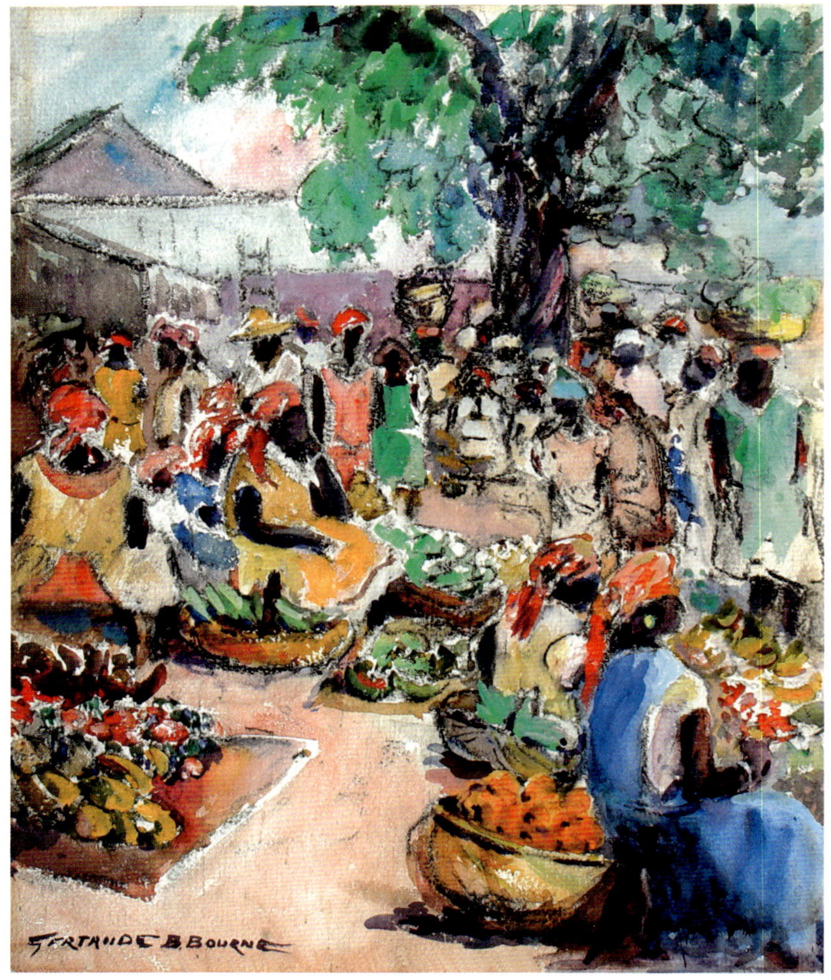

above: ***Kingston Market, Jamaica***, 1931.Watercolor and charcoal on paper, 19 1/2 x 16 inches. Exhibited at the American Water Color Society, 1931. Here Bourne uses the mosaic-like patterning observed in the later work of Maurice Prendergast, similarities which reviewers noted.
right: **Maurice Prendergast (1858-1924),** ***Park Gloucester***, 1920-23. Watercolor and pencil on paper, 13 3/4 x 19 3/8 inches.
Courtesy of Childs Gallery, Boston.

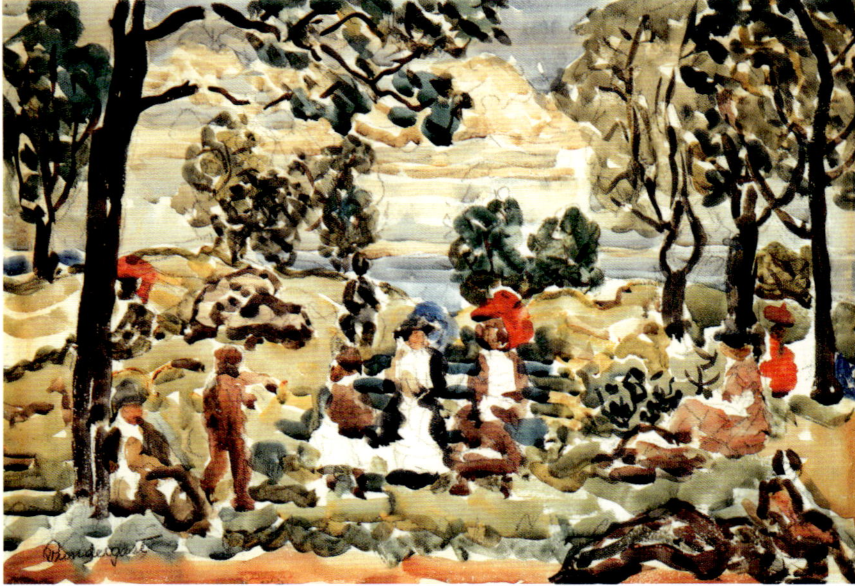

In January of 1931 Frank and Gertrude left Boston for a tour of the Caribbean, Mexico and the American Southwest, which was probably done mostly by ship. They visited Nassau in the Bahamas, Cuba (San Cristobal on February 22 and Havana on February 28) and Jamaica. They seem to have then gone on to Mexico to Cuernavaca and returned in April by way of San Antonio, Texas to Boston. In early September they visited New London, Connecticut, Block Island and Montauk and the Hamptons on Long Island. Gertrude lost no time in submitting her new work, sending *Kingston Market, Jamaica* to the annual exhibition of the American Water Color Society from October 20 – November 8. From December 3-27 she exhibited *Cymbals* and *Faun* at the Corcoran Gallery as part of the Washington Water Color Club exhibition.

Gertrude Bourne continued to exhibit her Caribbean and Mexican work at the 1932 Boston Art Club January 15 – 30 exhibition "Contemporary American Watercolor Painting" with *Pink Church, Cuernavaca*.

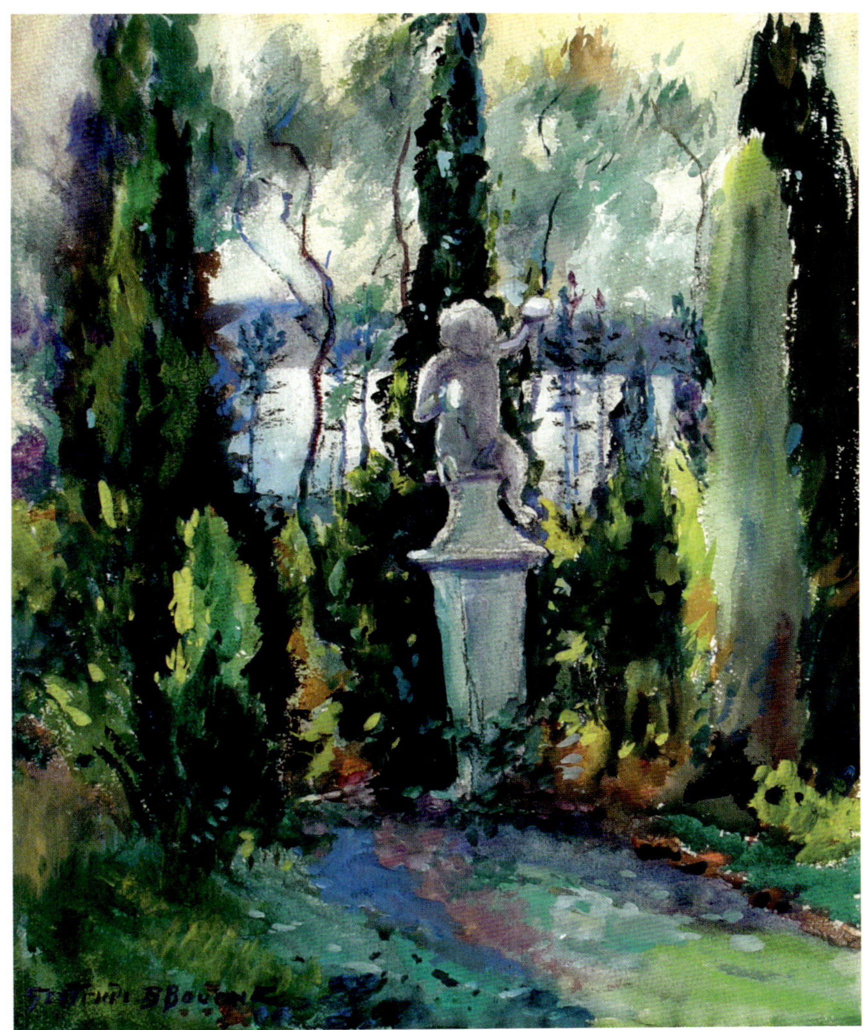

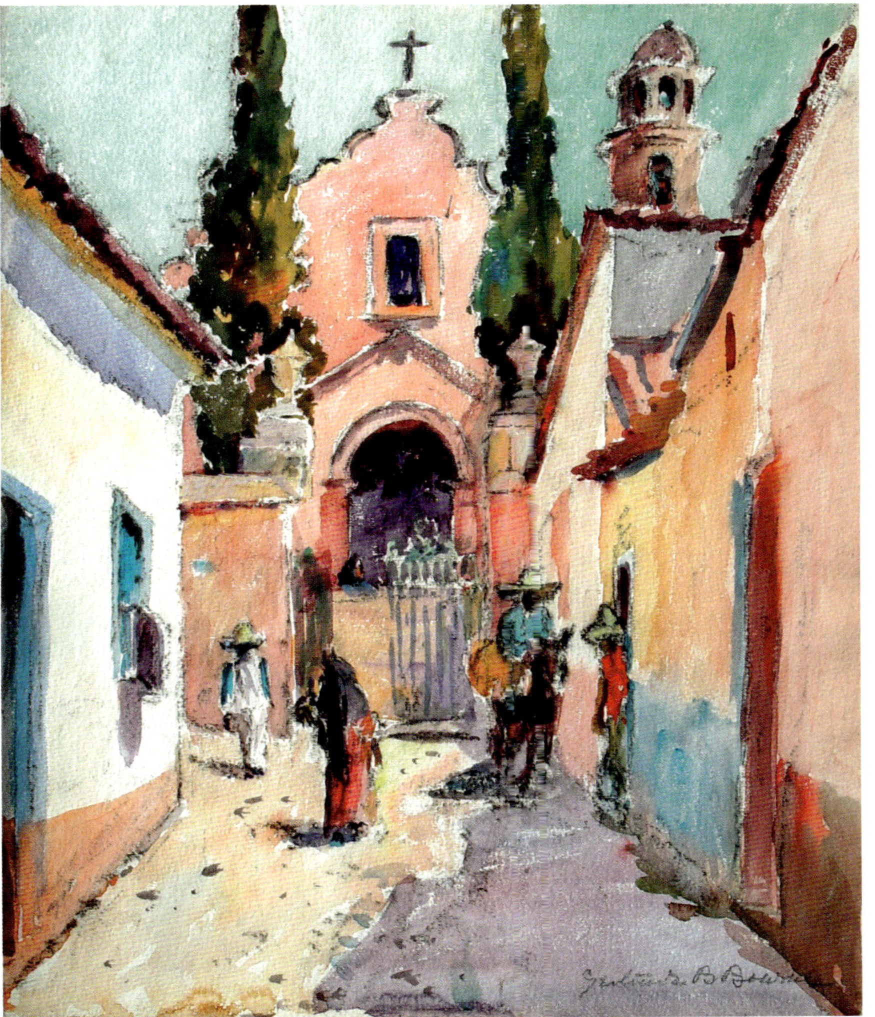

above: ***Pink Church, Cuernavaca***, 1931. Watercolor and charcoal on paper, 19 1/2 x 16 inches. Courtesy of Childs Gallery, Boston.

left: ***Cymbals***, c. 1931.
Watercolor on paper, 19 x 16 inches. Private Collection.

Frank and Gertrude Gain a Daughter-in-Law

Philip Bourne, having followed his father by studying architecture at M.I.T., met a fellow-student, George James Guthrie Nicholson, Jr. Nicholson's father was English, but young Nicholson grew up on his parents' ranch in

Wyoming. He also had cousins in Marblehead where he often went as a weekend respite from M.I.T. He invited Philip to go with him in either 1929 or 1930 and meet, among others, his sister, Mary. Philip and Mary hit it off. Mary was slim, attractive and well-born. Her mother was a cousin of Henry Francis Dupont's (and his sister, Louise Dupont Crowninshield's) mother. Mary remembered staying at Wintherthur, the Dupont country house, before Henry Francis inherited it and began the many enlargements to house his legendary collection of Americana. Mary also stayed with her cousin Louise when she visited Boston. In an odd coincidence, Louise Dupont Crowninshield (Mrs. Francis B.) owned 164 Marlborough Street which was directly across Marlborough Street from the complex which included Gertrude's childhood house, 328 Dartmouth Street.

Mary had been born in New York City in 1906, and so was a year older than Philip. Like her brother, much of her childhood had been on the Wyoming ranch; after a few years in California, Mary was living in New York. By 1930 her parents were divorced. She first met Gertrude when the Bournes senior were in New York City. According to Mary, Gertrude "thought we were too young to get married—he was an only child. But we finally did." Mary remembered her impressions of her new mother-in-law: "She was a bit overwhelming. She was the boss of the household, obviously. Mr. Bourne I liked very much but…he did what she said."[86] Philip Bourne and Mary Elliot Nicholson were wedded on June 15, 1932 at the exclusive Colony Club on Park Avenue in New York City. Mary remembered, "The first summer after we were married they went to Ireland and we had their house in Boston. When they came back in the fall we went to Holden Green which was Harvard housing. Phil was in Harvard graduate school in city planning."[87]

Mary Bourne recalled Gertrude's painting habits, "I saw the studio on the third floor, but she painted a lot when she was away."[88] The summer of 1932 again found the Bournes off to Europe. This time they started in Ireland where they viewed the Dublin Horse Show on August 3 and went on to Cobb, Mizen Head, and Cork in the far southwest of Ireland. Then they crossed the Irish Sea to Liverpool, and visited Wales before ending in England (the itinerary then went from St. David's to Oxford.) They may have returned in time for the October 27 – November 13 showing of *New England Garden* at the American Water Color Society's annual exhibition in New York.

In the winter of 1932-33 the Bournes went to the White Mountains, as Gertrude's winter paintings of New Hampshire indicated that they had often before. They stayed at the Glen House on the slopes of Mount Washington. At the 67th annual exhibition of the American Water Color Society from November 2 – 9 Bourne showed *Mt. Washington*. Other paintings from this Mount Washington trip would provide material for her next major exhibition.

Modernism in the Salons of America and Reaction in Boston

From April 9 – May 6 Bourne participated for the only time in the 1934 Salons of America at the Forum Gallery, R. C. A. Building, Rockefeller Center. The Salons of America, which had begun in 1922, and continued through 1936, had never before or after had such a large exhibition. They attracted 1504 artists—including 373 women—showed 4,719 works, nearly ten times the largest number of works shown in a previous Salon. Bourne submitted four works: *Mt. Jefferson*; *Mt. Adams*; *Mt. Errigal*; and *Mt. Washington* (p 102). The company included artists that were fairly conservative, such as Charles Gruppe, Gertrude Nason, Ogden Pleissner, William Merritt Post, Ernest D. Roth, and W. Lester Stevens. The Salon also represented women painters with whom she can be considered compatible, such as Anna Richards Brewster (daughter of William Trost Richards), and Marion Huse. The latter was an American Scene painter from Springfield who showed seven works—mostly of Vermont subjects, including *New England Church*. The Salons further included American Scene and Social Realist painters who were considered to be "moderns" in 1934 such as Audrey Buller, Lloyd Parsons, Joseph Margulies, John McCready, Jerome Myers, and Waldo Pierce. But it also included "radicals" such as Milton Avery, George Ault, Byron Browne, Werner Drewes, J. W. Golinkin, Adolf Gottlieb, Yasuo Kuniyoshi, Kyra Markham, William and Marguerite Zorach and M. Rothkowitz (who would shortly change his name to Mark Rothko). Members of the latter group were reducing discernable subject in their paintings to a much lesser role, or, in many cases, abandoning it altogether. This was interesting company for a proper woman from Beacon Hill, one of the few Bostonians represented; her work was relatively modern in Boston, but fairly conservative in this gathering. Some of the very few Boston women artists who also exhibited were Gertrude Nason, who while remaining representational, incorporated Modernism in her work and Molly Luce, an American Scene painter from Belmont, Massachusetts, who had been a neighbor of the Bourne's at 24 Garden Street on Beacon Hill from 1925-1928. One of the few other Boston-born artists was the sculptor Donald De Lue who had moved to New York and placed *Franklin Roosevelt,* his first work shown under his own name in this exhibition.

Bourne entered her work in the Salons of America exhibition just before her 66th birthday. It is difficult to assess how modern or radical she thought her work was. In Boston, her work, since the early 1910s, would be best placed with the more modern paintings in most exhibitions. Socially, she and Frank had chosen to associate with a more artistic crowd than was normal for a lady of her upbringing. Outside of Boston, in the various watercolor societies, her work would have been somewhere from the middle to more modern. But Bourne also submitted her work to distinctly modern venues or venues with very modern artists as part of their exhibitors. These included not only Salons of America, but the Gallery on the Moors and North Shore Arts Association. There her work would have looked quite conservative compared to the more radical entries. Boston was not the only place where art exhibits and associations were feeling the strains of division in the art establishment, but official Boston took a distinctly conservative position. The established museums, clubs, and societies were still firmly in the hands of administrators and artists with a conservative bent.

The battles that had recently taken place in Boston over divides between Impressionism and Post-impressionism were perhaps best skewered satirically by an article that appeared in the *Waterbury [Connecticut] American* in 1928 with the title "Boston Growing More Virtuous." It was reprinted in the *Boston Transcript*:

> After several years of bickering the recalcitrant art committee of the Boston Art Club has been purged of its liberal majority and reorganized under the conservative leadership of Hermann Dudley Murphy. This change marks the end of prolonged exploitation within the club of what Mr. Murphy eloquently describes as "that crazy stuff," more kindly referred to in other quarters as modernist art. To what purpose one can only wonder, but presumably to appease some of those whose works have been barred from exhibitions during this unhappy period.
>
> And who cares? Well, perhaps the episode is of little importance as it first appears, but viewed in relation to other manifestations of decadence in our charming center of culture, it may have a passing significance. For does it not, in fact, fit into a whole picture of a Boston gone myopic and moral. Granted there is such a thing as too much of any form of art, that even a small number of decorative geometric figures are more than adequate for the average artistic craving, we still nurse a suspicion that the art club is fairly typical of the current Boston mind in most matters.
>
> One recalls, for instance, the arrest on Boston Common when the chivalrous Mencken championed the cause of the lady, Hatrack. And one reflects sadly on the late Boston board of literary censorship composed of a police official and a preacher, a long-nosed Cyrano and a virtuous-faced Christian combining to pay court to a self-righteous Roxane.[sic] Is there not in the art club's revolt against post-impressionism a similarly affected hypersensitiveness.
>
> Interesting too, is that fact that among the new members of Mr. Murphy's renovated art committee is no less a person than his Excellency, Governor Alvan T. Fuller, to whom Elmer Davis has referred as "a good specimen of contemporary Boston" who "got rich selling automobiles." Plainly, Mr. Fuller will have something to say hereafter as to what does and what does not go into exhibition, which suggests that self-expression in art will hereinafter receive scant attention at the hands of the Boston Art Club.
>
> But why weep? Boston is still the seat of the baked bean legend, and as for freedom in art, we must, alas, pin our faith to the banner of the Waterbury Art School.[89]

Although there were venues for advanced art in the Boston area, such as the Harvard Society for Contemporary Art which had been founded in 1928 by Lincoln Kirstein, John Walker, and Edward Warburg, and Beacon

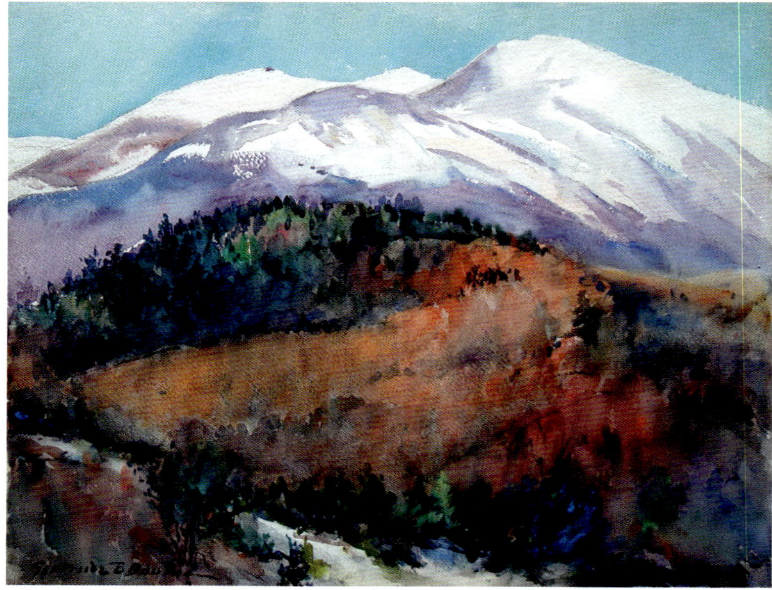

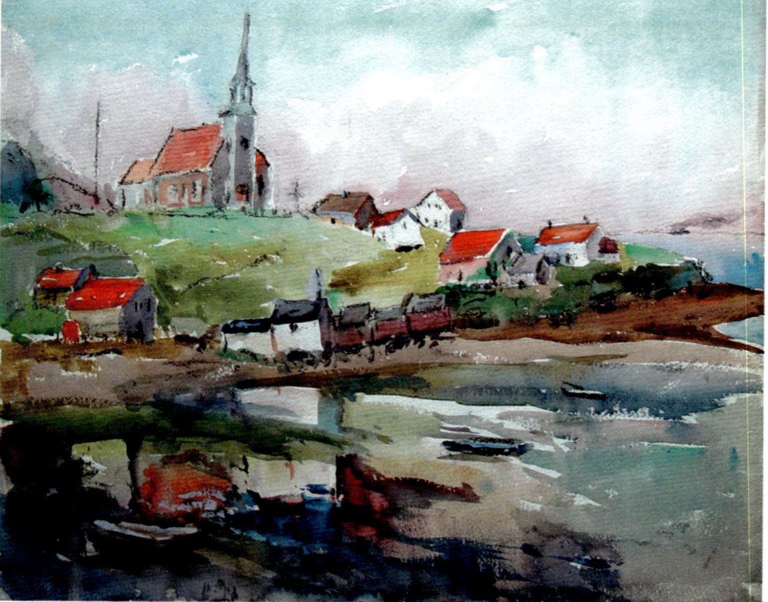

Hill's own Modernist "Barn Gallery," the Waterbury wit was fairly accurate in his assessment of the Boston establishment's resistance to the more radical examples of Modernism in the early 1930s.

How did Gertrude confront the extent of the newer means of expression, especially at venues in New York, while Boston collectors, critics, curators, and Bostonians in general had rejected them? Her first method seems to have been to send works to the Salons of America, the exhibition with the most radical art and artists to be compared with her own work, that were very well painted, but conservative even compared with her own recent work. She chose not to compete at all with her fellow-exhibitors who were at the most radical edge. She could have chosen to send Jamaica market scenes from 1931 which might have been compared with the late work of Maurice Prendergast, or her Gaspé works of 1930 with a light, John Marin-like, even tentative approach to the subject matter. Instead, she chose New Hampshire winter scenes of the White Mountains that could be understood by anyone as distinctly New England subjects handled by a distinctly New England painter. As her art advanced into more Modern expressions she did not have any compulsion to exhibit herself or her paintings as a statement of Modernism, but only as works of art demonstrating the personal advances that she had made in thought, choice of subjects, composition, and technique. Even if Boston was increasingly being seen by the contemporary art world as a backwater of stifling conservatism where anyone with get up and go got up and went, Bourne found her personal journey opened new prospects for her art. This was true even if her embrace of Modernism seemed modest as measured by the standards of contemporary New York. At the very end of Gertrude's life,

---

left above: ***Mt. Washington,*** 1933.
Watercolor and gouache on paper, 16 x 20 inches.
Exhibited: American Water Color Society 1933; Salons of America 1934.
Courtesy of Childs Gallery, Boston.

left below: ***Clorimonde, [Gaspé Peninsula, Province of Quebec]***, 1930.
Watercolor and charcoal on paper, 16 x 19 1/2 inches.
This may represent the town of Cloridorme, which Gertrude may have misremembered when she wrote the title verso.
Courtesy of the Bourne Art Trust.

artists in Boston like Andy Warhol would have to go to New York to achieve major success. Most of Boston had rejected Modernism—Bourne had not.

A Birth and a Death

Philip and Mary Bourne, were living in Washington, D.C. at 3802 T Street, when they announced the birth of their daughter, Sallie, on October 10, 1934. They had already had a child who had died at birth. Frank Bourne undertook a project as a gift for the infant Sallie—a project which he may have begun at about the time of the birth of the previous child.[90] He built Sallie a dollhouse, an architecturally correct Colonial Revival dollhouse, of two stories and six rooms that was fully furnished with furniture that Frank had made himself. Gertrude and Frank's artist friends became involved and made miniature paintings for the dollhouse. The overmantle panel in the living room, *Sea-side with Animals and People*, was by Charles Prendergast; other artists who provided paintings, in addition to Frank and Gertrude, included their neighbors Carroll M. and Sally Cross Bill.

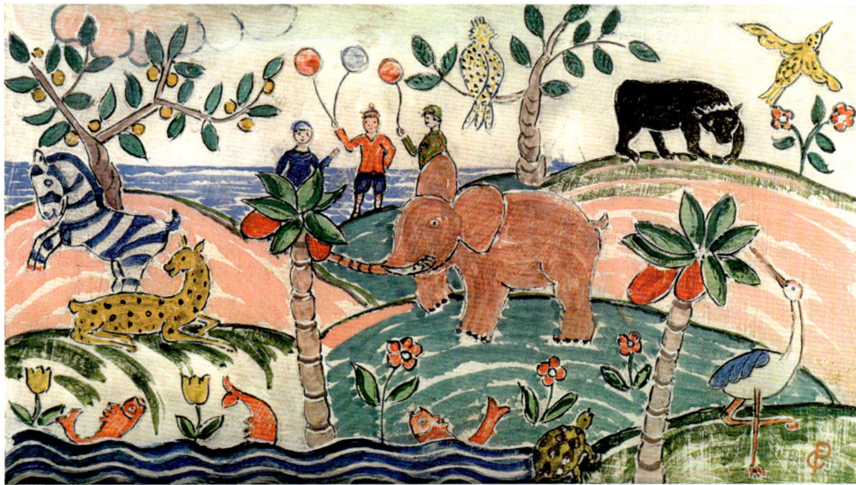

above: **Charles Prendergast (1868-1948), *Sea-side scene with Animals and People***, c. 1930.Oil on cardstock, 4 1/4 x 8 3/4 inches. Private Collection, courtesy of Childs Gallery, Boston.

right: ***Tea House at the Champion House, East Haddam, Connecticut***, c. 1934. Watercolor, gouache, and charcoal, 21 x 14 inches. Courtesy of the Bourne Art Trust.

In the winter of 1934-35 Gertrude Beals Bourne, age 66, sat for her portrait by Marie Danforth Page. She was shown with her cat Galusha (perhaps the cockatoo, Sir Harry, was too difficult as a sitter). Page, the wife of Dr. Calvin Gates Page, one year Gertrude's junior, nearby long-time resident of 128 Marlborough Street, was a popular, widely respected, and successful portrait painter. The two artists had been fellow-exhibitors at the Boston Art Club from the early 1890s and showed together in many other venues. Page was especially noted as a painter of children, but had recently done her self-portrait and exhibited it. Page thought enough of the portrait she had created of Gertrude to exhibit it in January of 1935 as *Gertrude and Galusha* at the 130th Annual Exhibition of the Pennsylvania Academy and again in Boston at the April annual Jordan Marsh Exhibition of Paintings. The painting shows a very comfortable-looking older woman nestled into and surrounded by fabric. Gertrude and the cat are both the picture of contentment.

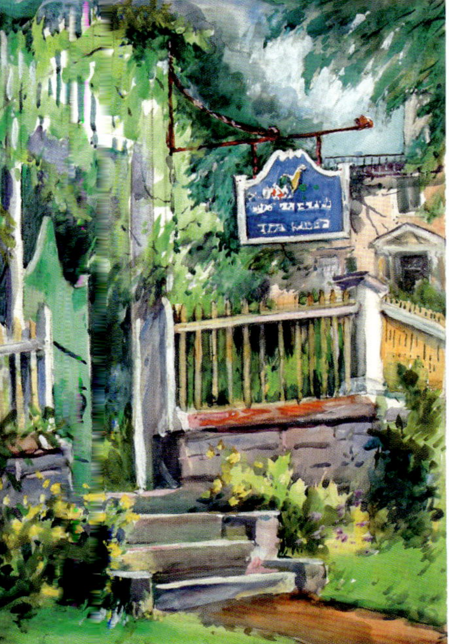

Gertrude showed *Garden – East Haddam* at the American Water Color Society 68th annual exhibition from October 26 – November 18, 1934. She had made a number of watercolors in East Haddam, Connecticut of the Ephtroditus Champion House (1794) and of the Tea House that had been established in Champion's former store—probably in the summer of 1934. Those watercolors continued Bourne's interest in Colonial and Colonial Revival subjects. In 1936 the American Water Color Society 69th annual exhibition was again moved to the beginning of the year (January 3 – 21) and Bourne showed *The Ancestor*. The latter was the final public exhibition by Bourne of a Colonial Revival subject.

On February 15th Frank A. Bourne died at age 65. His death was noted in the major American architectural publications. "Architecture" magazine reported in April of 1936:

> Among his better-known works are the Winchester Congregational Church, Bangor Congregational Church, St. Luke's in Chelsea, St. John's in Franklin, the Mission of the Epiphany in Dorchester, the Church of All Nations, Our Lady of the Snows in Dublin, N.H., the Ray Memorial School and Dean Academy Science Building in Franklin. Mr. Bourne also designed a score or more houses in Charles River Square.
>
> Mr. Bourne wrote many articles and several books, among them, "Study of the Orders of Architecture" and "Architectural Drawing" (with H. V. von Holst and F. C. Brown). He also compiled bibliographies on city planning and housing. Mr. Bourne was a member of the American Institute of Architects.

The extent of Gertrude's loss cannot be known. She was a strong and independent woman who had her own career and agenda. But to all evidence Frank Bourne had fitted into that world as her advocate and supporter, her traveling companion and comforter. Where she might have been a bit assertive or abrasive or a little too sure of herself, Frank was there to soften the edges. They had been married nearly thirty-two years and during that three decades she had achieved most of what she would do in her lifetime. They had chosen an eccentric house and made it into a center of social and cultural life on Beacon Hill. Together and separately they had advanced the rebirth of Beacon Hill as a prime neighborhood for proper Boston. They had traveled extensively together and separately as Gertrude had gone to Ireland, England, Wales, Sweden, Holland, France, Switzerland, Germany, Spain, the Azores, Italy, Dalmatia, Morocco, Cuba, Jamaica, and Mexico. They had also traveled widely in the United States and Canada. Frank had had a successful career as an architect and Gertrude had advanced her art in quality and in style and shown work across America and abroad. Together they had raised a son, had seen him graduate from M.I.T. and Harvard and follow in his father's profession as architect, and they had witnessed the birth of a grandchild.

Frank made Gertrude the sole beneficiary of his will, which showed that they held their assets separately and that she controlled the much larger sum.[91] There is no evidence that she ever considered re-marriage—Gertrude would spend the next twenty-six years in Sunflower Castle alone. She would continue to be a productive painter and a successful exhibitor. She would continue as an active member and promoter of the Beacon Hill Garden Club. She would continue to travel wherever and whenever she wanted, but she would limit her travels to the United States, the Territory of Hawaii, and Canada. And she would continue to cultivate her circle of friends in the arts and horticulture—no doubt with strong, warm, and positive memories of her partner, Frank.

NOTES, Chapter Three

1 John P. Marquand, *The Late George Apley* (Boston: Little, Brown and Company, 1937), 119.
2 Boston Vital Statistics, Marriage Record, Vol. 549, 116.
3 Frank A. Bourne, "In Appreciation of C. Désiré Despradelle."
4 Boston City Directory, 1897-99.
5 Douglass Shand-Tucci, *Built in Boston: City and Suburb 1800-1850* (Amherst, MA: University of Massachusetts Press, 1988), 63-65.
6 Mary Nicholson Bourne, interview with author, 10 November 1998 (hereinafter called Mary Bourne Interview).
7 Marquand, 121-22.
8 "Alterations on Acorn Street, Boston, Mass.," *The American Architect and Building News,* Vol.XC, No. 1614, 1 December 1906, 175.
9 "Harcourt Studio Fire," *American Architect and Building News,* Vol. LXXXVI, No. 1508, 19 November 1904, 57.
10 This may be Philip Hall Sharples of Cambridge whose sister, Sarah Hall Sharples is probably the same as the Sarah Hall Sharples who married Frederick Law Olmsted, Jr. in 1911.
11 *The Boston Globe,* 16 June, 1904.
12 American National Biography, Vol. 16 (New York and Oxford: Oxford University Press, 1999), 700-01.
13 National Cyclopaedia of Biography, Vol. A, 49-50. Perry had graduated from the University of Pennsylvania in 1891, but chose, by taking an additional one-year special course at Harvard to receive the same A.B. from the latter institution in 1892. He then entered the Episcopal Theological School in Cambridge, Massachusetts where he was ordained in 1895. Presumably he was in the same Harvard circle in those years.
14 National Cyclopaedia of Biography, Vol. 29, 243-244.

[15] "An Exhibition and Competition of Colonial Pictures under the auspices of the Colonial Dames of Massachusetts" [December 6-17], Boston, MA: Colonial Dames of Massachusetts, 1898. AAA MB506 7407-7411.
[16] "A Second Exhibition and Competition of Colonial Pictures under the Auspices of the Colonial Dames of Massachusetts" [December 2-16], Boston, MA: Colonial Dames of Massachusetts, 1899. AAA MB506 7412-7416.
[17] There seems to have been a female child born or still-born to Frank and Gertrude before Philip's birth. This child was never mentioned to Philip during his childhood. (Mary Bourne Interview.)
[18] "Miss Walley Dead at 96," *Boston Herald*, 25 June 1942, 19:3. "Miss Abigail Walley," *New York Times*, 25 June 1942, 23:5. (She died June 23, 1942.)
[19] Sallie Bourne Harrison, interview with the author, 18 March 1999 (hereinafter called Sallie Harrison Interview).
[20] Ibid.
[21] Gail Weesner. *Beacon Hill in the 1920s and 1930s: Rebirth of a Neighborhood* (unpublished mss., c.2001).
[22] Walter Firey, *Land Use in Central Boston* (Westport, CT: Glenwood Press, 1947),119-120.
[23] "Boat Shop is Now a Home,"*Boston Globe,*"Magazine Supplement, Part II, 12." 31 October 1909.
[24] Peter Hastings Falk, *The Annual Exhibition Records of the Art Institute of Chicago* (Madison, CT: Sound View Press, 1990),140.
[25] "Exhibitions Suggested" in *The Better City: Bulletin of the Metropolitan Improvement League*, Boston, 1909. "A 'Picturesque Boston' Exhibition", in *The Better City: Bulletin #2 of the Metropolitan Improvement League*, Boston, 1911. Frederick Law Olmsted, Jr., now Chairman of the Boston parks Commission, was one of the driving forces of the League. The League's plan for an exhibition seems to have been thwarted by difficulty in finding space at the preferred location at the old Museum of Fine Arts in Copley Square.
[26] "Paintings of Henry B. Snell," clipping dated 30 December 1922, in Fine Arts Reference, Boston Public Library.
[27] F. W. Coburn, "Watercolors at Milton," *The Sunday Herald, Boston,* 13 September 1914, Music and Drama section, D3.
[28] Letter from Abbie B. P. Walley to the Milton Public Library, April 15 [1914], in the historical records collection of the Milton Public Library.
[29] Suffolk County Massachusetts Probate (administrative) #166, 142. When Joshua's estate was probated the liquid assets of stocks, bonds and cash, amounting to $70,000 (approximately $1,303,400 in 2004 dollars) all went to Edith.
[30] Guest Register of Philbrook Farm (1900-October 1919), Philbrook Farm, Shelburne, New Hampshire.
[31] "At the Copley Gallery—Watercolors by Mrs. Bourne," *Boston Evening Transcript*, 22 April 1915, 15.
[32] "New Exhibitions Open in Art Galleries of Boston," *The Christian Science Monitor*, 21 April 1915, 4.
[33] "Mrs. Bourne's Water Colors," *The Sunday Herald*, Boston, 28 April 1915, Arts Section, 3.
[34] "Woodbury Exhibit Shows Much Life," *Boston Journal*, 21 April 1915, 6.
[35] Guest Register of Philbrook Farm.
[36] *Who's Who in Art,1917* lists her as a 1916 member of NYWCC.(MCL 223)
[37] In 1892 as Bourne first began exhibiting at the Boston Art Club, Dow's studio was located at 135 Huntington Avenue; Dow moved to the Grundmann Studios facing Trinity Church and the old Museum of Fine Arts in 1894.
[38] "Italians in Boston Get Warm Greeting," *New York Times*, 26 June 1917, 11.
[39] Boston exhibitors also included Jean Nutting Oliver, Mary Bradish Titcomb, Marion Power and Hannah Matthews Bryant. Other painters included Theresa Bernstein, Cecilia Beaux, Olive Parker Black, Lydia Field Emmett, Agnes Pelton, Ellen Emmett Rand, Margaret Sargent, and Jane Peterson. AAARoll N443 frames 1072-1101.
[40] "The Women Artists," *Boston Evening Transcript*, 1[illegible] April 1919, 15.
[41] "Makes A Triumphal Entry," *Boston Evening Transcript*, 24 February 1919, 6.
[42] "Work by Boston Contributor", undated and unidentified Washington newspaper clipping referring to the October-November 1919 Washington Water Color Club exhibition.
[43] Sidney Woodward, "Women Painters and Sculptors' Work Shown," *Boston Post*, 4 February 1920. (MH20)
[44] Gertrude Beals Bourne, "Letter to Sidney Woodward" Feb. 10, 1920.
[45] "Water Colors By Gertrude B. Bourne," *American Magazine of Art*, Vol. 14, May 1923, 260-61. Despite his premature burial in the *American Magazine of Art*, Henry W. Rice remained alive and well until 1934.
[46] The Eight were a group of New York painters of the early 20th century that included: Robert Henri (1865-1929), George Luks (1867-1933), William Glackens (1870-1938), John Sloan (1871-1951), Everett Shinn (1876-1953), Maurice Prendergast (1859-1924), Ernest Lawson (1873-1939), and Arthur Bowen Davies (1862-1928)
[47] Weesner.
[48] Weesner. [Text of the Manifesto] First: Restricting to residence use and against business [the entire district] excepting only Charles Street, keeping Beacon Street residential along both the Common and Public Garden.
Second: Restricting Charles Street to local business uses, confined to the first floor of buildings, if possible, so a to prevent in the future of a wall of buildings, cutting Beacon Hill off from the residential district between Charles Street and the Basin.
Third: Limiting the maximum height of buildings west of the State House to 65 feet and five stories, so as to protect light and air of the existing dwellings, and especially to prevent buildings from being erected along Charles Street and Beacon Street which would cut off the sun and breezes from the rest of the territory.
Fourth: Keeping any additional businesses from being introduced…, there being already sufficient neighborhood stores in this section.
Fifth: Regulating the construction of future apartment houses on Beacon Hill, so that they cannot cover so much of the lot as to deprive existing dwellings of adequate light and air.
[Signed] March G. Bennett, Guy W. Currier, Gerog[illegible] R. Nutter, Edward R. Warren, Frank A. Bourne, Chairman.
[49] Ibid.
[50] Ibid.
[51] Frank A. Bourne, in a now lost notebook, transcribed by Margaret Hanni, a copy of which is in the possession of the author.
[52] The National Gallery of Art, then in existence, became the National Collection of Fine Arts upon the founding of the "Mellon" Gallery in the 1930s and has now become the National Museum of American Art.
[53] "Mrs. Edith W. Beals Dead," *Boston Transcript*, 9 August 1927.
[54] Suffolk County Massachusetts Probate (administrative) #230, 282.The liquid assets of her estate were valued at $109,685 (approximately $1,[illegible]85,000 in 2004 dollars).
[55] "Goodspeed Exhibitions," *Boston Evening Transcript*, 14 March 1928, III, 6.
[56] "Lithographs and Etchings by Frank A. Bourne on Exhibition and Sale March 12—March 24," Goodspeed's Book Shop, (Boston: 1928).
[57] Frank A. Bourne, "Appreciation: Water Colors by Aiden L. Ripley Receive Enthusiastic Praise," *Boston Evening Transcript*, 7 February 1927, Section I, 10.
[58] Holmes, Sr. 272-73.
[59] Katherine Crosby, "High, Low and Hidden Gardens as They Bloom on Beacon Hill," *Boston Evening Transcript*, 4 August 1928, Magazine Section, 2.
[60] *Beacon Hill Garden Club-Minutes 1928-42* (Hereinafter referred to as *Garden Club Minutes*. Manuscript copy in possession of the Beacon Hill Garden Club), 25.
[61] Ibid., 22.

[62] Katherine Crosby, "Garlands From the Gardens of Beacon Hill," *Boston Evening Transcript*, 18 May 1929, Magazine Section, 1, 3.
[63] *Garden Club Minutes*, 49.
[64] Ibid., 44-45. Fletcher Steele was the most important figure in American landscape architecture for bringing about the transition from Beaux Arts design to modernism. At the time of the talk, Steele, who lived at 48 Beacon Street on Beacon Hill, had already established himself as one of the most prominent landscape architects in America. In 1926 Fletcher Steele met Mabel Choate who became his more important client. Aged 56, to his 41, she was about to inherit the family fortune and Naumkeag. Stanford White (McKim's partner) had been her mother's architect and Mrs. Choate knew how to work with designers. The Afternoon Garden (c1930) was her first project with Steele. In 1934 they extended the garden, with bold flowing curves, into the South Lawn. A Chinese garden was made (1937-9) and stimulated their interest in colour. In 1938 they worked on what became Steele's most famous project, the Blue Steps at Naumkeag. The Oxford Companion to Gardens describes this beautiful design as follows: 'In the Blue Steps (of concrete painted light blue) rising in sweeps over small cascades through a birch wood, which he created, selecting trees of various sizes, he has successfully re-interpreted Renaissance forms in terms of the modern concern for values of space, form, texture and colour'. Bourne, who became friends with Mrs. Choate, would use the dramatic vistas and enclosures of Naumkeag as the subject for many of her watercolors.
[65] Ibid., 95.
[66] Ibid., 96.
[67] Ibid., 59.
[68] Letter from Frank A. Bourne to Dana Somes, 25 March 1932 as quoted in Weesner.
[69] *Garden Club Minutes*, 271.
[70] Ibid., 114.
[71] Ibid., 149-150.
[72] Ibid., 36.
[73] Ibid., 92.
[74] Ibid., 95.
[75] Ibid., 169.
[76] Ibid., 182.
[77] Ibid., entry for April 11, 1939.
[78] Ibid., 201.
[79] Ibid., entry for February 4, 1931.
[80] Ibid., entry for April 25, 1935.
[81] Ibid., 213.
[82] Ibid., 115-130.
[83] Ibid., 229.
[84] Katherine Crosby, "Woman the Ceaseless Apartment Seeker, Drives Art First from Beacon Hill, the from the South End to Fine Privacy Near the Copps Hill Graveyard," *Boston Evening Transcript*, 5 October 1927, Section III, 2.
[85] *Art Digest*, 15 November 1930, 8.
[86] Mary Bourne Interview.
[87] Ibid.
[88] Ibid.
[89] "Boston Growing More Virtuous,"*Boston Evening Transcript* (reprinted from the *Waterbury American*), 15 September 1928, Book Section, 8.
[90] Mary Bourne Interview.
[91] Suffolk County Massachusetts Probate #273, 416 (Frank A. Bourne). Gertrude was the sole beneficiary of his will—his liquid assets amounted to $13,817.40 (approximately $186,300 in 2004 dollars).

Fishelson's [Charles Street, Boston], c. 1934-38.
Watercolor and gouache on paper, 19 x 23 3/4 inches.
Courtesy of the family of Phillip E. Bourne.

About 1918 Fishelson's florist shop moved from Boylston Street to 25 Charles Street—about two blocks from Gertrude Bourne. As a lover of flowers and gardens she must have found them a great resource, for the Fishelsons were early direct importers of flowers and exotic plants. By 1934, proprietors Max and Rebecca Fishelson (109 Mount Vernon Street) and Nathan and Sarah Fishelson (45 River Street) were also neighbors of the Bournes. (The shop later moved to 34 Charles Street.)

This painting was exhibited at Doll and Richards in 1939.

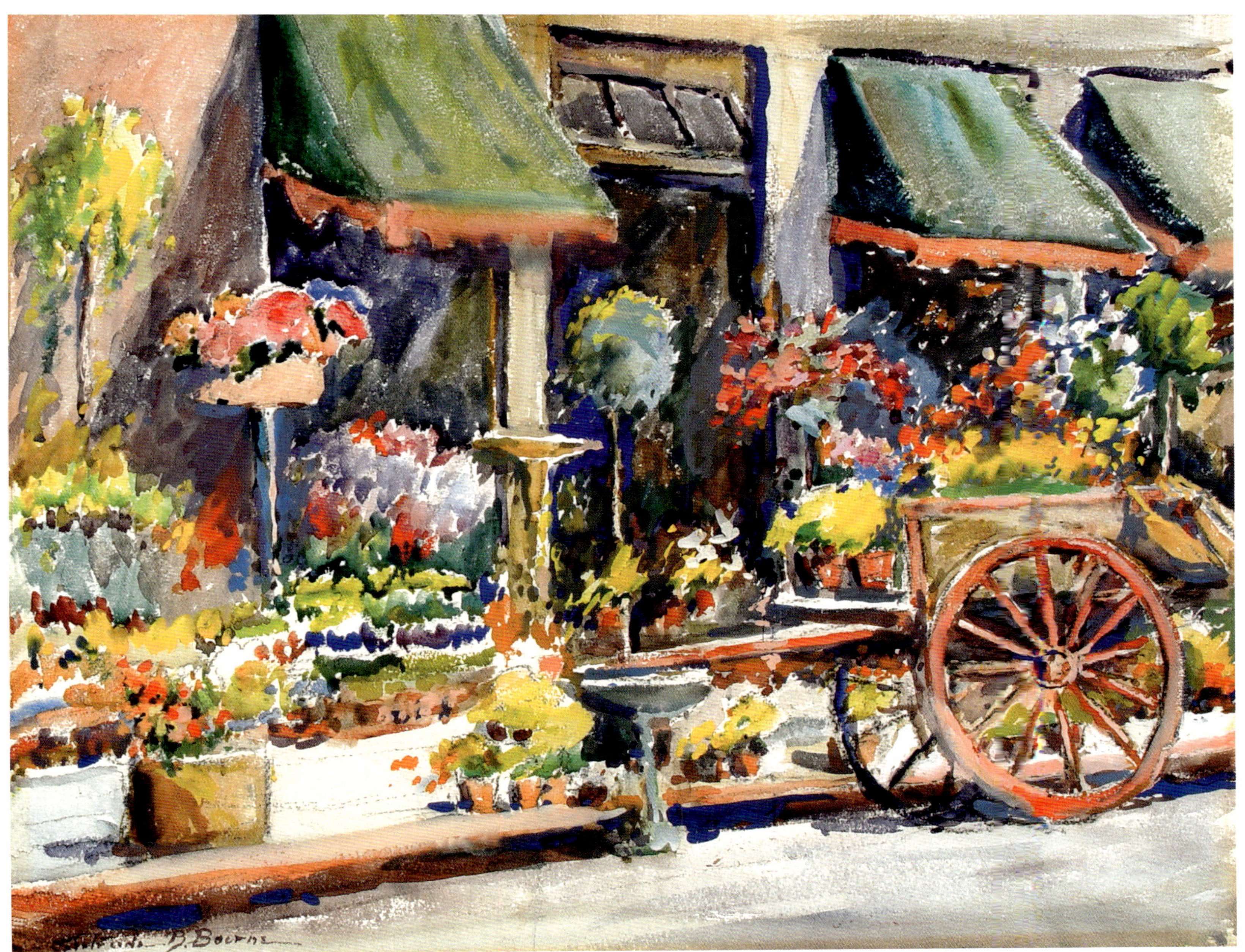

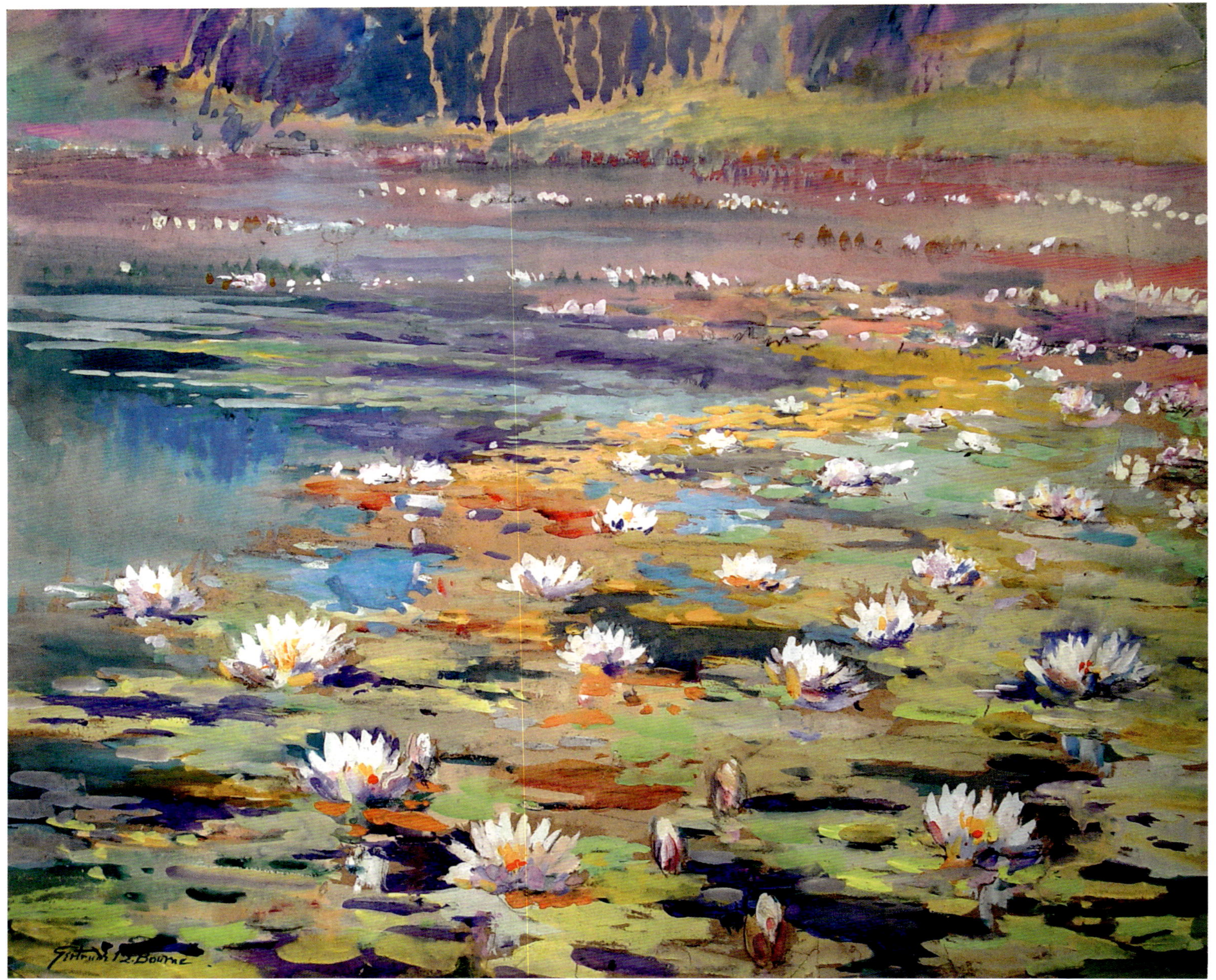

CHAPTER FOUR

The Widow of Sunflower Castle

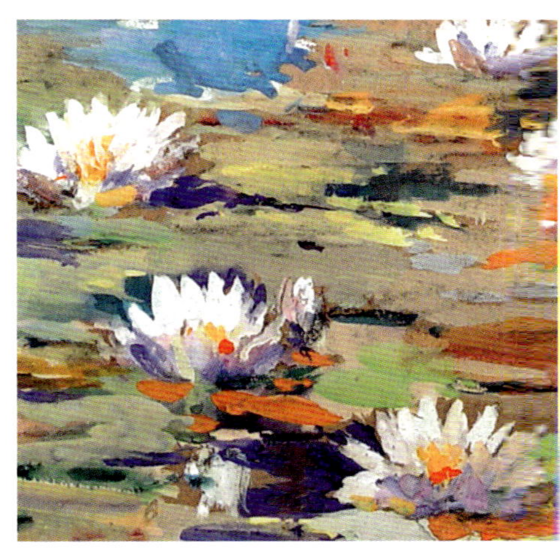

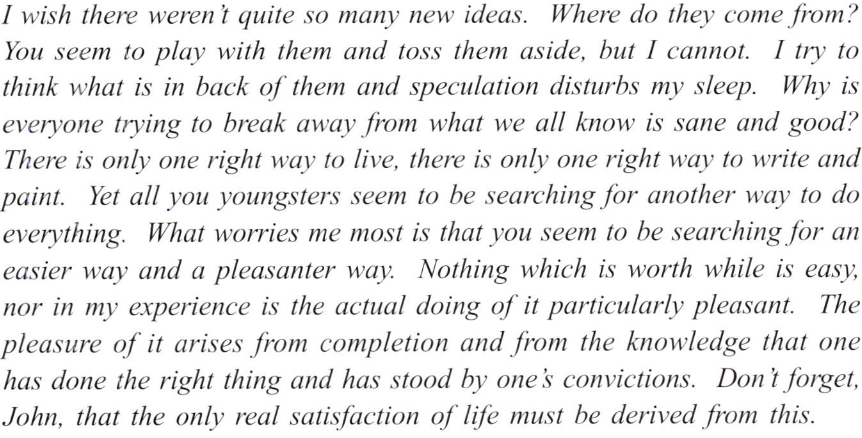

I wish there weren't quite so many new ideas. Where do they come from? You seem to play with them and toss them aside, but I cannot. I try to think what is in back of them and speculation disturbs my sleep. Why is everyone trying to break away from what we all know is sane and good? There is only one right way to live, there is only one right way to write and paint. Yet all you youngsters seem to be searching for another way to do everything. What worries me most is that you seem to be searching for an easier way and a pleasanter way. Nothing which is worth while is easy, nor in my experience is the actual doing of it particularly pleasant. The pleasure of it arises from completion and from the knowledge that one has done the right thing and has stood by one's convictions. Don't forget, John, that the only real satisfaction of life must be derived from this.

I do not want to be an "old fogey." I try to keep my mind open to everything. This afternoon your sister invited Hopkins and me to an exhibition on Newbury Street in which she seems to be deeply interested. Of course, I have heard of Cubism before the War and have laughed as heartily as anyone at the Nude Descending the Staircase, but now to see supposedly intelligent people gaping at a wall full of paint slobbered willy-nilly over canvas makes me feel that the world is going mad. Eleanor, who appears to have read about it endeavored to explain something of the theory, but the Monets at the Art Museum are radical enough for me.[1]

George Apley, writing to his son, John
— John P. Marquand, *The Late George Apley*

Waterlilies, c. 1920.
Watercolor and gouache on paper, 24 x 29 inches.
Exhibited: Baltimore Water Color Club, 1921; Washington Water Color Club, 1923.
Private Collection.

Had Monet been Gertrude's ideal in the 1890s when she first became an artist? Did she first see Monet's work at a three-man exhibition in 1891, *The Impressionists of Paris: Claude Monet, Camille Pissarro and Alfred Sisley* at the J. Eastman Chase Gallery in Boston? Or did she notice Monet when he first had a one-man exhibition of 23 works in Boston at the St. Botolph Club in 1892 , or during a later exhibition of 27 of his works at the same location in 1895? In 1911, the Museum of Fine Arts, Boston had been the first American museum to devote an exhibition to Monet—with forty-five works. The Brooks Reed Gallery in Boston showed seven of Monet's Venice paintings in 1912 and continued exhibiting his works regularly until 1923. Monet's popularity in Boston, even in comparison to his French colleagues, is indicated by an 1892 article in the *Boston Evening Transcript*:

> As long as Monet spells money, [dealers] may be depended upon to keep up the furor to the best of their ability...Boston is still a good buyer of Monet's, and every dealer in town makes it a point to have 'a fine example' under a curtain in the back room. Prices range from $1,000-$1,500, with an upward tendency, proving that the demand is lively. The other Impressionists are not so much in favor.[2]

Monet's death in 1926 did not end his influence on American painters, but beginning in the 1880s when his work first began to be shown in Boston, through at least 1910, Monet was the single most important influence on Boston's American Impressionist landscape painters.

The evidence of her own paintings from the 1890s would suggest that even if Gertrude admired Monet, she was not yet attempting to emulate his work of that period. However, as his work progressed and his painting in the twentieth century became more loose and abstracted, Gertrude's work progressed in a similar vein. Her London paintings of the Thames River of 1923 show a reference to Monet's Thames paintings that were first shown in America in 1902, and, may have been seen in private Boston collections or during Bourne's travel in European museums and galleries. By the late 1930s a case could be made that Gertrude was especially influenced by Monet's waterlilies, however Bourne also shared with Monet an interest in conventional flower gardens with paths, architecture, and arbors.

The famous painting *Nude Descending a Staircase* by Marcel Duchamp-Villon which George Apley mocked, was part of the Armory Show of 1913 that awakened America to many of the newer and more radical directions in art. While controversy focused on a few of the most extreme paintings and sculptures shown in New York, many have now forgotten that this pivotal show, after closing in March 1913 at the 23rd Street Armory in New York went on to be shown later in the year at the Art Institute of Chicago and Copley Hall in Boston. Also infrequently remembered is the wide range of contemporary American and European art that was exhibited, including five paintings by Monet, and five paintings by Dodge Macknight.

To be sure, Monet was primarily a painter in oil and Bourne a dedicated watercolorist, but his influence as a landscape painter in America in general and Boston in particular in the first forty years of her painting career was perhaps the greatest for an artist primarily concerned with landscape, as she was. Were "the Monets at the Art Museum radical enough for" her? The answer is yes in two different ways. If one means that Bourne did not feel a need to experiment with Cubism or Dada or complete abstraction in her paintings in any significant way—the answer is "yes." If, however, one means that Monet was being seen late in Bourne's career as the most radical of his peers, the answer may be "yes" again. When one looks at the Monets which were entering Boston collections after 1900—the Monets owned by the Alexander Cochranes at 257 Commonwealth Avenue: *Water Lilies*, and *The Grand Canal*, [3] or those owned by Governor Alvan T. Fuller at 150 Beacon Street: *The Waterlily Pond*—then one can discern a "Modernism" that radically changes the way paint is applied. In many ways Bourne increasingly adopted that freedom of color and brushwork in watercolor which Monet had pioneered for many artists in oil. By the end of Bourne's career, New York critics were rehabilitating Monet as a radical and making him part of the ancestry of the Abstract Expressionists.

Bourne made a similar passage to the one made by Monet, albeit about two decades later. Like Monet, Bourne always painted her surroundings and was a direct observer of nature. While corrections may have been made in the studio, there is no feeling in her work of assembled "easel" paintings. Her media themselves, watercolor and gouache, were conducive to spontaneity, and the watchword of much criticism in watercolor was to keep "freshness" of paint and color. She was interested in many of the same subjects as Monet, and while she did not often paint great cathedral façades—one of Monet's signature subjects—Bourne was interested in architecture for its historical associations, its picturesqueness, and its formal utility for composition and color. She was not interested in social realism or "The American Scene," but in the pure picturesque or compositional quality of her figures (*Marines February 24, 1919* (p. 4) and *Kingston Market Jamaica* (p. 98)) and the referential

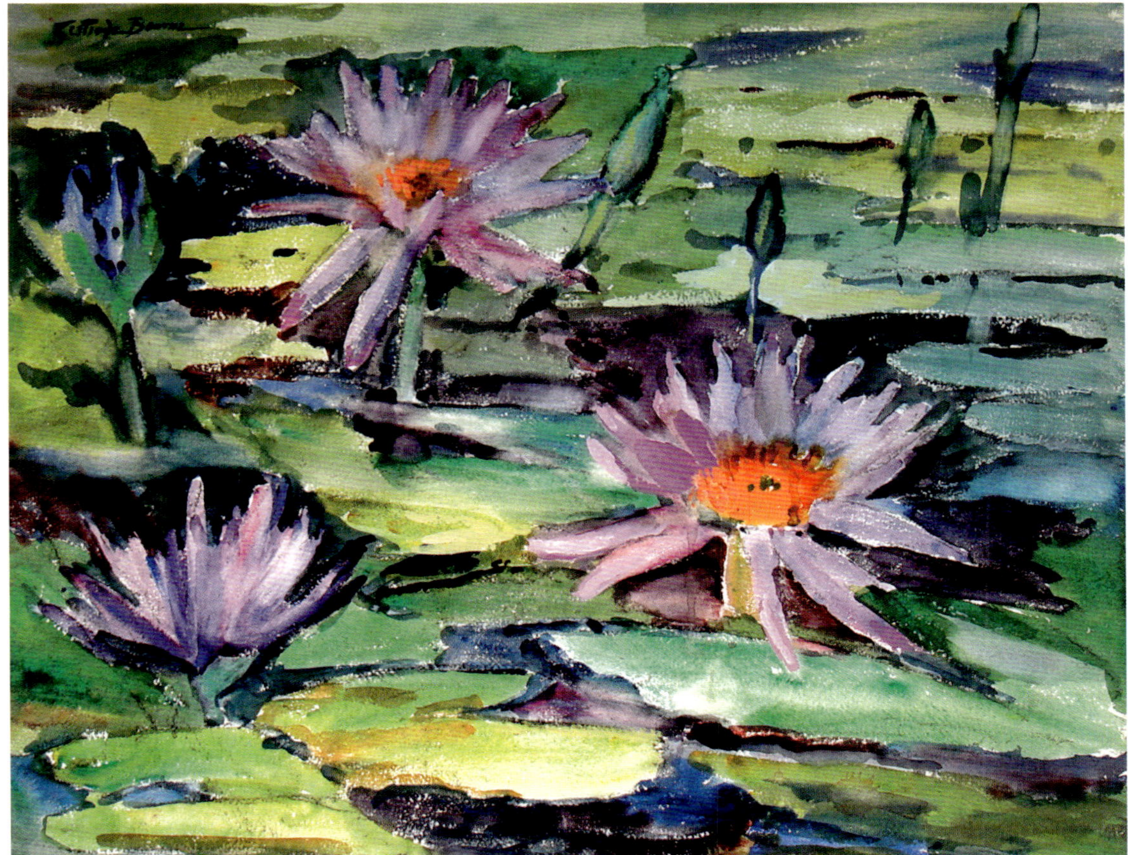

Pond Lilies (Purple Nymphaea), 1939.
Watercolor, gouache, and charcoal on paper, 20 x 24 inches.
Bourne could hardly have missed the association of this painting of waterlilies with Monet's nymphaea series (including the use of the botanical name). Exhibited: Doll and Richards, Boston 1940.
Private Collection.

quality of some of her subjects (*Colonial Houses, House of Seven Gables, Federal Churches, Ann Hathaway's Cottage*). In referential architecture she only occasionally ventured away from her native New England. She was, however, interested in the picturesque exotic. If occasionally her style and subject seemed to relate to The Ash Can School, it was in the darker, grittier whole of the environment and not focused on the individual souls in the street. Gardens and flowers may have been her greatest love and she lavished her attention on both paintings and originals. As a good New Englander, Gertrude Bourne made harbors, docks, and boats part of her subject matter. It did not matter to her whether the boats were in the harbors of Rockport or Ragusa, but it did matter if they made a good composition.

If part of the message to be apprehended in Monet's "Grandes Décorations" was simplified form and the glorification of color and pattern, then Bourne would move to a similar message in "Petites Décorations," her flower paintings of the late 1930s. Perhaps, however, American Modernism, rather than French Modernism, was her primary guide in these latter works as her boldness in color, composition, and application of paint resembles her fellow-New Englander Marsden Hartley more than Monet. Bourne would have known Hartley's bold flower still life painting of the 1930s and 1940s, which related to her own journey into Modernism. In addition, she might have been thinking of the paintings of single blossoms by Georgia O'Keeffe which were carefully designed to be in the forefront of Modernism in the 1920s and 30s. In each case the American painters created bold decoration on a small scale.

When Gertrude Beals Bourne was widowed she was not yet 68 years old. Her son Philip had followed in his father's footsteps: he had become an architect and was married with his own child. But Gertrude continued to be actively involved in the Beacon Hill Garden Club, and she seems to have increased her visits to friends. Miss Mabel Choate at Naumkeag in Stockbridge, Massachusetts and Miss Gertrude Shurcliff in Ipswich were among those who shared Gertrude's interests in gardening and flowers and whom Gertrude would often visit. Naumkeag was an estate developed in the nineteenth century by Miss Choate's father; the design included a house by Stanford White and landscaped gardens. Between 1926 and 1956 the gardens were transformed by Fletcher Steele (who had been an early lecturer at the Beacon Hill Garden Club) into a showplace for both the landscape architect and owner. Mrs. Shurcliffe, on a somewhat more modest scale maintained impressive gardens in Ipswich. Gertrude knew both ladies well and was welcomed to visit and paint the glories of the flowers and gardens. In the case of Mrs. Choate, Philip Bourne became a friend as well and was a welcome visitor in his own right.

At the time of Frank's death friends and family were worried that Gertrude might become a recluse. Their worries were unfounded. Despite the loss of her husband and travel partner, Frank, Gertrude hardly slackened either her exhibition schedule or her travel. Her travel now, however was confined to North America and a single trip to Hawaii. Arrangements had already been made before Frank's death for her showing of *The Ancestor* at the Washington Water Color Club exhibition at the Corcoran Gallery from February 9 to March 1, 1936, and *Susquehanna River* was shown in April at the New York Water Color Club. The following year Bourne showed *Dining Room in the Arbo* at the American Water Color Society from January 7-21 in New York, and *Dupont Circle [Washington, D.C.]* at the New York Water Color Club in April. In the summer or fall of 1937 Gertrude Bourne made a trip to the Canadian Rockies, Pacific Northwest (including Washington State and parts of the Cascade Range), and southern California. In December 1937 she presented *Mount Shasta, California* at the New York Water Color Club as the first of the western works. At the American Water Color Society exhibition January 27 to February 12, 1938, she exhibited *Glacier and Frozen Lake* from the same trip.

Unless she returned to these western sites in 1938, the 1937 trip formed the basis for her exhibition of twenty-seven watercolors at Doll and Richards from January 2-14, 1939. Like the Copley Gallery before it, Doll and Richards had a long and impressive history of representing many of the most prominent American painters of the nineteenth and twentieth centuries, and the gallery remained a force in Boston art in the 1930s. Gertrude's exhibition there was divided into four parts: California and the South West, Boston, Nantucket, and seven miscellaneous watercolors. In addition to the most recent work of her western trip from 1937, the other works, some of which had been previously exhibited, help to form a retrospective of at least five previous years of work. The writer for the *Boston Sunday Herald* was enthusiastic:

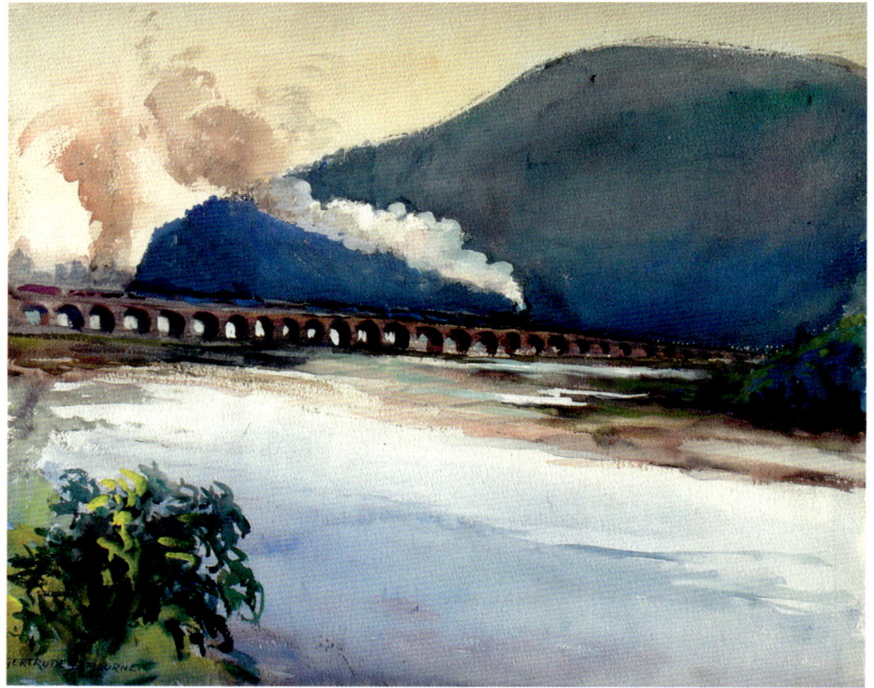

Susquehanna River, c. 1935-36.
Watercolor and gouache on paper, 20 x 24 inches. Exhibited: New York Water Color Club, 1936. Courtesy of the Bourne Art Trust.

> At Doll & Richards, Gertrude Beals Bourne, widow of a well-known Boston architect, proves in 27 enthusiastic and colorful papers that she has been hiding her light under a bushel on Beacon Hill. She is pupil of Henry Snell and H. W. Rice; she is a member of the New York and Washington Water Color societies and the American Water Color Society, but this is her first Boston exhibition. Views around the Hill where she makes her home, of

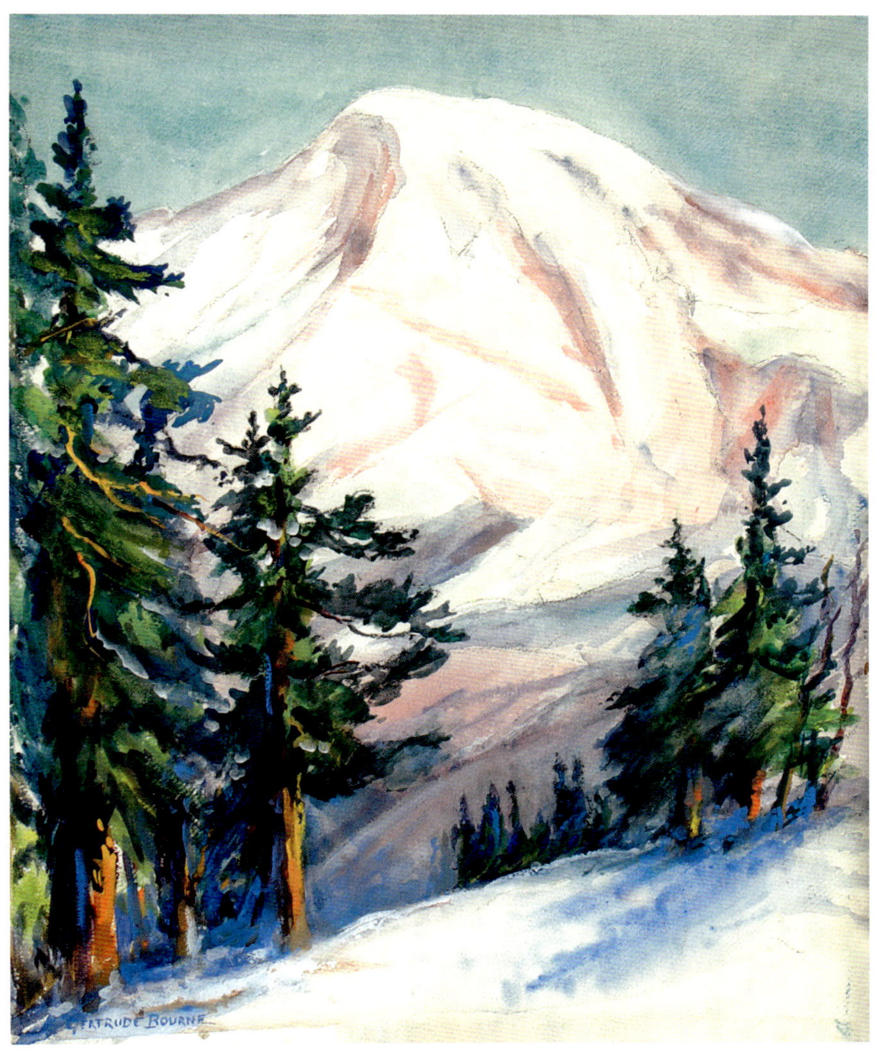

Mt. Rainier, c. 1937
Watercolor, gouache, and charcoal on paper, 23 3/4 x 19 inches.
Exhibited: Doll and Richards, Boston, 1939. Courtesy of the Bourne Art Trust.

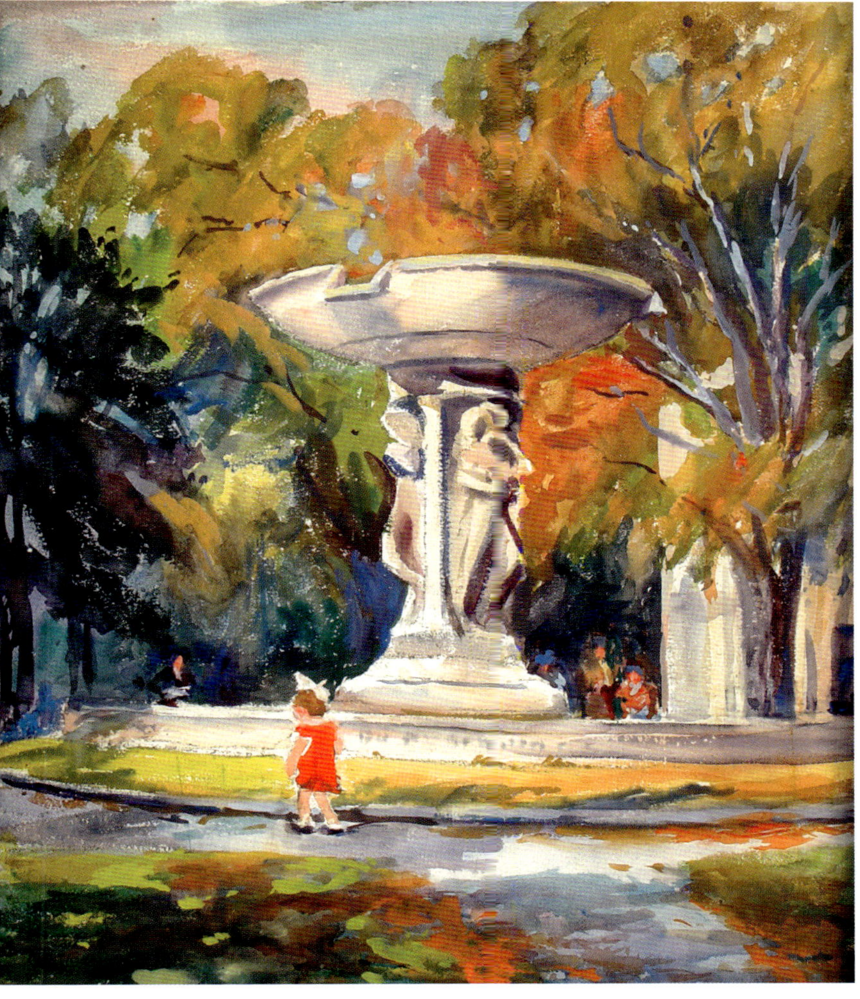

Dupont Circle [Washington. D.C.], c. 1936.
Watercolor, gouache, and charcoal on paper, 2[illegible] x 20 1/8 inches.
Exhibited: American Water Color Society 193[illegible]. Courtesy of Childs Gallery, Boston.

> Nantucket and California make up the exhibition. A sure awakener of spring fever is her *Public Garden Swanboat*. Somewhat reminiscent of Prendergast, it is therefore delightfully animated in treatment.[4]

The reviewers for the *Boston Evening Transcript* and the *Christian Science Monitor*, similarly approved of the work, but in their critical notes, they seem to have liked more and liked less opposite parts of the exhibition. The *Transcript* writer observed:

> Among the best are the California and the Nantucket views, the still lifes and flowers. The artist paints in the traditional Boston water color style and is very competent in her handling of washes.[5]

Dorothy Adlow in the *Christian Science Monitor* found fault with the "larger scenes" in California which the *Transcript* writer had especially liked, and she suggested that specificity and arrangement of details were Bourne's particular skills:

> Mrs. Bourne is ingenious in her choice of subjects, such for example as *Frog Pond in August* and *Public Garden Swanboat*. She seems happier in these, working more upon characteristic details than in larger scenes such as the flower fields of Bakersfield, Calif. The more formidable subject robs her of special skill in description.[6]

Although the *Herald's* writer was mistaken that this was Bourne's "first Boston exhibition," he would have been correct in observing that she had not had a solo exhibition in Boston since the Copley Gallery exhibition of 1915—a space of twenty-four years. He might also have noted that except for a 1932 watercolor exhibition at the Boston Art Club and a few other local showings, she had not shown in Boston group exhibitions for more than a decade, but far from "hiding her light under a bushel," Bourne had been an active exhibitor in venues across the United States as well as in London.

Bourne was very satisfied with the exhibition. She wrote to her son and daughter-in-law in Washington, D.C. on January 2: "My exhibition has kept me busy—Hung it on Saturday, and Mr. McKean [Director of Doll and Richards] was very complimentary about the exhibit. I myself am quite pleased and wish you could be here to see it. Miss Murdock took some little photos—which I will enclose for you to visualize a little of the way they are hung—27 in the gallery & 2 in the window. … I forgot to say the four women in New York were successful in seeing a number of exhibitions & met Mrs. [William] Glackens at the Whitney Museum. … Tomorrow I am dining at Fenway Court with the Morris Carters—Saturday night with the Grays—Thursday a trip with Aunt Alice up to Peterborough. So it goes—all very interesting."[7] The 70 year-old widow was conducting her social life at a furious pace, with visits to New York, New Hampshire and dinner at the Isabella Stewart Gardner Museum with the director and his wife. She socialized, at least briefly, with the recently widowed Mrs. William Glackens and maintained an intense interest in the art world.

The one-man exhibition was immediately followed by the combined New York Water Color Club and American Water Color Society Exhibition from February 10-26 where she again exhibited *Public Garden Swanboat*. By 1939 Gertrude was listed as a "Life Member" of the American Watercolor Society and may be counted among those who had "arrived" in that organization.

Much of what we know about Gertrude Beals Bourne's personality comes from accounts by her daughter-in-law, Philip's wife, Mary Nicholson Bourne, and Gertrude's eldest grandchild, Sallie Bourne Harrison, both of whom knew Gertrude later in her life. Neither was particularly fond of her, which colors their commentary. Gertrude and Mary Bourne were both strong personalities and both were in love with and possessive of Philip. Mary, who retained a perfect figure at 92, referred to Gertrude as "a very heavy woman." Mary Bourne, however, respected her mother-in-law and her talents. According to Mary, Gertrude "took her painting seriously. Very seriously! [and] I think she was a good mother."[8] As a girl, teenager, and young woman, Sallie conflicted with her grandmother on many issues. Gertrude was interested in classical music and thought that Sallie should play the piano: Sallie liked to play the piano but did not like being made to do so every time that she saw her grandmother. Gertrude thought Sallie should be able to converse with her in French—Sallie couldn't. Gertrude defined herself as an artist and was passionate about art—Sallie wasn't. But there was one thing on which they could agree when Sallie was a girl: "Her garden! And that meant a lot to her. I used to love

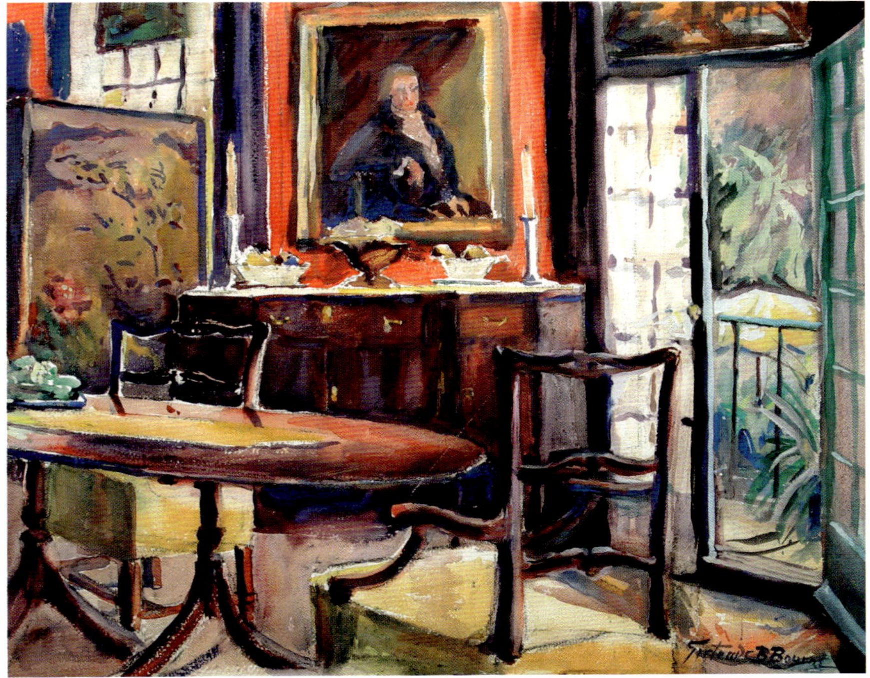

above: ***The Ancestor***, 1935-36.
Watercolor, gouache, and charcoal on paper, 19 x 23 1/2 inches.
This shows the very settled interior of "Sunflower Castle" and the entry to the garden staircase that was purchased at the 1929 Flower Show. Courtesy of the Bourne Art Trust.

right: ***Gertrude Beals Bourne** (left), **Sallie Bourne, Philip W. Bourne, Philip E. Bourne, and Mary N. Bourne on the Beach near Honolulu***, summer 1939. Courtesy of the Bourne Art Trust.

to go in her garden in Boston. It was very small, but really lovely. I think she was knowledgeable about flowers. She didn't have a gardener; she did it herself. The space was small with beds, a fountain…that's where she had her cockatoo. His name was Sir Harry…He goes back as far as I remember. He was known to like to bite fingers so we were never allowed near him."[9]

Despite her artistic achievements, Gertrude Bourne was no Bohemian. Her favorite brother, Sidney, who had become a very proper gentleman, married a woman of whom Gertrude did not approve. Nevertheless, when they divorced, Gertrude never spoke to Sidney again—at least in part because of the divorce. Even a personality as conservative as the fictional Bostonian, George Apley, when confronted with his son John marrying a divorced woman made accommodations:

> From all I have been able to gather, Mrs. McCullogh comes of a reasonably good New York family, but this is not the point. The point is that Mrs. McCullogh was in Reno, Nevada, six months ago, where she obtained a divorce from her husband, on the grounds of cruel and abusive treatment. Although I cannot and will not believe that John, in any way whatsoever, had anything to do with this divorce, at the same time the matter presents an aspect which makes me glad at last that John's activities are centered about New York instead of here. I had hoped that he might be back with us again but now this will be impossible, at least for several years.[10]

It appears, however, that Sidney's transgression was too much for Gertrude to accommodate and she refused to reconcile with him.

In early 1938 Philip and Mary Bourne, who had been living in Washington, D.C., moved to Honolulu, Hawaii. Philip was working as an architect and planner for the Roosevelt administration in the National Housing Administration for subsidized housing projects. In the summer of 1939 Gertrude arrived for a month's stay to visit the family and to paint. To her daughter-in-law's relief, the elder Mrs. Bourne stayed in a nearby hotel. Mary Bourne remembered that "she changed her painting. She took to painting [typical Hawaiian] flowers." She fell in love with Hawaii and native customs and

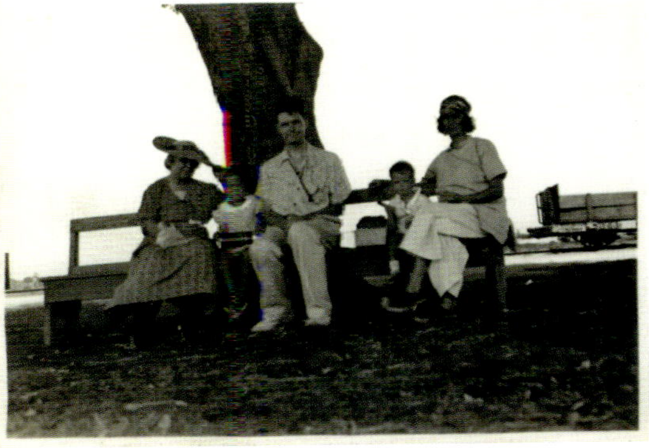

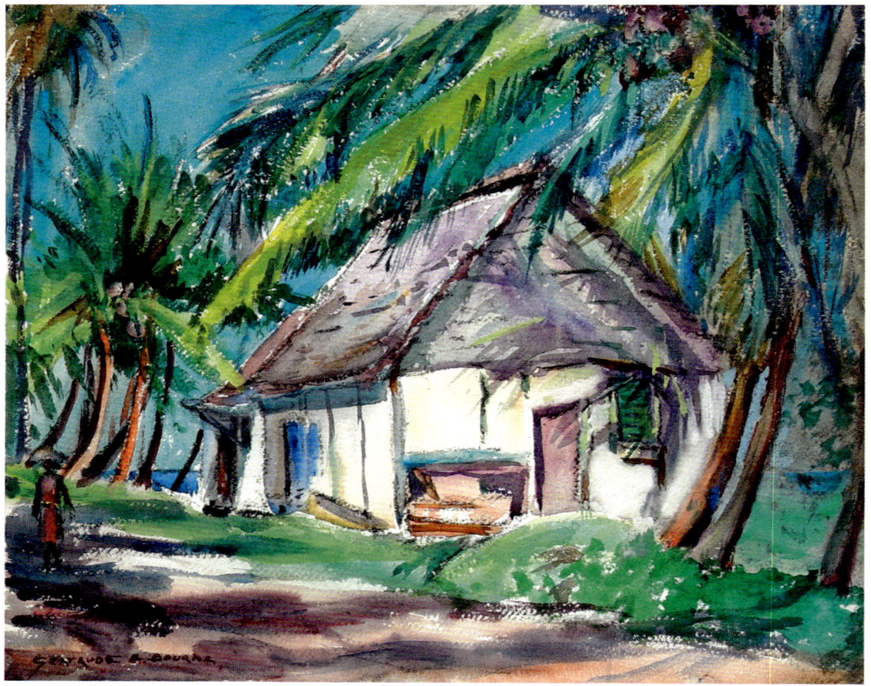

dances. Gertrude painted Robert Louis Stevenson's hut, which was built in native style and had been preserved. Mary Bourne noted that "she loved the hula and native flowers, [and that one day she nearly drowned]. She hopped off a rock and some man pulled her out and she gave him a gold watch…for saving her life. [The gift] stuck in my mind because it was unique. She also probably could not afford it."[11] Gertrude's grand-daughter, who was almost five at the time, remembered her in Hawaii, "She always had her paints with her. She had a little silver watercolor box with many compartments in it, which were always full. She was always sitting down to paint something. I remember several picnics in Hawaii where she'd sit there—she always had a hat on and dressed as though it were wintertime—and she'd paint. Of course, I was only four at the time." Sallie continued, "She always seemed to have masses of clothes on—layer upon layer with a hat on... In one photograph on a beach, she's all dressed up and everyone else has on shorts."[12]

The paintings of Hawaiian flowers were a departure from anything that Gertrude Beals Bourne had done previously with the subject. Unlike her carefully considered flower still-lifes of the 1890s or her flowers in natural garden settings in the intervening years, the new works of Hawaiian blossoms were fierce statements of single blossoms close up. There were precedents for her new direction. Gertrude might have known the William Sharp chromolithographs, made in Boston in 1854, of the giant Victoria Regia waterlilies that had been discovered in the Amazon. And she almost certainly knew the uncompromising still life floral paintings recently made by Marsden Hartley. That Gertrude was able in her early seventies to reform her painting into a level of boldness and uncompromising power previously unseen in her work was a testament to her ability to grow and adapt within her times and in response to Modernism.

Gertrude returned to Boston ahead of Philip's family, who were in Washington by August where Philip was completing his work in public housing and planning. The importance of a house as the hearth and lodestone of a family in Boston, especially at the time it welcomed a new member of the family, was noted by George Apley:

> I cannot understand why you have insisted on the newfangled idea of having my grandson—because I know he will be a boy, since something must work out sometime—brought into the world in the delivery room of a

---

left: ***Stevenson's Grass Hut***, 1939.
Watercolor, gouache, and charcoal on paper, 16 x 19 1/2 inches.
Exhibited: Doll and Richards, Boston, 1940. Bourne demonstrated her internalization of Sargent's watercolor technique. This watercolor suggests Sargent's *Corfu: Lights and Shadows*, Museum of Fine Arts, Boston. Courtesy of the Bourne Art Trust.

right: ***Heliconia (Lobster Claws)***, 1939.
Watercolor, gouache, and charcoal on paper, 20 x 25 inches.
Bourne demonstrates her most aggressive and sweeping Modernism in this work with simple subject and bold design.
On paper watermarked "AQUERELLE ANSON FRANCE." Exhibited: Doll and Richards, 1940. Courtesy of the Bourne Art Trust.

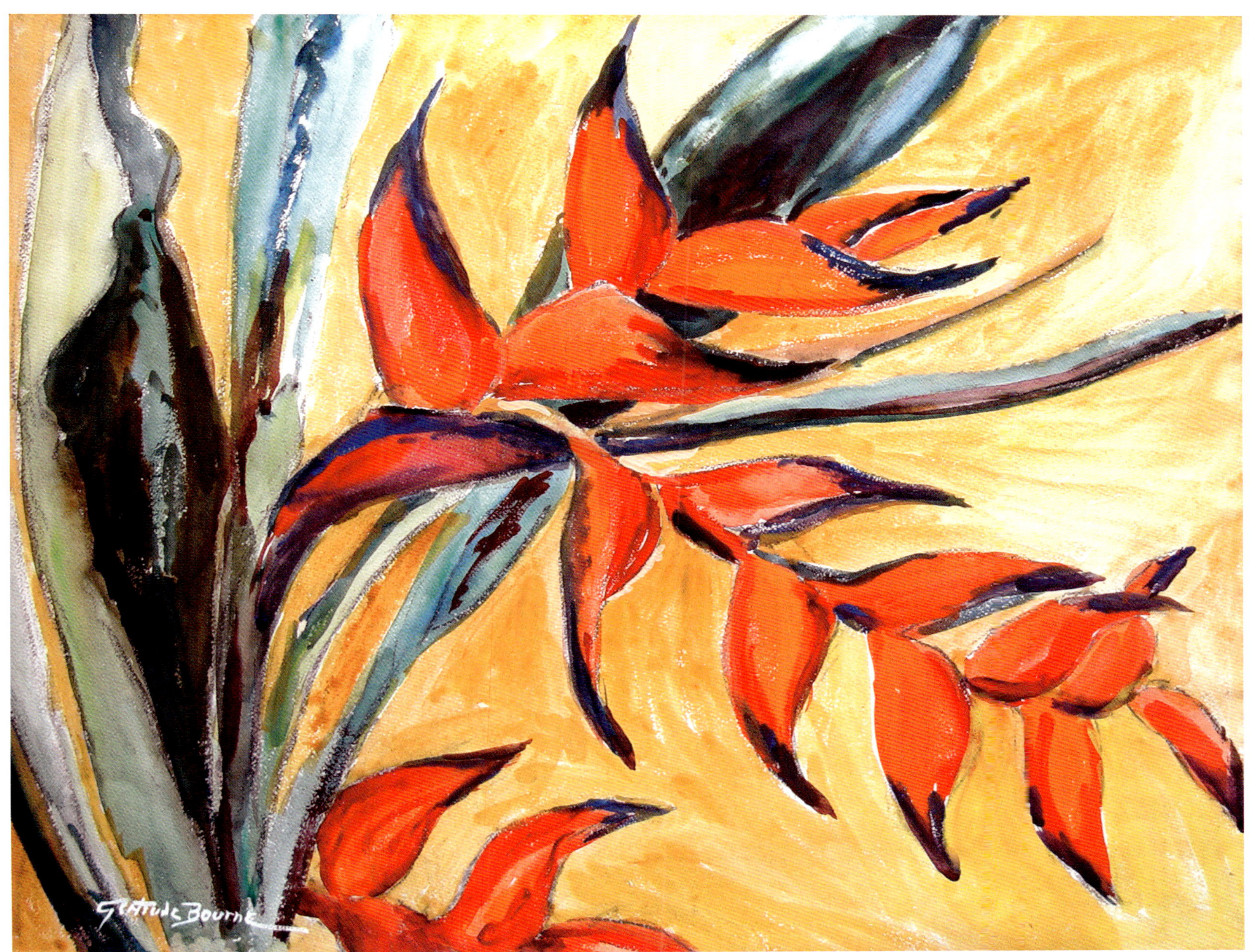
Gertrude Bourne

hospital. Your mother and I had both hoped that dear Louise might be induced to come to Hillcrest to be cared for by Doctor Hadley, who brought you into the world...Of course the christening will be held at Hillcrest and my own dear mother's lifelong friend Mr. Pettingill will perform the ceremony, if his health will permit him.[13]

In September Gertrude was awaiting the birth of her second grandchild. According to Mary Bourne:

> I was living in Washington. I flew up to Boston to have [Jonathan] and then I flew back to Washington. She wanted Jonathan born in 'our house' at 130 Mount Vernon Street...she loved the house. [Gertrude said] 'just have him born there and you can take him to the hospital.' But I stayed there until I had to go to the hospital. And that wasn't the easiest. She was sort of flustery. She wanted to plan everything and control everything and she did. And I'm pretty strong-willed myself, but I kept it serene.

Jonathan Bourne arrived in Massachusetts General Hospital on September 25, 1939. Soon the Philip Bournes moved from Washington to Salem, Massachusetts, and later, in 1948, they bought 93 Hale Street in Beverly, Massachusetts. Philip established his own architectural practice in the same Boston offices that his father had occupied. This meant that Philip could be near his mother and that he would be working in Boston most weekdays.

The Hawaiian trip resulted in a second exhibition of her work at Doll and Richards from April 8 to 20, 1940. The exhibition of twenty-eight watercolors included topographical sites such as *Diamond Head*, *Stevenson's Grass Hut*, and *Thomas Square*, Hawaiian genre such as *Lei Makers* and *Hula Girls*, but the preponderance of the exhibition was of the exotic flowers of the islands. Elizabeth M. Bowser reported in the *Boston Evening Transcript:*

> Gertrude Beals Bourne reports on a visit to Hawaii in her flowers and sketches in water color which are on view at Doll & Richards. These exotic, tropical blooms are seen in the vividness and brilliance of their natural color, that remind us what pale sisters some of our own garden variety are, compared to the purple pond lilies, the scarlet orange Heliconia, the brilliant bird-of-paradise and the yellow Alamandas.
>
> Mrs. Bourne handles them quite broadly, on a large scale in keeping with their striking color and forms, and she often stresses their eminently decorative quality as in Stercula Foetida, which seemed to us the nicest of all, with its brilliant orange and green blue against a cream background.
>
> When the artist becomes involved in leaves and stems as in *Hawaiian Bouquet,* she loses the clarity and essential forms, brought out so sharply in such a painting as the Heliconia (or lobster claws) seen against intense yellow. There are only a few of the landscape sketches, which are colorful but not as interesting, possibly because of their juxtaposition with the exuberant floral arrangements.[14]

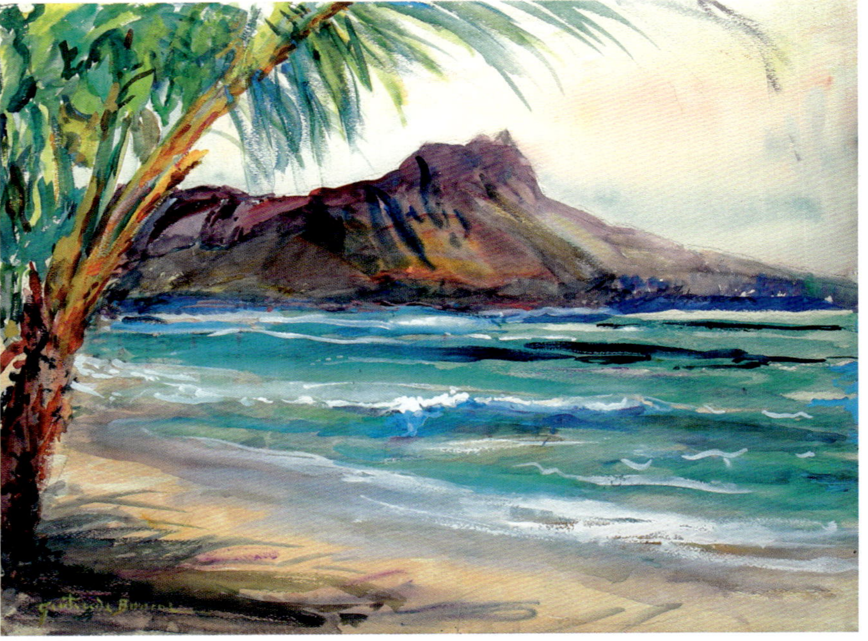

Diamond Head, 1939.
Watercolor, gouache, and charcoal on paper, 19 3/4 x 26 1/8 inches.
Exhibited: Doll and Richards, Boston, 1940.
Courtesy of Childs Gallery, Boston.

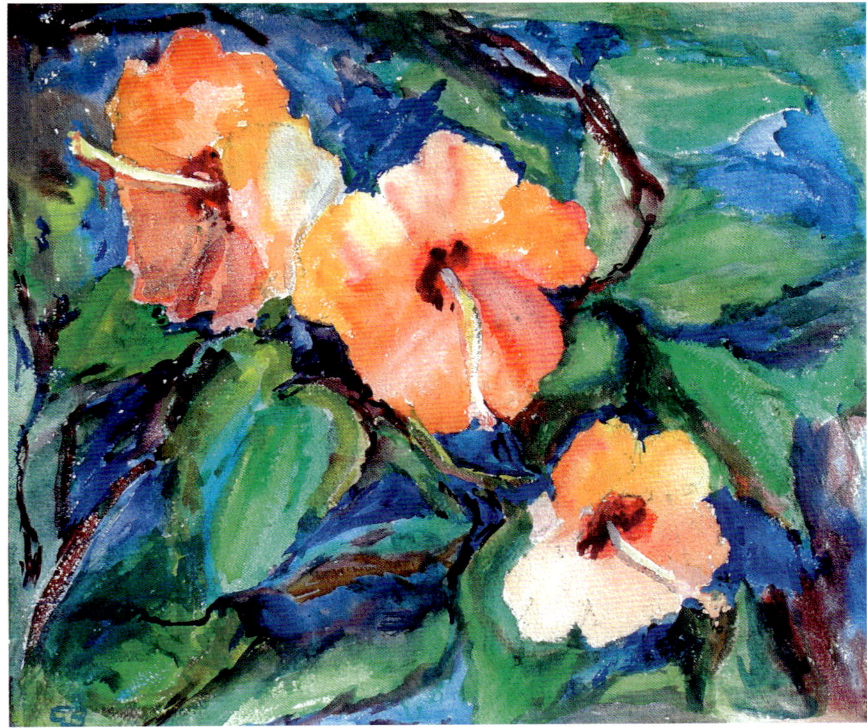

Orange Hibiscus, 1939.
Watercolor, gouache, and charcoal on paper, 16 1/2 x 18 1/4 inches.
Exhibited: Doll and Richards, Boston, 1940.
Courtesy of Childs Gallery, Boston.

Dorothy Adlow of the *Christian Science Monitor* reported in a similar vein:

> Mrs. Bourne shows her repertory, the startling shape of the Heliconia (Lobster Claws), charming yellow alma orchids, large purple pond lillies, large white night-blooming cereus. For the latter she sat up all night during the time of opening of the blossom, which she painted at 6 a.m. There are white and yellow plumeria, orange hibiscus, anthuriums, white bird of paradise, apé, alamandas, and torch ginger.
>
> Mrs. Bourne has done some tropical landscapes, showing the lei makers preparing the garlands, Stevenson's grass hut among the monkey pod trees, and the extinguished volcano, Diamond Head."[15]

In *Night Blooming Cereus*, *White Bird of Paradise*, *Heliconia*, and *Red Plumeria* she was able to find a subject both exotic and familiar to an avid horticulturalist and which inspired her to a brightness of palette and an expressionist freedom that had been incipient in her work but never before expressed to this degree. Mary Bourne noted that her work of this period was "different from what she used to paint."[16] In many of the Hawaii floral works, Gertrude filled the entire sheet of paper with only one or two blossoms. She combined the purples and oranges of Dodge Macknight and his freedom of brushwork with subjects such as *Pond Lilies (Purple Nymphaea)* that had obsessed Monet. This final solo exhibition was Gertrude Bourne's most expansive Modernist production.

Later in 1940 she exhibited again and for the last time with the Baltimore Water Color Club in the 43rd Annual Exhibition at the Baltimore Museum of Art from November 1-28, showing #28 *White Bird of Paradise* and #29 *Diamond Head, Hawaii*. The following year, 1941, she exhibited *Hawaiian Magnolia* at the American Water Color Society exhibition from February 7-23. In 1943 she exhibited again at the American Water Color Society *Kedron Brook* from March 24 to April 14.

In the 1940s Gertrude had friends in art circles in Boston, on Beacon Hill, and in the Garden Club. She remained active in the club by making Sunflower Castle available for meetings and by taking charge of the Bateman Cup that had been acquired by the club, making certain that it was available to each hostess for meetings. Gertrude continued to help plan programs and nominate new members. She helped to take charge of flower arrangement classes for the public at the Mechanics Building, and in 1946 inspected the club's progress and advised on plantings for the grounds of Old North Church.[17] Her son, Philip, would accompany her to symphony, and she probably went to musical events with other friends. She also had a handyman who did chores around 130 Mount Vernon Street and who would take Gertrude to the movies. And she had Sir Harry, the cockatoo, and her cat, Galusha.

Resembling tremendous stone mushrooms, and giving an oddly Japanese effect, are two concrete staddle-stones [sic] from England, and a bull-trough, now planted with flowers. A tremendous rhododendron tree dominates one side of the garden; thick bittersweet vines ascend roof-high and clamber over the tiled wall. Chrysanthemums, ivy and dwarf yews all add their accents to the garden, and near the center a great snow-vine breaks into white blossoms. A wide circular fountain, the water coming from the mouth of a head designed by the owner of the garden herself, has two handsome concrete ducks, also executed by Mrs. Bourne, standing guard. A stone in front of the pool holds the print of a dinosaur's foot, brought from Springfield where it was discovered. There is also a charming bronze birdbath. The delightful use of personal mementos in this sheltered garden gives it originality."[18]

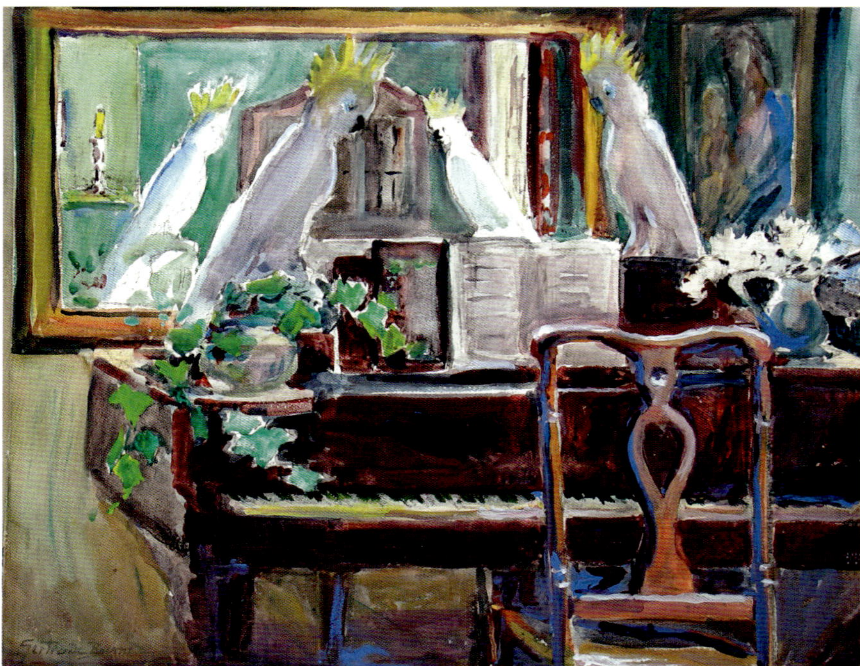

above: ***Cockatoos***, c. 1938.
Watercolor and gouache on paper, 19 x 23 1/2 inches. Sir Harry confronts his own image and that of a ceramic impostor. Exhibited: Doll and Richards, Boston, 1939.Courtesy of the Bourne Art Trust.

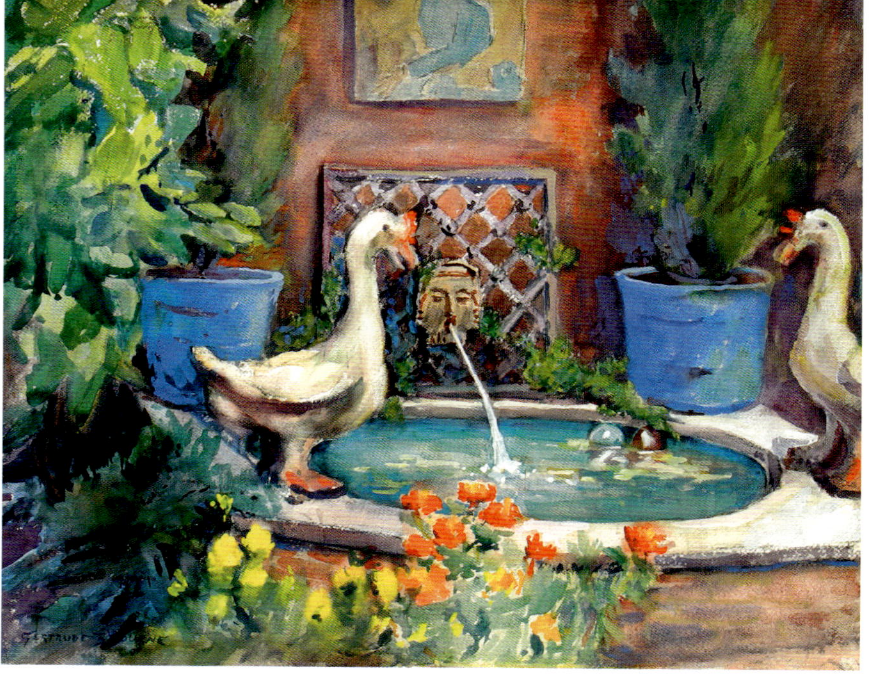

right: ***Ducks in My Garden***, c. 1938.
Watercolor, gouache, and charcoal on paper, 19 x 24 inches. Probably exhibited as *My Garden*, Doll and Richards, Boston, 1939. Courtesy of the Beacon Hill Garden Club.

The 1959 description of the garden suggests the eclectic combinations of art and artifact that interested Gertrude Bourne and notes the continuous updates and changes to the garden:

> Surrounded by a high tiled wall and approached from the house by a graceful curved iron stair, the garden has the curious charm of a child's fairy tale.

In Bourne's later years she continued to show her ability to improvise in order to paint what, when, and where she wanted. The family tells a story of Gertrude finding herself in a small town in Vermont or New Hampshire in the winter while she was in search of subjects. According to Mary Bourne: "There weren't any hotels that she could get to. So she went to the jail and said that she'd like to spend some nights…and they took her in! She spent two or three nights and finished her paintings. That was that! She got what she wanted!"[19]

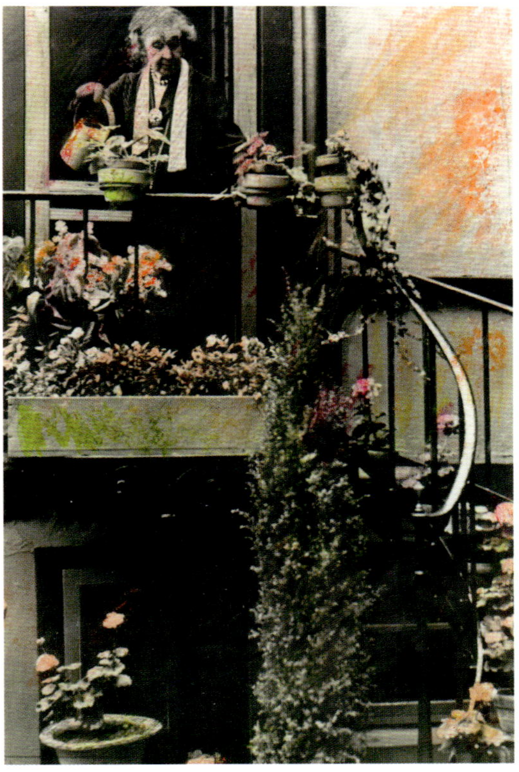

Gertrude Beals Bourne Watering Her Garden, c. 1950.
Hand-colored photograph.
Courtesy of the Bourne Art Trust.

Gertrude's granddaughter, Sallie Bourne Harrison remembered a similar story.

> It was remarkable. In 1959 when my son Peter was about three or four weeks old, at five in the morning, I looked out of the window and there was a checker cab. The driver came to the door and said 'I have a lady in the back of the car and need her fare.' The fare from Boston seemed enormous and I didn't have that much cash in the house. Grandma had just gone to Charles Street and picked up a taxi. She knew she wanted to go to 449 Hale Street in Pride's Crossing. I was astounded that she had reached us! But then she came to the door and said, 'Hello Mary, I've come to see the baby.' (She thought I was my mother.) I immediately called my father [Philip] and said 'Get over here and bring your wallet. I've got to bail out your mother.' I was horrified, but she was determined to see her great-grandchild.[20]

Edits, Resignation, and Prophecy

According to her family, Gertrude continued to paint even very late in her life. Sometime in the 1950s she engaged Philip to help her edit her paintings. She had a storage room, like most of proper Boston, in the Metropolitan Storage Warehouse next to M.I.T. She and Philip, according to Mary Bourne, went there to select which of her paintings would survive as her legacy. The others were ripped up and destroyed as unsuitable to represent the decades of her toiling for her art.

She may have continued to exhibit locally, but a key moment of retirement was in 1957 when she gave up her life membership in the American Water Color Society. After fifty-five years as a prominent and committed exhibitor and member, her resignation made clear that she no longer would compete for honor and attention in national venues. She, however, was still an active member of the Beacon Hill Garden Club. She was determined to remain independent and in control of her life.

Even as Gertrude became more dependent, she resisted the idea of leaving 130 Mount Vernon Street for an apartment or a retirement home. She began to accept interns from Massachusetts General Hospital who lived on the third floor of her house. They accepted at least some responsibility for caring for her, and she liked them and they liked her. However, as she aged, some of her eccentricities may have had them frustrated. She would wander off into the neighborhood, and when she had nurses, she would send them for a newspaper and then lock them out. Mary Bourne says that at that time, "she was a character."[21] About this time, when Gertrude was over ninety, her family and her doctors noticed that her mind was not as sharp as it had been.

However, she may have been tapping into special information. Gertrude Bourne's family was at first horrified and then puzzled by several incidents. Sallie Bourne related:

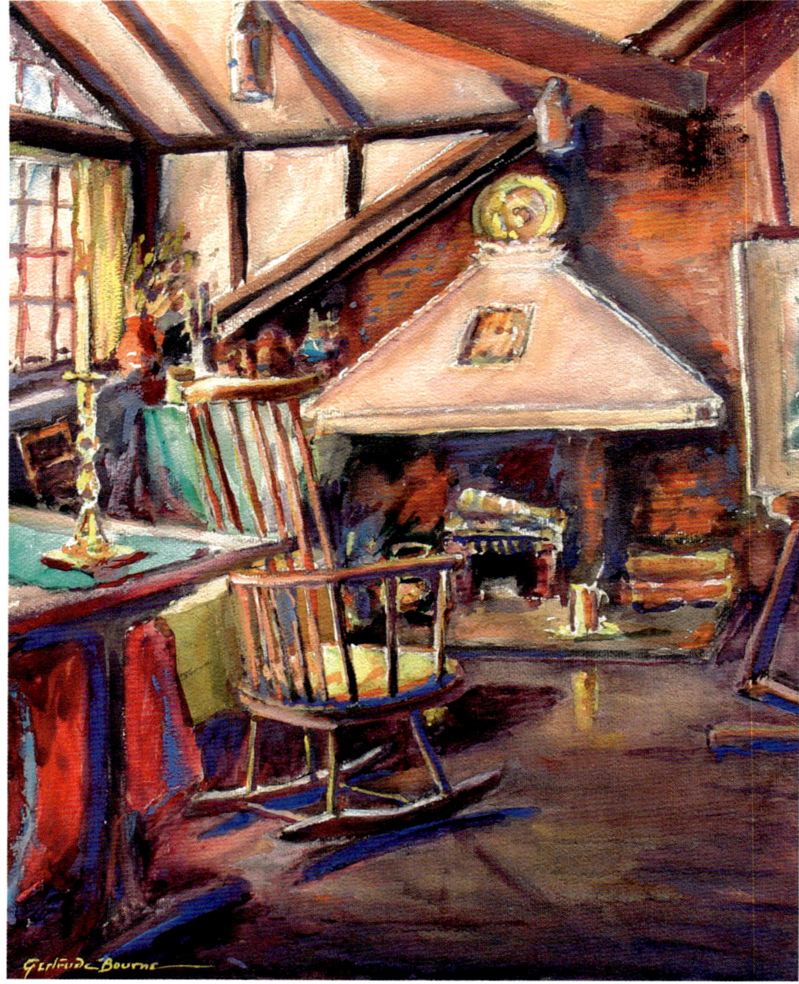

Studio Interior [Sunflower Castle], c. 1938.
Watercolor, gouache, and charcoal on paper, 24 x 18 3/4 inches.
Bourne's studio at 130 Mount Vernon Street in a late iteration.
Probably the painting exhibited as *Studio Interior* at Doll and Richards, Boston, 1939.
Courtesy of the Bourne Art Trust.

> We all heard the story about how she wandered into the bank—I think it was the Shawmut Bank on the corner of Charles and Beacon Streets. She walked in when she was nearly ninety and told them they were going to be robbed. And they looked at her and thought…'a wacky old lady.' But she was right! My God, they *were* robbed! And it couldn't have been grandma who robbed them, but we became concerned when we heard the story.
>
> And next she warned a merchant about a flood on Charles Street which actually happened. And then there was a third thing, which made my father think that we had better make certain that she stayed home. She had a kind of soft European gypsy woman look with layers and layers of clothes. The Marie Danforth Page portrait is a very good likeness. Later in her life with the shawl and clothing she might have been taken for a tea reader up to no good.[22]

After a number of incidents that made Philip fear for his mother, Gertrude was placed in a nursing home for her final few months. And Sir Harry went to the Stone Zoo in Stoneham.

Although her long life, in many ways, parallels the life of George Apley, Gertrude Bourne certainly lacked some of Apley's misgivings. Apley said, "When I stop to think of it, I had the unpleasant conviction that everything I have done has amounted almost to nothing…There has been too much talk in my life. There has been too little action."[23]

When Gertrude Beals Bourne, artist, died on May 23, 1962, two days after her ninety-fourth birthday, the obituary could not encompass all of her accomplishments. *The Boston Globe* noted high points.

> An eminent artist in her own right, her paintings were exhibited at shows in Boston, New York, Washington and London. Mrs. Bourne was active for many years in the American Water Color Society and the Washington Water Color Club. … She leaves a son, Boston architect Philip W. Bourne; three grandchildren and two great grandchildren, all of Beverly, and a brother, Sidney L. Beals of West Newton. Services will be held in Bigelow Chapel, Mt. Auburn Cemetery, Cambridge. Burial will be in the family plot there.[24]

Although her daughter-in-law, Mary Bourne, thought Gertrude was "not a wealthy woman," she left a respectable estate as the daughter and grand daughter of successful Boston merchants and businessmen.[25] Her son, Philip, was her sole heir. She left a legacy, however, much greater than probate records would indicate. Gertrude Bourne had led a life of action and accomplishment. In addition to living the life of a Boston lady, keeping a house, nurturing a husband, raising a son, attending symphony, and pouring tea, Gertrude Bourne left a collection of hundreds of finished watercolors that shows the development of her thought, style, and skills, but which also reflects the development of art in New England during the same period. She left a legacy of observations of Beacon Hill and Boston and of places far afield in New England and abroad. She showed a constant interest in and great knowledge of flowers and gardens and made them the subjects of many of her paintings. And she founded the Beacon Hill Garden Club and helped create the renaissance of Beacon Hill that gave it the character that it enjoys today.

Her grand-daughter, Sallie Bourne Harrison made an assessment that would have pleased Gertrude:

Every time I saw her she made a statement that she was first and foremost an artist. "That's what I do." I can see her sitting in the Martha Washington chair in the living room where she had painted friezes around the top, and she said: "I am an artist." She **was** *an artist first and foremost. That I am sure of. And she took it very seriously. It was her raison d'être.*[26]

NOTES, Chapter Four

1 Marquand, 294-95.
2 "Monet Spells Money," *Boston Evening Transcript*, 15 April 1892, 7.
3 Paul Hayes Tucker, et al. *Monet in the Twentieth Century* (Boston: Museum of Fine Arts Boston, 1998). See Cover illus, cat. 33, 51.
4 "Holidays Bring Art Exhibitions," *Boston Sunday Herald*, 8 January 1939, 39.
5 *Boston Evening Transcript,* 7 January 1939, part 3, 6.
6 Dorothy Adlow, "Three Water Color Exhibits," *Christian Science Monitor,* 11 January 1939, 14.
7 Gertrude Beals Bourne, letter to Phillip and Mary Bourne, 2 January 1939. Bourne Family Archives.
8 Interview between D. Roger Howlett and Mary Bourne, 10 November 1998. (Mary Bourne Interview).
9 Sallie Bourne Harrison Interview.
10 Marquand, 306-07.
11 Mary Bourne Inverview.
12 Sallie Bourne Harrison Interview.
13 Marquand, 324-25.
14 Elizabeth M. Bowser, "Gertrude Beals Bourne," *Boston Evening Transcript*, 13 April 1940, V, 7.
15 Dorothy Adlow, "Gertrude Beals Bourne," *Christian Science Monitor*, 10 April 1940, 12.
16 Mary Bourne Interview.
17 *Garden Club Minutes.*
18 Beacon Hill Garden Club, *Hidden Gardens of Beacon Hill*, (Boston: The Beacon Hill Garden Club, Inc., 1987).
19 Mary Bourne Interview.
20 Sallie Bourne Harrison Interview.
21 Mary Bourne Interview.
22 Sallie Bourne Harrison Interview.
23 Marquand, 344.
24 *The Boston Globe*, 24 May 1962.
25 Suffolk County Massachusetts Probate, #418,714.The liquid assets of her stock, bonds, and cash were valued at $99,450.67 (equal to $613,610.63 in 2004 dollars)
26 Sallie Bourne Harrison Interview.

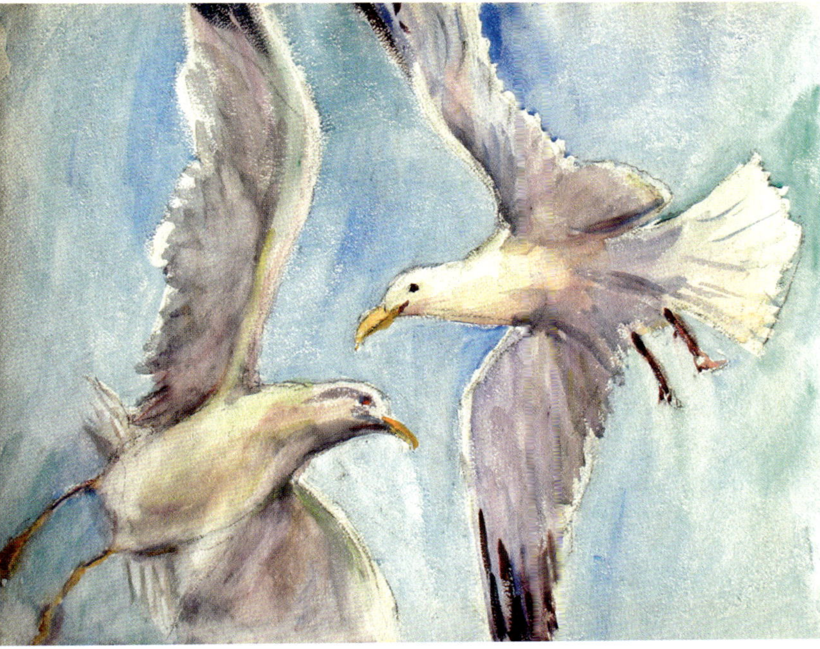

Seagulls, c. 1945.
Watercolor, gouache, and charcoal, on paper, 20 x 25 inches.
Courtesy of Childs Gallery, Boston.

CHRONOLOGY

1836 –August 25, Joshua Gardner Beals (Gertrude's father) born, in Boston.

1845 –Edith Ware Simmons (Gertrude's mother) born in Boston.

1858 –Joshua Beals graduates from Harvard University with an AB degree.

1859 –Joshua Beals leaves Harvard Law to join the *Boston Post*.

1861 –Joshua Beals receives AM from Harvard.

1865 –October 25, Joshua Beals and Edith Simmons marry at New South Church on Church Green, Summer St., Boston. He becomes a publisher of the *Boston Post*.

1868 –May 21, Gertrude born in Boston at 8 Pemberton Square on Beacon Hill.

1869 –Joshua Beals and family move to 419 Beacon Street in Back Bay, Boston.

1870 –William Beals (Gertrude's grandfather) dies.
–John Simmons (Gertrudes' great-great uncle) dies.

1871 –January 14, Frank Augustus Bourne (F.A.B.) born in Bangor, Maine.

1872 –November 9, Great Boston Fire begins.

1873 –January 14, Gardner Beals (Gertrude's brother) born.

1875 –Joshua Beals and family sell out interest in *Boston Post*

1876 –Dolly Whitney Beals (Gertrude's grandmother) dies.

1878 –Joshua Gardner Beals and family move to 41 Park Row, New York City; Joshua becomes a partner in Beals & Foster.

1879 –Boston Art Students Association founded.

1880 –April 22, Sidney Lane Beals (Gertude's brother) born.
–St. Botolph Club founded.
–Joshua Beals and family return to 419 Beacon Street in Boston and retires from active business.

1881 –Boston Art Club begins its new clubhouse at Newbury and Dartmouth Streets.

1882 –December 14, George W. Simmons (Gertrude's grandfather and noted New England clothier) dies in Boston. Leaves two large Nahant properties.

1883 –The "Foreign Exhibition" held in Boston.

1883-84 –Gertrude studies at Miss Ireland's School, 9 Louisburg Square, Boston.

1885 –According to family belief, Gertrude begins her watercolor studies while summering on Nahant.

1886 –The Beals family moves to 328 Dartmouth Street, Boston.

1887 –Boston Water Color Club organized for women.
–August, Gertrude summers with family in Dublin, N. H.

1888 –January-February, Dodge Macknight's first Boston exhibition at Doll and Richards.

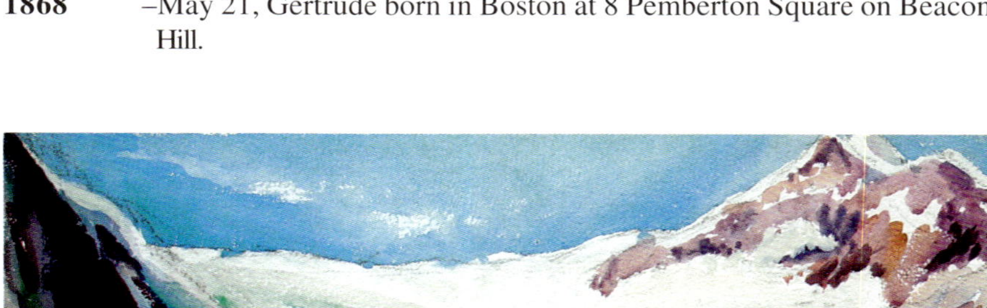

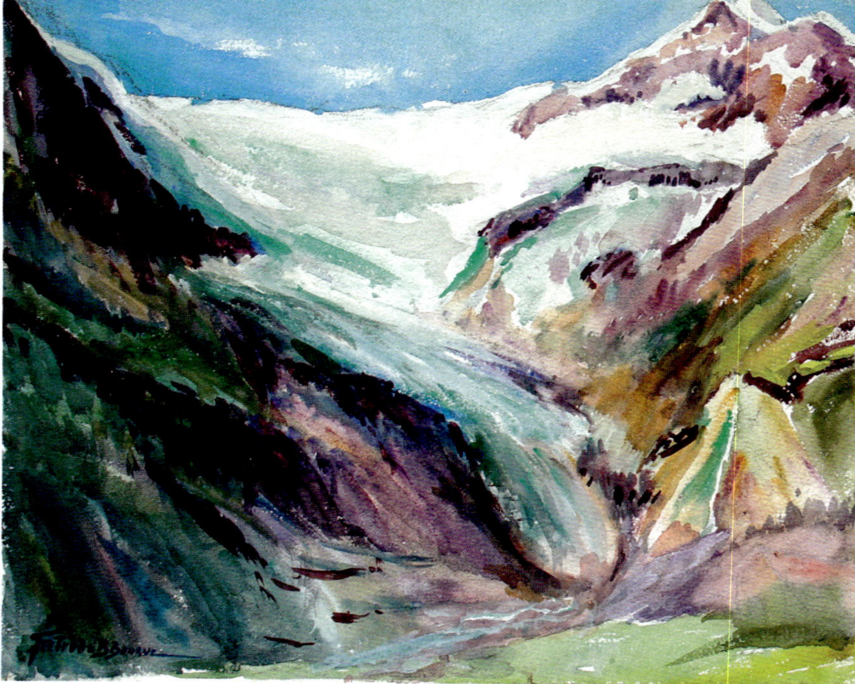

Alp Grüm and Glacier, Switzerland, c. 1929.
Watercolor, gouache, and charcoal on paper, 16 x 19 1/2 inches.
Albert Bierstadt painted at this site nearly three quarters of a century earlier.
Courtesy Bourne Art Trust.

–Summer, Gertrude travel to London, Paris, and Geneva, Switzerland with her parents and brothers.

1888-89 –Henry W. Rice hired to teach Gertrude Beals watercolor painting.

1889 –F.A.B. enters the University of Maine.

1889-90 –Henry W. Rice moves his studio from 18 Highland Street, Boston Highlands to the Harcourt Building, 23 Irvington Street in the Back Bay.

1890 –May, Boudin exhibition at J. Eastman Chase Gallery, Boston.

1891 –April 4-25, Exhibits at Boston Art Club (BAC) (44th) (watercolors): #142 *Azaleas.* (JE 160) (Henry Rice and Henry Snell also exhibit.)

–F.A.B. enters Massachusetts Institute of Technology.

1892 –April 2-23, Exhibits at BAC (46th) (watercolors): #146 *Geraniums.*

–*May-June, Sold for the (Otto) Grundmann Studio Building Fund: *Roman Anemones* $15.00; *Old House Marion* $18.00.

–Monet exhibition at St. Botolph Club, Boston.

–May 6-September 18, Gertrude travels to Paris, Normandy, Brittany, Switzerland, and Germany with her parents and brothers.

1893 –April 8-29, Exhibits at BAC (48th) (watercolors): #85 *Clock Tower—Dinan*; #187 *Arches and Shrine—Dinan.*

–August-October, Gertrude travels with her parents and brothers to Maine, Montreal, Quebec City, Kingston, Toronto, and Niagara Falls.

1894 –Joshua Beals belongs to the University Club, and remains a member until his death in 1914.

1895 –April 6-27, Exhibits at BAC (52nd) (watercolors), #46 *June.*

–Monet exhibition at the St. Botolph Club, Boston.

–Frank A. Bourne graduates from MIT.

1896 – F.A.B. receives his Master's degree in Architecture from MIT.

–F.A.B. joins the architectural firm Shepley, Rutan, and Coolidge.

1897-98 –Gertrude makes trip to Bermuda.

1898 –April 2-23, Exhibits at BAC (58th) (watercolors), #369 *A Cottage by the Sea, Bermuda.*

–F.A.B. studies architecture at Harvard and boards at 17 Marlboro St.

–Joshua Beals purchases part of the G. W. Simmons estate in Nahant.

–Gertrude makes a trip to Nantucket.

1899 –April 1-22, Exhibits at BAC (60th) (watercolors), #52 *In Old Nantucket.*

–Gertrude makes a trip to England.

–Gertrude listed in the Boston City Directory as "artist" at 289 Boyston Street, home remains 328 Dartmouth St.

– F.A.B. establishes his own architectural firm at 850 Tremont.

–Simmons College founded under the provisions of the will of John Simmons (Gertrude's grandfather).

1900 –April 7-28, Exhibits at BAC (62nd) (watercolors): #144 *In Clovelly*; #149 *Ann Hathaway's Cottage.*

– F.A.B. moves to 105 Mount Vernon Street.

1901 – F.A.B. rooms at 20 St. Botolph. Designs his first major building which is built in Bangor, Maine (First Congregational Church).

1902 –April 21-May 4, Gertrude exhibits at American Water Color Society (AWS) 35th Annual Exhibition: # *Doorway—Dedham.*

–Gertrude travels to Norway.

1903 –April 4-25, Exhibits at BAC (68th) (watercolors): #99 *Valders Valley, Norway.*

– F.A.B., with the help of Joshua Gardner Beals, purchases 130 Mount Vernon Street.

–Maurice and Charles Prendergast move to 56 Mount Vernon Street.

1904 –Gertrude joins the Copley Society of Boston.

– F.A.B. moves his office to the Mason Building at 70 Kilby Street.

–June 15, Gertrude, age 35, marries Frank Augustus Bourne at 328 Dartmouth St., usher Frederick Law Olmsted.

–Frank and Gertrude move to 130 Mt. Vernon St. (where she maintains a studio until her death.)

–Summer, Frank and Gertrude Bourne honeymoon in Italy (Venice, Florence, Cortina).

1905 –April 7-29, Exhibits at BAC (72nd) (watercolors): #168 *Plazzo Daris, Venice.*

–November 11-December 3, exhibits at New York Watercolor Club (NYWCC) 16th Annnual Exhibition: #205 *Golden Glow, Garden of Weld, Brookline* $50 (not a member)

–Gertrude listed in *The Artists Year Book* for 1905, published in Chicago.

1906 –April 6-28, exhibits at BAC (74th) (watercolors): #44 *Villa D'Este.* -Summer, Rochester, NH Fair: *Summer Garden*; *Azalea Path Arboretum.*

–November 10-December 2. Exhibits at NYWCC (17th): #323 *Lily Pond* $75.

–F.A.B. publishes architectural book, *A Study of the Orders,* with Frank Chouteau Brown.

1907 –March 15-April 6, Exhibits at BAC (76th) (watercolors): *A Corner in Rothenburg.*

–May 7-June 16, Exhibits at Art Institute of Chicago (AIC) (19th) (watercolors): #18 *Villa d'Este*, #19 *On the bank of the Artichoke.*

–Summer, Exhibits at Rochester, NH Fair: *Rhododendrons.*

–November 2–24. NYWCC (18th): #105 *Rhododendron in the Arboretum* $125

–November 30, gives birth to Philip Walley Bourne.

1908 –November 3-December 20, exhibits at the Philadelphia Water Color Club (Philadelphia WCC) at the Pennsylvania Academy of the Fine Arts: #48 *The Wide Spreading Pond*; and #250 *Satuit Brook.*

1909 –Gertrude and Frank Bourne purchase and renovate a boat shop at Scituate Harbor, Massachusetts at the edge of Satuit Brook.

–Exhibits at Philadelphia WCC (at the Pennsylvania Academy of the Fine Arts): *A New England Porch.*

–F.A.B. designs Charles River Square.

1910-11 –Gertrude submits at least two watercolors to the Metropolitan Improvement League "Picturesque Boston Exhibition," *Judas Tree in the Public Garden*; and *Hotel Somerset From the Fenway.*

1911 –Frank, Gertrude, and Philip Bourne travel to England and are there for the coronation of George V—June 22, 1911 (Westminster Abbey). F.A.B. goes to Germany while Gertrude & Philip go to France.

–August, Monet exhibition at Museum of Fine Arts, Boston (first American museum exhibition devoted to the artist).

1911-14 –Gertrude studies with Henry B. Snell. Stylistic changes in her watercolors suggest that she did not study with him before 1911 and had the opportunity to study with him by mid-1914.

1912 –May 7-June 5, exhibits at AIC (24th) (watercolors): #16 *A New England Porch.*

–Monet exhibition at Brooks Reed Gallery, Boston.

–Museum of Fine Arts, Boston acquires their first John Singer Sargent watercolors, which Gertrude copies in the museum in the next few years.

1913 –March and later, Armory Show in New York, Chicago, and Boston.

1914 – F.A.B. publishes "Architectural Drawing."

–April, Gertrude visits Charleston, South Carolina and paints azaleas in bloom.

–July 14, Joshua Gardner Beals dies from heart failure at his residence, 328 Marlboro St., Boston.

–September 9-30, Two-woman exhibition at the Milton Public Library, Milton, Mass. (with Abigail B. P. Walley). Gertrude shows: *A. Ward's Pond* $35; *B. Rear View of State House* $75; *C. Bridge on the Charles River* $50; *D. The Fountain (Mr. Newton's Garden)* $50; *E. The Blacksmith's Shop, Egypt (Loaned by Mr. Luther Smith)*; *F. Foxgloves* $50; *G. Magnolia Gardens, South Carolina* $75; *H. Cohasset Garden* $50; *I. New Castle, N. H.* $60; *J. Iris* $40; *K. Sea From the Garden* $50; *L. A Century Old* $50; *M. Rhododendrons and Pond Lilies* $60; *N. End of the Pond—Sargent's Place Brookline* $40; *O. Muddy Brook*; *P. John Alden House, Duxbury* $50; *Q. Rhododendrons* $50; *and R. Scituate Light (with frame)* $100.

–Exhibits at the Philadelphia WCC (at the Pennsylvania Academy of the Fine Arts)*: A New England Garden*; *Rhododendrons*; and *Laurel Phlox.*

–Maurice and Charles Prendergast move to 50 Washington Sq. S. New York City.

1915 –February 18, Gertrude arrives at Philbrook Farm, Shelburne, N.H. for several weeks of painting.

–February 20-March 11, exhibits at WWC: #97 *Phlox* ($75); and #264 *Rhododendrons* ($100).

–April 20-May 1, exhibits at Copley Gallery, Boston in solo exhibition: 1.*The Ravine*; 2. *Edge of the Woods*; 3. *Melting Snow*; 4. *Adams and Madison*; 5. *The Brook*; 6. *Birches*; 7. *Willows*; 8. *The Hillside*; 9. *New England Garden*; 10. *Phlox*; 11. *Rhododendrons*; 12. *The Fountain*; 13. *The Magnolia Gardens*; 14. *A Southern Home*; 15. *Hanging Moss and Azaleas, Charleston, SC*; 16. *Looking Toward Portsmouth*; 17. *Autumn at Wildwood*; 18. *A New England Farmhouse (House with Green Shutters?);* 19. *Church in Alexandria*; 20.*Rocks, Lowtide*; 21. *Old Fashioned Garden.*

–*American Federation of Arts founded. Gertrude exhibits: *Christchurch, England*; *Mt. Washington from Sugar Hill.*

–May 13-June 13, Exhibits at AIC, 29th Annual: #51 *New England Garden*; #52 *The Fountain.*

–Exhibits at Philadelphia WCC (at the Pennsylvania Academy of the Fine Arts): *Adams and Madison.*

–December 31, 1915-January 20, 1916, Exhibits at WWC 20th Annual Exhibition at the Corcoran Gallery: #259 *Church of Alexandria* ($85); #260 *Birch Trees in Winter* ($100).

1916 –January 24, Gertrude arrives at Philbrook Farm, Shelburne, N.H.. Dodge Macknight arrives there to paint January 25.

– Exhibits at the Baltimore WCC: *Birch Trees in Winter.*

–*Concord Annual Exhibit shows *The Brook, January*.

–February 3-27, Exhibits at the AWS 49th Annual Exhibition: *A Newburyport Garden*; *A New England Garden*.

–Gertrude joins the New York Watercolor Club as a member.

–F.A.B. joins the Harvard Club.

–November 4 – 26, Exhibits at the NYWCC (27th): #36 *February, Cape Cod*; #43 *Birch Trees, Winter*; # 58 *The Cove*.

–*Joins NYWCC.

1917 –February 1-24, Exhibits at the AWS 50th Annual Exhibition: *February*.

–Exhibits at WWC: #54 *February*, *Cape Cod* ($125); #133 *The Cove* ($100).

–May 4-June 3, Exhibits at AIC (29th) (watercolors): #33 *The Deep Pool* ($100); #313 *February* ($125).

–June 25, Prince Ferdinando di Savola di Udine visits Boston's North End. Gertrude records the event as seen on Salem Street in *When the Italian Prince Came to Boston.*

–Perhaps the Bourne's first time summering in Ipswich; they rent part of the Emerson Howard House, Turkey Shore Road from Arthur Wesley Dow.

–August 23-September 15, "exhibited at least one painting" at the Gallery on the Moors.

–November 3-25, Exhibits at the NYWCC at the Fine Arts Building: 4 works, #60 *Green Street Bridge [Ipswich]* ($125); #89 *The Deep Pool* ($100); #209 *A Cape Ann Garden* ($80); #240 *South Green Church, Ipswich* ($100).

–First year as a member of the New York Water Color Club.

–November 17-December 5, Exhibits at WWC: #40 *Noonmark Mt., Adirondacks* ($125); #57 *The Old Wharf* ($125).

–Exhibits at Philadelphia WCC (at the Pennsylvania Academy of the Fine Arts): *February, Cape Cod*; *Gardens Sentinels*; and *Birch Trees in February.*

1918 –Bourne family summers in Ipswich at Emerson Howard House.

–August 15-September 5, Exhibits at the Gallery on the Moors: *The Brook and The Ravine*; *Fitzwilliam Church.*

–November 2-24, Exhibits at the NYWCC at the American Fine Arts Building: #47 *The Ravine*; #264 *New Hampshire Village in Winter*; #275 *Salem Street Where the Italian Prince Came to Boston*; #310 *Fitzwilliam Church*; #314 *Ipswich River*.

1919 –February 15-March 3 , Exhibits at the National Association of Women Painters and Sculptors, 28th Annual, at the Fine Arts Building, New York City: *#26 A Garden*; *#141 The Cobbler's Shop*; *#148 The House at the End of the Bridge; #S206 The Garden Gate*; *#S261 A Holiday.*

–Joins the National Association of Women Painters and Sculptors, helps to organize the Boston Chapter, * and becomes the chapter secretary.

–February 24, President Woodrow Wilson disembarks at Boston on his return from the peace arrangements after World War I. Gertrude records the event as seen on Beacon Street.

–March 17-31, Exhibits at WWC: #165 *Green Street Bridge , Ipswich* ($150); #166 *South Green Church, Ipswich* ($100).

–April 14-26, Exhibits at National Association of Women Painters and Sculptors, Copley Gallery, Boston: #3 *Winter Wanes*; #4 *February 24, 1919.*

–May 15-June 15, Exhibits at AIC 31st Annual Exhibition (watercolors): #12 *The Bridge*; #13 *New England Church*; #190 *The Lavender Door*.

–July 12-29, Exhibits at Art Association of Newport (Newport Art Association) 8th Annual Exhibition of Pictures by American Painters: #19 *Boston's Welcome Home to the 26th Division*; #20 *Brook in the Ravine*; #21 *Ipswich River* #22 *Marines February 24th, 1919*; #23 *Winter Wanes*.

– Summers at the Emerson Howard House, Turkey Shore Road, Ipswich, Massachusetts (perhaps her last summer in Ipswich).

–August, Exhibits at Duxbury Art Association: *Marines February 24, 1919*; and **Ipswich River.*

–*August 21-September 10, Exhibits at Gallery on the Moors: *The Old Stone Bridge.*

–October 31-November 23, Exhibits at WWC: #39 *The End of the Day* ($150); #51 *The Bridge, Low Tide, Cos Cob* (#150); #60 *Hillside in March* ($125).

–November 1-23, Exhibits at NYWCC, at the American Fine Arts Building, 215 W. 57th St. 5 watercolors: #21 *Guinea Boats* ($150); #118 *Boston's Welcome to the Return of the 26th Division* ($150); #145 *Boatbuilding Rockport* ($100); #164 *Drying Sails* ($150); #173 *A Cincinnati Market* ($150).

–Exhibits at the The Pennsylvania Academy of the Fine Arts and the Philadelphia Water Color Club 17th Annual Exhibition *Boston [Marines] February 24th, 1919.*

1920s –*Exhibits at the Halcyon Gallery, London.

–*Exhibits at the James Newman Gallery, 24 Soho Square, London.

–*Secretary of the National Association of Women Painters and Sculptors (NAWPS) (Boston Chapter).

1920 –February 3-14, Exhibits at the NAWPS at the Grace Horne Gallery in Boston: *Stone Bridge, Ipswich* (and one other painting).

–February 4, article published in Boston Post by Sidney Woodward about NAWPS show.

–February 10, Letter to Mr. Sidney C. Woodward.

–February 18, Gertrude loans *Boat Building, Rockport*; *The Kitchen Door, Coscob*; and *River at Coscob* for the Copley Society Exhibition at the Museum of Fine Arts, Boston.

–April 10-May 1, Exhibits at NAWPS 29th Annual, at Fine Arts Building, NY: *Nocturne*; *A Blue Garden.*

–*Exhibits at Duxbury Art Association: *White Sulpher Porches.*

–*Exhibits at Baltimore WCC: *The Ravine.*

–May 11-June 6, Exhibits at AIC (32nd) (watercolors): #26 *Rockport Drying Sails.*

–August 4-23, Exhibits at Gallery on the Moors: 'No title'

1921 –*Exhibits at Baltimore WCC: *Waterlilies.*

–*February 4-23, Exhibits at WWC: #47 *Nocturne* ($150); #94 *The Lavender Door* ($150).

–BAC and Copley Society exhibit Homer, Sargent, and Macknight.

–*August 5-21, Exhibits at Gallery on the Moors: *Mt. Adams and Mt. Madison.*

–December 31, 1921-January 15, 1922, first combined exhibition of NYWCC and AWS. Gertrude exhibits *House at Boothbay Harbor; Mt. Adams and Mt. Madison*; *A Wiscasset Garden.*

1922 –Paints a series of winter views of the East River and Manhattan skyline.

–Joins AWS and exhibits regularly through 1943, remains a member until 1957.

–*February 11-March 5, Exhibits at WWC: #117 *Waterlilies* ($200).

–April, F.A.B. helps found the Beacon Hill Association.

–April 4 – 15, Exhibits at NAWPS 31st Annual, at Anderson Galleries, New York: #29 *Peck Slip*; and #33 *Skyscrapers.*

–July 15-August 12, Art Association of Newport, #27 *Cornish Garden*; #23 *Golden Screen.*

–North Shore Arts Association founded.

–August 5-27, Gallery on the Moors, *Peck's Slip*; and *Brooklyn Bridge.*

–October 18-30, Exhibits at NAWPS, 32nd Annual, at the Fine Arts Building, New York: #19 *Pond Lilies.*

– December 22, 1922-January 9, 1923, Exhibits at NYWCC: #265 *East River* $200; #437 *New Years Day, Boston* $250.

1923 –Both Gertrude and Frank join North Shore Arts Association (NSAA), Gloucester, Massachusetts as first year members.

–*January 6-28, Exhibits at WWC: #75 *Monhegan Harbor* ($200); #79 *Spring Garden* ($200); #85 *Trinity After Snowstorm* ($250).

–March-April. Solo Exhibition at the Arts Club of Washington.

–April, F.A.B. moves his office to 177 State St., Room 700.

–May, published in *American Magazine of Art.*

–*July 15-September 15, Exhibits at North Shore Arts Association First Annual exhibition: #83 *Waterlilies.* F.A.B exhibits: #173 *House at Rockport (Sketch)*; #207 *Charles Street Meeting House, Boston (sketch).*

–*June 7-September: Frank, Gertrude, and Philip go to Europe: Britain—London, Oxford (June 20), Wroxham; France—Paris, Concarneau, Nantes, Tours, Bordeaux, Angoullemes, Perigueux; Italy—Florence, Piacienza (August 29); Switzerland—Geneva, Montruex, Vevy; Nantua and Langeais, France again—Chillon, Rhone glaciers (Sept 4), Moret (Sept 23); Sweden. In Paris: see the Salon of 1923 and an exhibition of American artists: Sargent, Homer, Macknight, and Manship.

–*[Circa 1923] Exhibits at least 12 paintings at James Newman Gallery, 24 Soho Square, London, including: *Wet Pavements—Washington [Square] Arch*; *Waterlilies*; *Morning Sunlight, East River*.

–October 16-30, Exhibits at NAWPS, 33rd Annual, at the Fine Arts Building, New York: #33 *Court Yard in Spring*; #34 *Morning Light Sent Rest.* [sic].

–*October 27-November 20, Exhibits at WWC: #162 *The Brook in February* ($150); #199 *Thorn Mountain* ($200).

–December 28, 1923-January 15, 1924, Exhibits at the combined exhibitions of NYWCC and AWS: #164 *St. Paul's from Tower Bridges*; #168 *Flower Vendor, Paris*; #431 **Morning Light East River (this is not in American Watercolor Exhibitions. 1900-1945)*; *London Bridge* #21a.

1924 –*Travels with Philip to Yugoslavia—Ragusa, Sarajevo, Mostar; Italy—Ravello; Trieste; France—Paris; Holland—Volendam; Coast of Dalmatia on the Adriatic.

1925 –*Travels to Britain—Skipton Court, Wraxton, Chelsea, Oxford.

–March 1-14, Exhibits at NAWPS, 34th Annual, New York; #161 *Wine Boats, Ragusa*; #162 *Oleanders*; #163 *Ragusa.*

–*July 11–September 6, Exhibits at NSAA 3rd Annual Exhibition: #284 *Ragusa, Dalmatia*; #300 *Winter in Vermont.*

1926 –February 16-March 21, Exhibits at Baltimore WCC (30th annual), Baltimore Museum of Art: #168 *Winter in Vermont* ($200); #173 *Winter—Vermont* ($200).

–*February 5-28, Exhibits at National Gallery of Art with the WWC: *Between Voyages.*

–*Frank and Gertrude go on driving trip of Europe with a model T Ford, and are joined by Philip when a classmate (with whom he was traveling independently) contracts typhoid fever.

–*July 10–September 6, Exhibits at NSAA—Gloucester 4th Annual Exhibition: #203 *The Flower Show 1926*; #308 *Wine Boats, Ragusa, Dalmatia.*

1927 –*March–June, Visits Europe: Azores, Morocco—Marrakesh, Fes; Spain—Algericas, Loja, Ronda, Tepa, Granada, Alhambra, Lobrija; Italy—Florence, Rome, Pisa, Ravello (April); Switzerland (June); #199Britain—Winchester, Penshurst, Burrswood, Southampton; Paris—Le Havre (June 8).

–*Exhibits at Boston Women's City Club: *A New England Church.*

–*Exhibits at Baltimore WCC: *Market ,Ragusa, Dalmatia.*

–*Boston Art Club exhibits work from her travels to Morocco: *Fundouk Nejjarine*; *Souk, Fes*; *Grain Markets, Fes.*

–August 9, Edith Ware Beals dies at her residence, 65 Mount Vernon Street.

1928 –January 4-17, Exhibits at combined NYWCC and AWS exhibitions: *Polperro Harbor No. 1*; *Polperro Harbor no. 2.*

–March 6-April 1, Exhibits at Baltimore WCC (32nd annual), Baltimore Museum of Art: #149 *New England Church* ($200); #196 *Some Pumpkins* ($200).

–March 14-24, F.A.B. Exhibits etchings and lithographs at Goodspeed's Print Shop, Boston.

–April 9-May 7, Exhibits at NAWPS, 37th Annual, at Brooklyn Museum: #24 *Spring in Spain*; #25 *Backyards*; #26 *Heel Mountain.*

–June 19-July 31, Exhibits at Copley Society of Boston's "Exhibition of the Work of Painters and Sculptors of Boston and the Vicinity": *Afternoon, February*; *Brook Wilton.*

–Exhibits at Corcoran Gallery, WWC: #1 *Afternoon February*; #13 *Brook, Wilton.*

–July 7-September 3, Exhibits at NSAA: #319 *Some Pumpkins*; # 321 *A New England Church*; # 323 *The Wayside Inn.* F.A.B. exhibits: #282 *Fairlawn—The Survival*; #286 , #286 *Puit Cluny.*

–September 26, Gertrude founds the Beacon Hill Garden Club.

–October 10, Gertrude elected first President of the Beacon Hill Garden Club.

1929 –January 3-20, Exhibits at the combined NYWCC and AWS exhibitions: *The Brook, Wilton*; *Afternoon, February*; *A New England Church.*

–January 6-February 3, Exhibits at Corcoran Gallery with the WWC: #148 *A City Yard Garden* ($200); #172 *A Cohasset Garden* ($200); #174 *Some Pumpkins* ($200).

–February-April, Exhibits *Ragusa Market* in Copley Society Exhibition at the Museum of Fine Arts, Boston.

–March 19, Beacon Hill Garden Club exhibits "Back Yard Garden" at the Centennial Exhibition of the Massachusetts Horticultural Society.

–Spring, Gertrude tours gardens in Virginia.

–May 20 & June 3, first Beacon Hill Garden Club Tours.

–July 6-September 2, Exhibits at NSAA, #350 *City Yard Garden.*

–August, Gertrude Visits Paris (19th), Zurich (29th), Britain—Bibury.
–*December, Exhibits at NYWCC: *Winter's Coldring.*
–*December 8-29, Exhibits at Corcoran gallery, WWC: #58 *The Farm in Winter* ($200); #104 *My Yard Garden* ($200).

1930 –*August, trip to the Gaspe Peninsula (1st) through Maine.
–*Fall, trip to Connecticut—Litchfield, Marble head; Newport, RI; Wiscasset (Sept) (House of the Seven Gables cockatoo sketches).
–Gertrude and Frank give up membership at NSAA.
–October 10, Gertrude retires as president of Beacon Hill Garden Club, becomes 1st Vice President.
–October 23-November 16, Exhibits at NYWCC and AWS combined exhibition, *The Cockatoo's Garden*.
–Last listed as a member of NAWPS, 1930-31.

1931 –January–March: *Visits Nassau, Cristobal (Feb. 22) Jamaica (Feb.), Cuba—Havana (Feb. 28) and Mexico where Gertrude reported on Mexican gardens.
–*April, Visits San Antonio, Texas.
–*September 5-8, Visits New London, CT; Block island; Montauck; Southampton, Long Island.
–October 8, Gertrude shows Mexican sketches at Beacon Hill Garden Club.
–October 20-November 8, Exhibits at AWS 65th: *Kingston Market Jamaica*.
–*Exhibits at Portland Society of Art: *Garden in Cotswolds.*
–*December 3-27, Exhibits at Corcoran Gallery, WWC: #16 *Faun* ($200); #23 *Cymbals* ($150).

1932 –January 15-30, Exhibits at Boston Art Club, "Contemporary American Watercolor Painting": #146 *Pink Church Cuernavaca.*
–April 22-May 9, Exhibits at NYWCC 43rd Annual: #30 *Cymbals.*
–June 15, Gertrude and Frank's son, Philip Walley Bourne, marries Mary Elliot Nicholson at the Colony Club in New York City. The newlyweds live at 130 Mt. Vernon Street while the Bournes Sr. are in Europe.
–August-October, Frank and Gertrude visit Ireland—Dublin Horse Show (Aug 3), Cobb, Cork, Mizenhead ("the Bull"); Wales; Liverpool; Oxford.
–Philip Bourne enters the School of City Planning at Harvard University, lives with his wife at Holden Green in Cambridge.
–Philip begins work at Frank Bourne's architectural firm at 177 State Street.
–October 27-November 13, Exhibits at AWS 66th, *New England Garden*.

1933 –* Winter of 1931-32 at Glen House, an inn on the slopes of Mt. Washington in the White Mountains.
–*Exhibits at BAC: *Cymbals*.
– November 2-9, Exhibits at AWS 67th Annual Exhibition: *Mt. Washington*.

1934 –April 9–May 6, Exhibits at Salons of America, NYC: #431 *Mt. Jefferson*; #432 *Mt. Adams*; #433 *Mt. Errigal*; #434 *Mt. Washington*.
–October 10, birth of grand-daughter, Sallie Bourne.
–October 26–November 18, Exhibits at AWS 68th Annual Exhibition: *Garden—East Haddam.*

1934-35 –Gertrude sits for her portrait, *Gertrude and Galusha,* by Marie Danforth Page.

1935 –January, Philip and Mary Bourne leave for Washington, D. C. where Philip has a job in city planning with the National Housing Administration.
–*Exhibits at NYWCC: *Garden in Weston.* [submission not accepted?]

1936 –BCD 1936 shows Gertrude and Frank at 130 Mt. Vernon, and Philip and Mary at: 202 E Holden Green, Cambridge, and Philip's office at 177 State St. Room 700.
– January 3-21, Exhibits at AWS 69th: *The Ancestor*.
–February 15, Frank Augustus Bourne dies.
–February 9-March 1, Exhibits at WWC at Corcoran: #13 *The Ancestor.* (Illustrated in catalogue).
–April 16-30, Exhibits at NYWCC 47th Annual: # 50 *Susquehanna River*.
–Listed as a Life Member of the American Watercolor Society.

1937 –BCD shows Philip and Mary E. Bourne living at 130 Mt. Vernon St and his office at 177 State St. Room 700 (they are actually in Washington D.C.).
–January 7-21, Exhibits at AWS 70th: *Dining Room in the Arbo.*
–February 14-28, Exhibits at NYWCC 48th Annual: #377 *Dupont Circle*, $150.

–Trip to the Canadian Rockies, The Pacific Northwest, and southern California.

–December 4-22, Exhibits at NYWCC 49th Annual: #336 *Mount Shasta, California*, $250.

1938 –January 27-February 12, Exhibits at AWS 71st: *Glacier and Frozen Lake.*

1939 –January 2-14, Solo exhibition Doll and Richards Gallery in Boston: "Water Colors by Gertrude Beals Bourne" **California and the South West** 1. *Mt. Shasta*, 2. *Pala Mission* [near San Diego]; 3. *Desert Near Palm Springs*; 4. *Ramona's Wedding Place*; 5. *Purple Thistles, Bakersfield*; 6. *Poppies and Lupin, Bakersfield*; 7. *Mt. Rainier*; 8. *Lake Louise (frozen lake)*; **Boston** 9. *Frog Pond in August*; 10. *Public Garden Swanboat*; 11. *Cockatoos*; 12. *Ancestor*; 13. *Kitchen Fireplace, Paul Revere's House*; 14. *Fishelson's*; 15. *October*; 16. *My Garden*; 17. *Autumn*; **Nantucket** 18. *Arbor dining room "The Wood Box"*; 19. *Windmill*; 20. *Nantucket Boat*; and seven miscellaneous watercolors 21. *Still Life*; 22. *Blue Vase and Chrysanthemums*; 23. *Snowberries*; 24. *Delft Lion and Chrysanthemums*; 25. *Susquehanna River*; 26. *Studio Interior*; and 27. *"Popo," Mexico.*

–February 10-26, Exhibits at NYWCC and AWS combined exhibition: #152 *Public Garden, Swanboat* $200.

–Summer, visits Philip W. Bourne and family in Honolulu, Hawaii for about one month and paints Hawaiian landscape and flowers extensively.

–September 25, birth of grandson, Jonathan Bourne, in Boston.

1940 –April 8-April 20, solo exhibition at Doll and Richards, Boston, "An Exhibition of Water Colors—Hawaiian Flowers and Sketches by Gertrude Beals Bourne": 1. *Anthuriums*; 2. *White Bird of Paradise*; 3. *Belladona Lilies (Datura)*; 4. *Lei Makers*; 5. *Hula Girls*; 6. *Magnolia*; 7. *Cactus* Flower; 8. *Night Blooming Cereus*; 9. *Apé*; 10. *Bird of Paradise*; 11. *Hawaiian Bouquet (Mountain Ginger, Torch Ginger, Anthuriums)*; 12. *Pond Lilies (Purple Nymphaea)*; 13. *Stevenson's Grass Hut (Monkey Pod Trees)*; 14. *Night Blooming Cereus No.2*; 15. *Night Blooming Cereus No. 3*; 16. *Heleconia (Lobster Claws)*; 17 *Torch Ginger*; 18. *Alamandas*; 19. *Lotus*; 20. *White Plumeria*; 21. *Red Plumeria*; 22. *Hibiscus*; 23. *Orchids, Alma*; 24. *Royal Poinciana Trees*; 25. *Thomas Square;* 26. *Stercula Foetida*; 27 *Thunbergia*; 28. *Diamond Head.*

–November 1-28, Exhibits at Baltimore WCC (43rd Annual) Baltimore Museum of Art: #28 *White Bird of Paradise* ($300); #29 *Diamond Head, Hawaii* ($250).

1941 –February 7-23. Exhibits at NYWC and AWS combined exhibition: *Hawaiian Magnolia.*

1942 –Submits *Anthuriums* to AWS.

1943 –March 24-April 14, Exhibits at AWS: *Kedron Brook.*

1957 –Resigns membership with the American Watercolor Society.

1959 –Birth of great-grandson, Peter.

1962 –May 23, Gertrude Beals Bourne dies in Cambridge.

1987 –May 4-29, Exhibition at the Trustman Gallery, Simmons College: *Sailboats and Wharf*; *Corner Bridge, Ipswich, MA*; *Red House with Ivy*; *New York Harbor*; *Birch Trees*; *Barret Mountain*; *Mt. Washington from Sugar Hill*; *Winter Mountains*; *The Brook, Wilton*; *Poppies (Cape Ann Garden)*; *Purple Azaleas, Arboretum*; *Autumn Glory*; *Garden and Harbor, Ipswich*; *Fall Garden*; *Pink Clouds*; *Hoag Island, Ipswich*; *Blue and Orange Marsh Landscape*; *Palms, Marakech*; *White Dome in Morocco*; *Boats, Ragusa, Dalmatia*; *Fishing Fleet, Concarneau*; *Boats on the Thames*; *Ships Waiting.*

1988 –March 6-May 1, Exhibition, *An Essex County Collection: the watercolors of Gertrude Beals Bourne*, at the Essex Institute, Salem, MA.

1990 –March 13-30, Exhibition, *Women Artists in the White Mountains: 1840-1940*, at the Hopkins Center, Dartmouth College, Hanover, N.H. *Mt. Monadnock and Maple Grove* and *Winter, Presidential Range.*

1995 –September 5-30, Exhibition, *Mainescapes: Women Artists, 1900-1995*, at the Ogunquit Museum of Art, Ogunquit, Maine. *Peospect Harbor, Maine.*

–December 19, Death of Phillip Walley Bourne.

1997 –August 2-October 18, Exhibition *Emile Gruppe and his Contemporaries* at the North Shore Arts Association, Gloucester, MA. *North Shore Garden.*

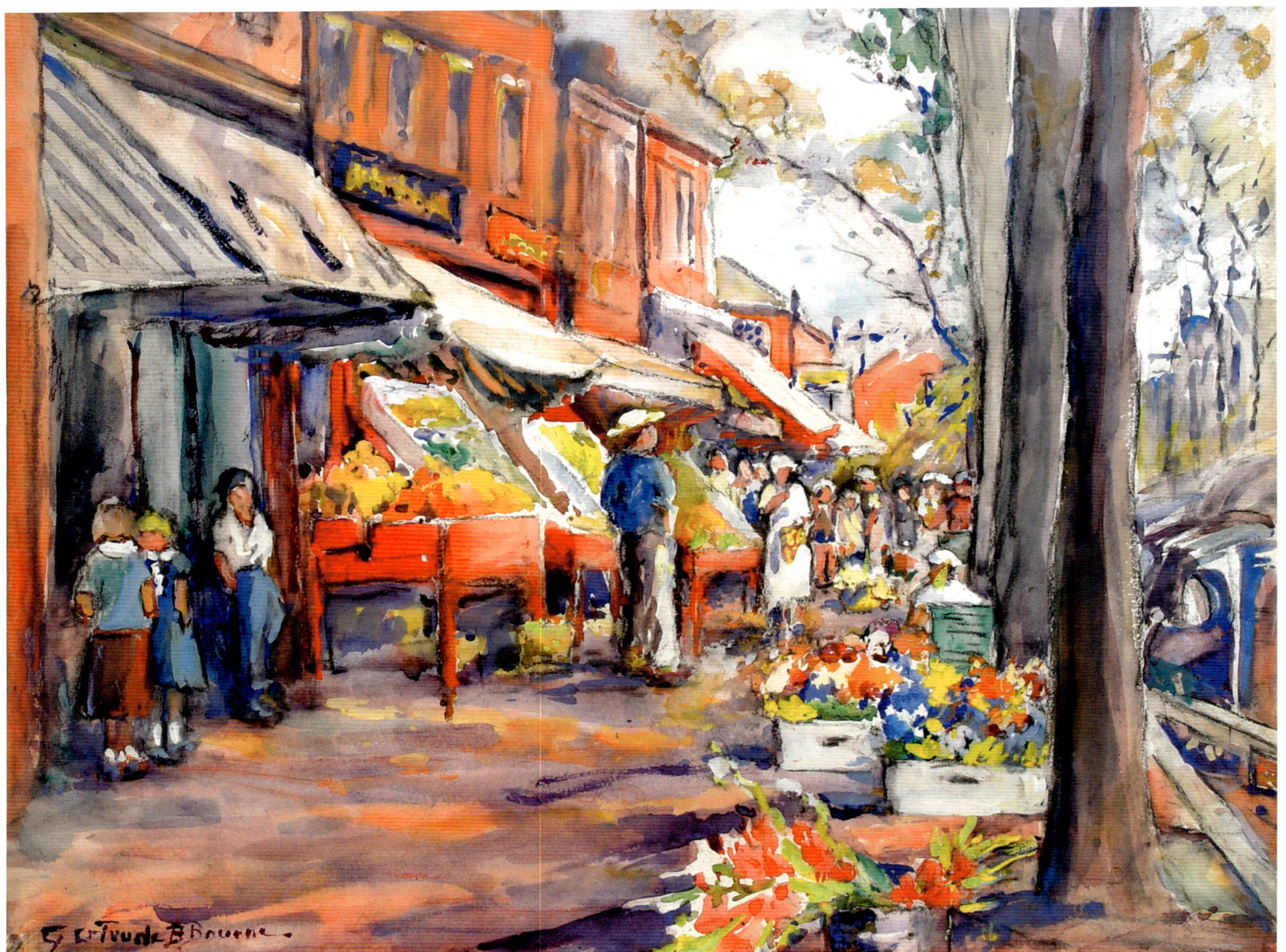
Gertrude B Bourne

BIBLIOGRAPHY

Books:

Adams, Henry, et al. *American Drawings and Watercolors: In the Museum of Art, Carnegie Institute.* Pittsburgh: University of Pittsburgh Press, 1985.

Adams, Russell B., Jr. *The Boston Money Tree*. New York: Thomas Y. Crowell Company, 1977.

Beacon Hill Garden Club. *Beacon Hill Garden Club: 75 years.* Boston: The Beacon Hill Garden Club, 2004.

Beacon Hill Garden Club. *Hidden Gardens of Beacon Hill*. Boston: The Beacon Hill Garden Club, Inc., 1987.

Bénézit, E. *Dictionnaire des Peintres, Sculpteurs, Dessinateurs et Graveurs.* Paris: Editions Gründ, 1999.

Bunting, Bainbridge. *Houses of Boston's Back Bay: An Architectural History, 1840-1917.* Cambridge, MA: Belknap Press, 1967.

Carter, Morris. *Isabella Stewart Gardner and Fenway Court.* Cambridge, MA: The Riverside Press, 1925.

Chadbourne, Janice H. et al. eds. *The Boston Art Club: Exhibition Record, 1873-1909.* Madison, CT: Sound View Press, 1991.

Cikovsky, Nicolai, Jr. *Winslow Homer.* Hew Haven, CT: Yale University Press, 1995.

Flower market, Boston, c. 1930.
Watercolor, gouache, and charcoal on paper, 19 x 23 3/4 inches.
Courtesy of the Family of Philip E. Bourne

Clement, Clara Erskine and Laurence Hutton. *Artists of the Nineteenth Century and Their Works.* Boston: Houghton Mifflin and Company, 1880.

Curry, David Park. *Childe Hassam: An Island Garden Revisited.* Denver: Denver Art Museum, 1990.

Fairbrother, Trevor J. *The Bostonians: Painters of an Elegant Age, 1870-1930.* Boston: Museum of Fine Arts, 1986.

Falk, Peter Hastings, ed. *The Annual Exhibition Records of the Art Institute of Chicago.* Madison, CT: Sound View Press, 1990.

————. *Who Was Who In American Art, 1564-1975: 400 Years of Artists in America.* Madison, CT: Sound View Press, 1999.

Firey, Walter. *Land Use in Central Boston.* Westport, CT: Glenwood Press, 1947.

Gerdts, William H. *American Impressionism.* New York: Abbeville Press, 1984.

Giffin, Sarah L., and Kevin D. Murphy, eds. *"A Noble and Dignified Stream": The Piscataqua Region in the Colonial Revival, 1860-1930.* York, Maine: Old Historical Society, 1992.

Green, Eleanor. *Maurice Prendergast.* College Park, Md.: University of Maryland, 1976.

Green, Martin. *The Problem of Boston: Some Readings in Cultural History.* New York: W. W. Norton & Company, Inc., 1966.

Hanni, Margaret. *An Essex County Collection: The Watercolors of Gertrude Beals Bourne 1867-1962.* Salem, MA: Essex Institute, 1988.

Harris, Leon. *Only to God: The Extraordinary Life of Godfrey Lowell Cabot.* New York: Atheneum, 1967.

Hirshler, Erica E. *A Studio of Her Own: Women Artist's in Boston 1870-1940.* Boston: MFA Publications 2001.

Holmes, Oliver Wendell, Sr. *The Autocrat of the Breakfast Table*. New York: Dutton, 1970.

Howard, Frances Minturn. *Beacon Hill: Hub of the Universe*. Dublin, NH.: Yankee, Inc., 1977.

Hopkins Center, Darmouth College. *Women Artists in the White Mountains 1840-1940* (Exhibition Catalogue). Hanover, NH: Dartmouth College, 1990.

Hoppin, Martha J. *Marie Danforth Page: Back Bay Portraitist*. Springfield, MA: Springfield Library and Museums Association, 1979.

Howe, Helen. *The Gentle Americans 1864-1960: Biography of a Breed*. New York: Harper & Row, 1965.

Kenny, Herbert A. *Newspaper Row: Journalism in the Pre-Television Era.* Chester, CT: Globe Pequot Press, 1987.

Joseph, Jonathan J. *Jane Peterson: An American Artist*. Boston, MA: Privately Printed, 1981.

Langtry, Albert P. *Metropolitan Boston: A Modern History Volume II.* New York: Lewis Historical Publishing Co., 1929.

Li-Marcus, Moyling. *Beacon Hill: The Life and Times of a Neighborhood.* Boston: Northeastern University Press, 2002.

Loria, John, and Warren A. Seamans. *Earth, Sea and Sky: Charles H. Woodbury.* Cambridge, MA: The MIT Museum, 1988.

Marlor, Clark S. *The Salons of America, 1922-1936.* Madison, CT: Sound View Press, 1991.

Marquand, John P. *The Late George Apley.* Boston: Little, Brown, and Company, 1937.

Moffat, Frederick C. *Arthur Wesley Dow (1857 – 1922).* Washington, D.C.: Smithsonian Institution Press, 1977.

Moore, Barbara W., and Gail Weesner. *Beacon Hill: A Living Portrait*. Boston: Centry Hill Press, 1992.

Moore, Barbara W., and Gail Weesner, eds. *Hidden Gardens Of Beacon Hill.* Boston: Beacon Hill Garden Club, Inc., 1999.

Patterson, Stanley C., and Carl G. Seaburg. *Nahant on the Rocks.* Nahant, MA: Nahant Historical Society, 1991.

Ratcliff, Carter. *John Singer Sargent.* New York: Abbeville Press, 1982.

Rowe, Henry. *Ancestry of John Simmons.* Cambridge: Riverside Press, 1933.

Sammarco, Anthony Mitchell. *The Great Boston Fire of 1872*. Dover, NH.: Arcadia Publishing, 1997.

Saeaburg, Carl. *Boston Observed*. Boston: Beacon Press, 1971.

Shand-Tucci, Douglass. *Boston Bohemia: 1881-1900.* Amherst, MA: University of Massachusetts Press, 1995.

————. *Built in Boston: City and Suburb 1800-1950.* Amherst, MA: University of Massachusetts Press, 1988. —

Simmons, Linda Crocker. *American Drawing, Watercolors, Pastels and Collages in the Collection of the Corcoran Gallery of Art.* Washington, D.C.: Corcoran Gallery of Art, 1983.

Stebbins, Theodore E, Jr. *American Master Drawings and Watercolors: A History of Works on Paper from Colonial Times to the Present.* New York: Harper and Row, 1976.

Strickler, Susan E. *American Traditions in Watercolor: The Worcester Art Museum Collection.* New York: Abbeville Press, 1987.

Treutner, William H., and Roger B. Stein, eds. *Picturing Old New England: Image and Memory.* New Haven, CT: Yale University Press, 1999.

Tucker, Paul Hayes. *Monet in the 20th Century.* Boston: Museum of Fine Arts, 1998.

Tuckerman, Henry T. *Book of the Artists*. New York: James F. Carr, 1966.

Van Rensselaer, M.G. *Six Portraits: Della Robbia, Correggio, Blake, Corot, George Fuller, Winslow Homer*. Boston and New York: 1911.

Weinberg, H. Barbara, Doreen Bolger, and David Park Curry. *American Impressionism and Realism: The Painting of Modern Life, 1885-1915.* New York: The Metropolitan Museum of Art, 1994.

Weesner, Gail. *Beacon Hill in the 1920s and 1930s: Rebirth of a Neighborhood.* (unpublished mss., c. 2001).

Wilmerding, John. *Winslow Homer.* New York: Praeger Publishers, 1972.

Articles:

Adlow, Dorothy. "Three Water Color Exhibits." *Christian Science Monitor,* 11 January 1939, 14.

————. "Gertrude Beals Bourne." *Christian Science Monitor*, 10 April 1940, 12.

Bowser, Elizabeth M. "Gertrude Beals Bourne." *Boston Evening Transcript*, 13 April 1940, V, 7.

Bourne, Frank A. "Appreciation: Water Colors by Aiden L. Ripley Receive Enthusiastic Praise." *Boston Evening Transcript*, 7 February 1927, Section I, 10.

Crosby, Katherine. "High, Low and Hidden Gardens as They Bloom on Beacon Hill." *Boston Evening Transcript*, 4 August 1928, Magazine Section, 2.

————. "Garlands From the Gardens of Beacon Hill."*Boston Evening Transcript*, 18 May 1929, Magazine Section, 1, 3.

————. "Woman the Ceaseless Apartment Seeker, Drives Art First from Beacon Hill, the from the South End to Fine Privacy Near the Copps Hill Graveyard." *Boston Evening Transcript*, 5 October 1927, Section III, 2.

Greta. "Art in Boston." *Art Amateur* 20 (January 1889): 28.

————. "Greta's Boston Letter," *Art Amateur* 5 (July 1881): 30+.

Philpott, A. J. in *Exhibition of Water Colors by the Late Henry W. Rice, Dec. 9-28*, Robert C. Vose Galleries, Boston (undated c. 1934).

Pipkin, Erin. "'Striking in its Promise': The Artistic Career of Sarah Gooll Putnam" in *The Massachusetts Historical Review* (Massachusetts Historical Society) 3 (2001): 89-115.

Shillaber, R. P. "Personal Reminiscences." *Boston Post Semi-Centennial Supplement*, 9 November 1881.

Woodward, Sidney. "Women Painters and Sculptors' Work Shown," *Boston Post*, 4 February 1920.

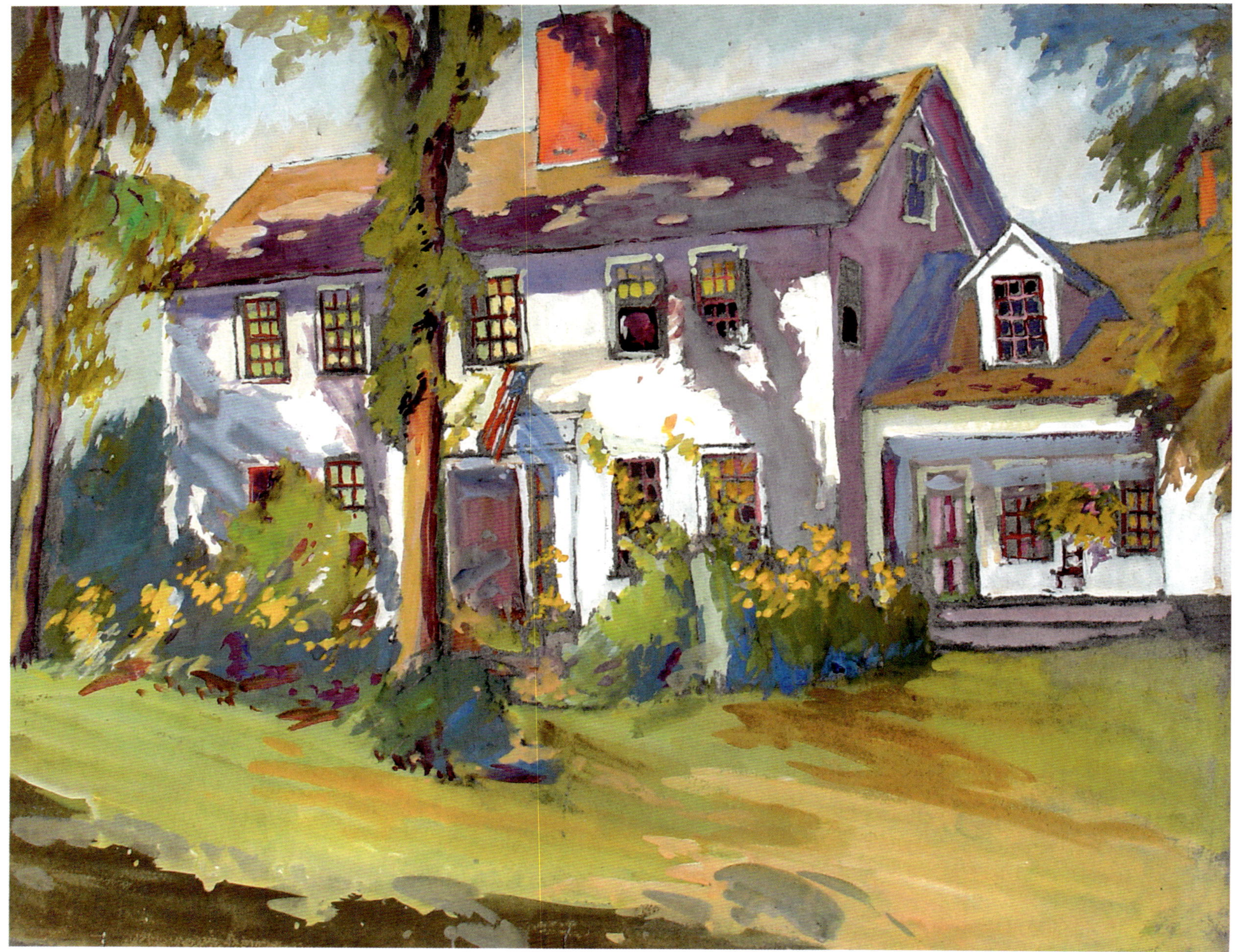

INDEX

Colonial House, c. 1917-19.
Gouache on gray paper, 20 x 25 inches.
Courtesy Childs Gallery, Boston.

PHOTO CREDITS:

All photographs courtesy of Liam O. Toomey and Gabriel B. Connolly except as noted in captions or as noted below:

Bourne Art Trust, pp.22 (*Gertrude, age 9*), 23, 36, 38 (*Dinan - La Tour de l'Horloge*), 42, 46, 60, 65 (*Joshua Gardner Beals at Home*).
D. Roger Howlett, pp. 18, 22 (*328 Dartmouth Street*).

In 1932, Stanley Morison designed the typeface Times New Roman for the Monotype Corporation, Ltd. for use in the London Times newspaper. It was crafted to be highly legible, and classically handsome. Morison was so successful that the English Linotype Company issued it simultaneously, a rare event in type founding. Later phototypesetting systems, and then CRT systems, adapted Morison's font. This book has been set "in house" at the Copley Square Press using Adobe Pagemaker software and its version of Morison's masterpiece.

Printing and binding are by the South China Printing Company (1988) Ltd. of Hong Kong.

In 1990, Richard C. Bartlett created the design for *William Partridge Burpee: American Marine Impressionist* by D. Roger Howlett. For this book, Bartlett's design has been adapted and executed by Liam O. Toomey.